get J. & Thomson on Cas[illegible] [illegible]rew
Critique of [illegible]

[illegible]adage
maxim: 64-65

include: 7, Jackson Essay on Bible (Bible link to NL)
10 work in Chuangtze & Holmes

LEGAL KNOWLEDGE AND ANALOGY

Law and Philosophy Library

VOLUME 13

The titles published in this series are listed at the end of this volume.

LEGAL KNOWLEDGE AND ANALOGY

Fragments of Legal Epistemology, Hermeneutics and Linguistics

edited by

Patrick Nerhot

European University Institute, Florence

KLUWER ACADEMIC PUBLISHERS

DORDRECHT / BOSTON / LONDON

Library of Congress Cataloging-in-Publication Data

Legal knowledge and analogy : fragments of legal epistemology, hermeneutics, and linguistics / Patrick Nerhot (ed.).
p. cm. -- (Law & philosophy library ; v. 13)
Includes bibliographical references and index.
ISBN 0-7923-1065-9 (HB : acid free paper)
1. Law--Interpretation and construction. 2. Law--Language. 3. Jurisprudence. I. Nerhot, Patrick, 1953- . II. Series: Law and philosophy library ; v. 13.
K296.L44 1991
340'.014--dc20 90-22507

ISBN 0-7923-1065-9

Published by Kluwer Academic Publishers,
P.O. Box 17, 3300 AA Dordrecht, The Netherlands.

Kluwer Academic Publishers incorporates
the publishing programmes of
D. Reidel, Martinus Nijhoff, Dr W. Junk and MTP Press.

Sold and distributed in the U.S.A. and Canada
by Kluwer Academic Publishers,
101 Philip Drive, Norwell, MA 02061, U.S.A.

In all other countries, sold and distributed
by Kluwer Academic Publishers Group,
P.O. Box 322, 3300 AH Dordrecht, The Netherlands.

Printed on acid-free paper

Printed in the Netherlands

TABLE OF CONTENTS

PATRICK NERHOT

INTRODUCTION

Reasoning by analogy, or the type of reasoning traditionally presented as the one in which one moves from one object to another on the idea that there is "something in common" between them, remains a fairly mysterious type of reasoning. The two definitions we shall offer, from Cornu and Gény, two famous French lawyers[1], will not really eliminate this sense of mysteriousness.

The former defines analogy as "the resemblance or conformity of several things among themselves", which may appear to be a minimalist approach, and considers reason by analogy as "a classic process of rational interpretation forming part of the exegetic method"[2]. The latter, traditionally presented as the decisive opponent of the French exegetic school, nevertheless locates the procedure of analogy at the very heart of what must according to it be a true science of law[3]. There is therefore a sense of mystery about a process of reasoning that is nevertheless common, since we very frequently establish a "resemblance" between two different objects and use the more

1 It should be easy to find equivalent definitions in other national legal cultures.

2 G. Cornu, *Vocabulaire juridique*, Association H. Capitant, P. U. F. , 1987, "Analogie".

3 F. Gény, *Sciences et Technique en droit privé positif*, 1922, I; esp. p. 158ff.

accessible of the two to make the other one more comprehensible. There is no need for surprise, then, if this concept has had a "wretched" reputation[4] and has been regarded as a "vague, soft, polymorphous, treacherous" concept[5]; Bachelard and Canguilhem have shown how analogy could in certain cases become an "epistemological obstacle". Conversely, the "analogical imagination", as Bachelard said, could play a constitutive role for a determinate science by helping to split up the area of investigation and suggest images that could each become concepts[6]. Analogy, accordingly, very clearly goes beyond the play of mere metaphors, and can act as an intermediary between already constituted disciplines and a newly constructed reality[7].

But what does it amount to in legal science?

The whole set of texts we are offering has, it seems to me, the considerable interest of fairly substantially covering the major questions that analogical reasoning poses for us. We have thus a diversity of proposed approaches, though all with a common referent, the clearest expression of our modern legal culture (19th and 20th centuries), namely that of law conceived of as a full discourse. Not that our authors, any more than myself, put the question

[4] *Recherches interdisciplinaires du Collège de France*, Vol. I, Aspects historiques "Analogie et Connaissance" sous la direction de A. Lichnerowicz, F. Perroux, G. Cadoffre, Introduction p. 5.

[5] *Ibid.*

[6] E. g. C. Ménard, "L'analogie de l'équilibre économique exclut-elle l'histoire?", in *Analogie et Connaissance, Recherches Interdisciplinaires du Collège de France*, *op. cit.*, p. 208.

[7] Thus Kepler, cited by D. Walker, in "Kepler's musical theories and analogy" in *Analogie et Connaissance*, *op. cit.*, p. 65ff., who shows belief in an analogical structure of the universe and of history: "the movements of the heavens are nothing other than a perpetual symphony (rational, not vocal) which moves, through dissonances, through as it were certain suspensions or cadential formulae (through which men imitate the natural dissonances) towards definite, prescribed cadences, each chord being made up of six terms (as it were six voices), and by these marks (cadences) it divides and distinguishes the immensity of time; so that it is no longer astonishing that Man, the ape of his Creator, should finally have invented this way of singing in several parts, unknown to the Ancients...".

of law as an object that has always already been there, systematic and complete. Quite the contrary. Some, indeed practically all of us, reject this sort of epistemology of law, and where the hypothesis of the coherence of the legal universe is put forward, this is in order to define it in very noticeably different terms from those traditionally used in legal scholarly accounts.

If this referent, the law presented as a full discourse[8], runs through all of the contributions, this is because reasoning by analogy has to be found its specific place within this legal culture. It is the place to locate the problem of "lacunae" in law, which at bottom allows our various contributions to be classified. With Zaccaria and Maris, the question of lacunae is accepted as such (this is, we might say, the "traditionalist" aspect of these two articles, which is counterbalanced by – keeping to the same terminology – "modernist" emphases, sometimes Dworkinian in nature), and becomes the backdrop for considerations of purely hermeneutic type, in Zaccaria, extended in Maris to the field of ethics. The papers from Lenoble and Jackson, the former philosophical and the latter semiological, take as their main target this legal knowledge where the theory of lacunae finds its place. Then come legal epistemological contributions from Villa and Nerhot, the question of the whys and hows of such a theory being taken as the object of consideration; and Dean Broekman then invites us, as it were, to change universes radically, to ask ourselves about this mysterious operation, which traditional legal methodology dodges, known as "legal qualification".

Among these various positions, then, we select our order of presentation of the various authors, with the honour of kicking off going undisputedly to Ladeur. He offers us in particular a historical survey of the use of reasoning from analogy in German legal culture, accompanied by a brief quantitative overview; this history fits in perfectly, in our view, with the special features of our European legal culture over these last two centuries.

8 A totality which has in the course of the last two centuries in Europe taken on various forms, since, very schematically, in an initial period (say the last two-thirds of the 19th century) we perceive it as the completeness and systematic nature of law, while in a second period (late 19th century, first four decades of this century more or less, with some divergence from one country to another) it appears as law's vocation towards completeness and system, and finally comes to be conceived of as coherence (perhaps for the first time in Betti, "Teoria Generale della Interpretazione", A. Giuffrè, Milan, 1955), law's systematic nature.

While, for instance, the Volksgeist expressed the unity of law while analogy brought about the *continuity of identity* of the overall legal system, let us not forget that during the same period the so-called exegetic method was also expressing this unity of law, and Cornu[9], moreover, today sees reasoning from analogy as "a classic process of rational interpretation forming part of the exegetic method". This comparative type of treatment I permit myself is not entirely innocent, since it seeks to show that two theories always regarded as very different nevertheless come together to express something identical, and quite fundamental. I am thus inviting the reader, and we shall return to this point later, to seek to understand these theories, Volksgeist and exegesis, not as something to be regarded as the completed expression of some fundamental legal knowledge, but on the contrary as *secondary, derived creations*, more or less a trace of something more general, more systematic, more profound: "an order of knowledge" (using a phrase from M. Foucault, who saw what we know chronologically as the 19th century as an epistemological break, a new way of stating and knowing things).

We do not intend within the limits of this introduction to develop this hypothesis, but let us stress in this perspective that in the mid-19th century, more or less, Linnaeus's seemingly impossible enterprise was apparently accomplished. The botanist, by looking at a leaf or a fruit, can manage to *induce the whole* of the tree or plant. In a very interesting work, F. Dagognet[10] if even tells us that "with a few petals, Linnaeus unfolded the whole universe, since geo-botany had taught him that the plant implies a soil, a climate, an environment, a region". Cuvier too could describe the whole of an animal from a tooth or a bone. The science of nature ceased to be *descriptive* and came to constitute "a tight network through which it informed the living". The scientific spirit of the age, this profound break with the epistemology of the classical age, lay in this articulation of knowledge enabling *scientific prediction* of the future, describing "this world below" *even if not yet visible*, inductively filling every type of vacuum. Our idea is that we must seek to understand legal science of the time on the basis of

[9] Cornu, p. 1 above.

[10] F. Dagognet, *Le catalogue de la vie*, Presses Universitaires de France, 1970, p. 176.

this *episteme*. Totality, unity (and thereupon systematicity or completeness) certainty, prediction, were the categories on the basis of which this order of knowledge recognized itself. At bottom, what the rapid but instructive positive legal history of analogical reasoning presented by Ladeur invites us to do is, then, to follow these constant shifts in the order of knowledge on the basis of the traces which are the various succeeding doctrines in legal dogmatics up to the present. *Begriffsjurisprudenz* (particularly through Laband) conceived of analogy within a philosophy where legal institutions were compared to, treated in the same way as, natural laws (Ladeur)[11]. It was with the Weimar Republic that "the link between deductivism and the continuity of experience is broken" (Ladeur), and we then find Kelsen coming along to express the idea of incompleteness of the legal system. Here too, the argument is not typically German; it can be found particularly in France, despite the force of the civil-law tradition, in Italy etc., and once again what this should show us is what it more substantially reflected, this knowledge on the basis of which we recognize things.

The argument becomes increasingly broad: "the assumption of the logical-syntactical order of the legal system and the comprehension of legal practice as deductive rule-application and, ultimately, the presupposition of a system of legal rules which is not itself transformed by its own application are given up" (Ladeur). However, despite acceptance of this "openness", using an item from today's terminology, of the process of self-transformation of legal knowledge that leads the idea of unity of the legal system astray, it seems to us that Ladeur is right to stress that the *principle of unity* as such should not yet be abandoned on that ground[12]. Having made these three general methodological remarks, and roughly brushed over the main features of our cultural legal context, we may now present our various authors, with the questions they raise.

[11] Recall that Gény located the *Begriff* at the very heart of this "scientific search" for law, where the construct (i.e. legal institutions) expressed the datum (i.e. natural laws).

[12] In this connection, it would be fairly easy to show the broad lines of continuity between Kelsen and Luhmann, specifically on the basis of this idea of self-creation of norms conceived conjointly with the principle of unity. On this question of autopoeisis, see in particular some conclusions of Ladeur himself, and the work of J. Broekman.

First of all, how is the question of analogical reasoning presented by Zaccaria? Here we find Ladeur's conclusion, namely that, for Zaccaria, the speculative space of analogy consists in bringing to the surface the structure of being as such and in its relationship with totality. This means that "Rechtsfindung" is the progressive construction of the relationship between the correspondence of the normative datum and the actual datum. J. Broekman likewise orients his whole work around this "space" between legal reality and, let us say social reality. But Zaccaria admits on the one hand the issue of lacunae and the other the subsumptive form, in order for the question of analogy to be properly posed: on the basis of these two premises, analogy is conceived of as reasoning that allows our knowledge to be increased, that is, it comes along to fill lacunae. This author reminds us that the positive-law position that regarded analogy as an extremely rare technique to fill the very exceptional lacunae in the complete legal system must definitely be abandoned, since in our days the lacuna has become the rule. What is to be the rational basis on which analogical inference will be acceptable? It will be a principle of justice conceived as proportion, since what is at the basis of analogy is the principle of universality. This is very exactly C. Maris's starting-point: "whether a case not covered by the law should nevertheless be treated equally to covered cases, because it is similar in its relevant respects". A principle of justice must guide analogical inference, and any risk of arbitrariness will be set aside, since analogical reasoning is conceived of as "a specific application of the principle of universality" (Maris, Zaccaria). With Zaccaria – who at the very beginning cites A. Kaufmann[13], recalling that, for him, the application of law, or any search for law, consisted not in a conclusion of formal logical type but in organizing a process of analogical type – the logical form of analogy is in the last analysis based on a principle of *distributive justice*.

With Maris – who like Zaccaria accepts the distinction between *analogia iuris* and *analogia legis*, both to be evaluated on the basis of the *ratio iuris* of any legal rule – we start with a narrow application of the principle of universality in order steadily to extend it to the legal system conceived of as

[13] Whose famous text "Analogie und Natur der Sache, Zugleich ein Beitrag zur Lehre vom Typus" he takes as a basis.

a totality (an interesting example of our legal culture) and to finish with the broadest application of the principle of universality in the field of ethics.

With all the other authors, we shall see why among the five concerned Bankowski has an original place. The problem apparently raised by analogical inference changes completely, finding perhaps its best expression in a phrase from J. Lenoble: "Law is the interpretation that the community, through its judges, does not cease to give of its *own history*" (our emphasis). We find five variations on this theme.

B. Jackson very rightly points out that before one can speak of any sort of similarity, the type of discourse – like the datum on the basis of which decisions are taken – must be made clear here. This semiology will be applied on the basis of a model, that of the Bible. Through this detour, Jackson invites us to deal with the act of interpretation no longer on the basis of a conceptual, hierarchical model but in a literary, analogical way, that is, by looking at the actual surface of the text, its form, for the notion of meaning, a type of reading which enables us, Jackson tells us, to show that analogy is used in order to accentuate the *difference*, despite a similarity that is only *apparent*. The argument is extremely interesting, since it well shows the interdependence between reasoning by analogy and its interpretive context, even if we lack the justification, the explanation, of the type of interpretation proposed: in other words, a semiotic.

For J. Lenoble, consideration of analogical inference ought to enable some answers to be given to questions arising from the discussions which in recent years have involved such authors as K. Apel, J. Habermas, R. Dworkin and H. Hart. Thus, for Lenoble, the issues of "lacunae" or "imperfect resemblance" around which consideration of analogical inference traditionally turns perhaps arise from a "not fully thought out binding to the dogmatism that often continues to permeate the interpretation that the theory and practice of law give of the operation of applying a rule", and more fundamentally from what the meaning of a rule is.

For Lenoble, two authors are essential in this work of excavation. These are Kant, who offers an original perspective on analogical reasoning applied to moral judgement, whose originality of analysis Lenoble seeks in his paper to extend to legal reasoning, using the contemporary accomplishments of linguistic philosophy, and then Wittgenstein.

Villa and I myself keep to the question pointed out by Lenoble, but using a more epistemological approach. Villa locates the question of analogical inference by asking on the one hand about the notion of interpretation, and on the other about the notion of integration in legal science; this question is located by him in a constructivist perspective, undoubtedly close to ours, in particular when he tells us that "it is the background conceptual framework that determines the 'working pattern' for the evaluation of similarities" and puts forward the hypothesis of a "network of relevant similarities between legal analogy and analogy as it is used in scientific method". Villa's question, the answer to which will remain very abstractly "metatheoretical", to use his own term, will then consist in discussing these 'standard ways' in which some current theories of legal reasoning face the problem of legal arguments", just as he also asks us what the function of analogical inference for the "legal system" consists in. We can summarize his position on the basis of the following question: "Can legal analogy legitimately be characterized as part of legal interpretation, or else should it be treated as part of the creation of law?"

Following Lenoble, Jackson, Villa and Nerhot, but before Broekman, we felt it appropriate to bring in Z. Bankowski, who may perhaps seem more surprising. The reason is fairly simple: we have already sketched it out at the start of this introduction. The last four authors, like Dean Broekman, want to turn their backs on a certain legal tradition, or culture, or at least seek to analyse it, and the theory of lacunae is one interesting aspect of it. But what do we have with Bankowski? A specific culture, that of "common law", where analogical reasoning nevertheless remains central. This is further verification of what Ladeur said at the outset: no work can be done on analogy without previous work on interpretation. But what is an interpretation in Continental law or in a common-law "system"? Let us very roughly sketch out what in our view a study of comparative type between these two legal cultures – common law, Continental law – would have to deal with in relation to the question of interpretation. All "phenomenologism" must be avoided, since a primary observation is not a fundamental truth so that all brandishing of some sort of "code" on the one side or some sort of "body of precedents" on the other in order to prove a difference must stop. Putting it simply, the problem is not, does not consist in, deriving a legal culture from the presence or absence of a code, quite the contrary: what is this culture that makes the code win on one side, and not win on the other? Let us be quite clear. From the presence of a code or otherwise, undoubtedly, specific interpretive *techniques* will come to bear or not (the notions of "norms", various principles up to the very recent general principles, specification of the idea of totality, of legal order or of systematicity, or even of coherence in today's sense etc.); the point is not to deny that. What we mean, however, is that all that material is nothing but *traces* that one must know how to read. This is a hard task, since the principle of law, that whereby, through which, law is stated, is not, as it were, extirpated from the legal texts themselves. In other words, legal experience is characterized not by objects but by the way in which it constitutes them. This characterized the main feature of the method of this comparative study.

The fundamental hypothesis on what interpretation in law is, which we shall *do no more than sketch out* in this general presentation[14], is that Western rational knowledge is constituted through texts, around texts, on texts, which have acted as starting-points for an *enquiry into truth*. Theology has never raised only theological questions: scholastic method, medieval Bible exegesis, philology, erudition, hermeneutics and linguistics were (and are) successive methods through which truth was stated and was recognized. Legal culture was constituted around, through, and on the basis of these various types of knowledge just as it was able to stimulate them. Truth was always to be produced through rational thought; it is never revealed. There is always a need to look for the pointers to it: our rational knowledge is organized around this *semiotics*.

This is the sort of question that we feel is raised by the problem presented to us by Bankowski. The phenomenological type of argument so often put forward by Continental legal scholarship when it has to express those interpretive principles thanks to which we state what the law is can clearly not be raised in the same way by common-law doctrine. The success Dworkin is having today is not to be explained solely by his manifest literary talent, and the questions raised by his philosophy of law are certainly questions that each of us recognizes as relevant, where he deals with the problem of knowing the law. Ultimately, it little matters what the answers are. The reason why we like Bankowski's paper so much is that it is a perfect example of this search-affirmation-limitation of the interpretive principle that leads to the "right" legal answer. Through these testimonies, these reconstructions of past events, the tracks are drawn on the basis of which a

14 See end of this introduction.

truth can be induced (in Bankowski's example, the principle of responsibility, the notion of third parties, the extent of a specific type of responsibility). Analogy will then relate to these first traces, these initial signs. Bankowski in fact tells us that: "... what we require is first of all a *basic line or point* (our emphasis) from which we can start and by reference to which we can compare". "Stare decisis", then, is nothing but this trace: the Continentals have their code, but it too is nothing without a semiotic.

Another interesting point about Bankowski's text, which brings us directly to Dean Broekman's work, is in showing that if one wishes to stress the "factual" aspect of legal reasoning by making more general, more abstract, these constituent elements of our perception of reality that we call "facts", then these factual categories no longer refer to legal rules but *are* those legal rules! Understanding analogical inference therefore requires, and it matters little whether we have to do with "common law" or not, an understanding of how the ordinary language of things mutates into legal language, which acts as the catalogue on the basis of which one can name the things themselves. This theme is the core of Broekman's work, though he himself is within a Continental tradition. Does a difference on this point between our two famous "traditions" still have legal tender?

As in Bankowski, in Broekman analogy is a "basic doctrinal operation which establishes legal discourse". If this operation is fundamental, it is by implicitly organizing a translation, a shift of meaning, between ordinary language and the language of legal scholarship. Broekman's work, then, will be located in this link, wrongly supposed to be easy to locate, known as legal description. The point of Broekman's method is that this translation cannot take place without prior acceptance of a fundamental analogy between everyday, let us say, reality and "the law". Broekman's paper very clearly poses this very difficult question raised by analogical reasoning: how and why should legal descriptions be constituted, how can jurists determine the exactness of their descriptions and how can they supply the necessary justification and legitimation for them. Everything is undoubtedly in these questions, even if the answers to what analogical inference organizes in the rationality of our knowledge nevertheless remain rather mysterious.

Consideration of analogy nonetheless leads us to what Foucault called an archaeology of our knowledge, and the contributions we present here, apart from what they furnish in terms of thinking about analogical reasoning as such, in our view allow us to see the fundamental epistemological questions raised by the comparison and understanding of the different *forms* of rational argument employed successfully by "Continental" and "common law" jurists.

In conclusion, I note that I have not really presented my own paper. This is perhaps because presenting oneself is too hard an exercise; either one displays excessive modesty and the picture one presents is obscured, or one tends to lack discernment towards oneself, which is always possible, so that what one says becomes frankly confusing. Be that as it may, I have no doubt unknowingly broadly sketched it out throughout this introduction. What I have certainly to clarify is that my paper is part of a broader study on interpretation in legal science (due to appear as a monograph some time in 1990), a study that asks some questions and seeks to give some elements of answers to them. Perhaps the extract we present here shows more the questions than the elements of answer. Though all that, then, may be unimportant, the main point was in any case, through this work, to begin to sketch out new pathways.

This study aims to contribute to a precise field primarily concerned with theoretical research and only secondarily with more "involved" interpretations of our legal culture (notably those which deal with concepts such as "l'Etat libéral" and the "welfare State")[15].

My work and the work of those eminent colleagues who have done me the honour of publishing under my editorship, are also part of a wider research project, the first results of which were published in the same series as the present volume[16], and constitute the premises of the current work. Our sole ambition has been to produce strictly epistemological work, even if some readers may give it an altogether different import.

Readers will notice that these contributions cannot be stamped French, Italian, German or English, etc..., they belong to a cultural sphere larger than the traditional national sphere and they attempt an analysis which is, perhaps, somewhat different from contemporary legal philosophy dealing with legal knowledge in the Western World.

15 It should be easy to find equivalent definitions in other national legal cultures.

16 P. Nerhot, *Law, Interpretation and Reality. Essays in Epistemology, Hermeneutics and Jurisprudence*, P. Nerhot, Gen. Ed. , Kluwer Academic Publishers, 1989.

THE ANALOGY BETWEEN LOGIC AND DIALOGIC OF LAW

KARL-HEINZ LADEUR

1. ANALOGY IN THE CLASSIC GERMAN LEGAL SCIENCE OF THE 19TH CENTURY

For the German legal science of the 19th century, analogy is a deductive procedure which, on the one hand, accepts the fragmentary character of the legal system and – in a paradoxical way – confirms the validity of the syllogistic reasoning on the other hand, i.e. the possibility of subsumption of the particular fact under the general law. The presupposed isomorphy of the case and the general law is supplemented by the possibility of relevance of the *similarity* between the normal case and the special case, and this method allows for a flexibility of the legal system which exceeds the limits of extensive interpretation and, at the same time, limits the constraint of explicit adaptation and transformation of law.

This method presupposes that – even if the law is fragmentary, as far as explicit textual expression is concerned – it has got the implicit autoproductive capacity, which needs activation from outside (the new case) but which is not informed by new situations because it constructs decisions and dogmatic options in its own forms.

Analogy and interpretation cannot easily be separated. Analogy – as opposed to interpretation – starts from the assumption that a law – according to its textual expression and its sense – does not apply to a particular case. Its practical relevance fluctuates with the transformation process of methodical orientations within the judiciary, e.g. its domain is dependent on the methodical choice of a reconstruction of the subjective historical will of the legislator or of the presumption of an objective will which is itself subject to historical change of time and situations and is therefore open to new social requirements[1].

The construction of the analogical reasoning is itself subject to controversy. According to Stammler[2], it is a third type of deductive procedure to be located between induction, the construction of a general norm from particular cases, and deduction in the proper sense, the construction of the particular decision from the general norm. That means, analogy is the construction of a particular normative hypothesis from other particular hypotheses. This assumption seems to be at least imprecise insofar as the new hypothesis won by analogy is not only deduced from other cases or hypotheses regulated by and won from the legal norm but analogy presupposes as well the existence of a relation between the normal case and the law on the one hand and a relation of *similarity* between the normal case and the special case on the other hand[3]. From these two relations the similarity or equivalence of a third relation is deduced, i.e. the relation between special case and special norm (constructed by analogical reasoning).

The explicit general law still functions as a kind of "attractor" – producing order in legal reasoning – insofar as analogy is restricted to borderline cases[4]. On the other hand, the attractor-role of the explicit law can even vanish if the norm itself appears to be nothing but a contingent expres-

[1] Cf. H. Coing, *Rechtsphilosophie*, 2nd ed., Berlin, 1969, p. 334 ss.; J. Esser, *Argumentations- und Stilwandel in höchstrichterlichen Zivilentscheidungen*, in: "Etudes de logique juridique", 1976, p. 53ss.

[2] R. Stammler, *Lehrbuch der Rechtsphilosophie*, 2nd ed., Berlin/Leipzig 1923, p. 270; cf. also W. Fikentscher, *Methodenlehre des Rechts*, vol. 3, Tübingen, 1976, p. 722; C.W. Canaris, *De la manière de contrôler et de combler les lacunes de la loi en droit allemand*, in: "Etudes de logique juridique", 1966, pp. 19, 27; K. Larenz, *Methodenlehre der Rechtswissenschaft*, 5th ed., Berlin etc. 1983, p. 365 ss.; U. Klug, *Juristische Logik*, 4th ed., Berlin, 1982, p. 118ss.

[3] Larenz, *loc. cit.* (Fn. 2), pp. 365, 368.

[4] Larenz, *loc. cit.* (Fn. 2), p. 368.

sion of a legal principle of a higher order[5]. In that case, the asymmetry[6] between the original relations disappears because the weight or number of the special cases becomes more important in comparison with the normal case. Then the original norm and the normal case seem to be nothing but one type among others and therefore lose their "attractor"-role[7].

The paradoxical role of analogical reasoning as a productive mechanism must be located between extensive interpretation of a norm in a "deviant" special case and the construction of norms from general principles by argumentative reasoning.

In the classical legal science, the properly constructive role of analogy is explained either with reference to natural law or to so-called legal "institutes" ("Rechtsinstitute") maintaining the unity and the systematic character of the law[8]. They form the "organic" capacity of the law integrating the "new" cases into the presupposed continuity of the system governed by a totalising idea ("Gesamtidee")[9] structuring the pyramidal layering of the legal system.

Analogy can proceed by transformation of the "original institutes" ("urbildliche Rechtsinstitute")[10] – this would be quite a rare case of a far-reaching change of law by this method. But, in general, analogy is characterised by the evolution of a new legal problem within a "known legal institute"[11]. Positive law according to Savigny exists in a deep relationship with the "spirit of the people" ("Volksgeist") which gives rise to an

5 Larenz, *loc. cit.* (Fn. 2), p. 372; Ch. Perelman/L. Olbrechts-Tyteca, *Traité de l'argumentation*, Brussels, 1970, p. 531.

6 Perelman/Olbrechts-Tyteca, *loc. cit.* (Fn. 5), p. 532.

7 A. Kaufmann, *Analogie und Natur der Sache,* reprinted in: *Rechtsphilosophie im Wandel*, Frankfurt, 1972, p. 310.

8 F. C. v. Savigny, *System des heutigen Römischen Rechts*, vol.1, Berlin, 1840, p. 290.

9 C. F. v. Gerber, *System des deutschen Privatrechts,* Jena, 1863, p. V.

10 v. Savigny, *loc. cit.* (Fn. 8), p. 290.

11 v. Savigny, *loc. cit.* (Fn. 8), p. 290.

"organic force" maintaining the inner unity of the legal system. And it is this force which helps integrate innovative steps into the continuity of the identity of the whole system by way of analogical reasoning[12].

In the later version of legal positivism and of "Begriffsjurisprudenz" (conceptual legal reasoning), the integrative force of the "Institute" inherent in positive law and proved by the continuity of practice is separated from its relationship to the history of ideas and of natural law. Now it refers rather to natural science for theoretical legitimation. Laband[13] compares legal institutes to natural laws: they allow for different forms as reflected in different codifications in France and in Germany, but they can ultimately be reduced to certain basic constructive principles, especially the logical-systematic order of elements and classes. These principles presuppose – drawing on the tradition of the Enlightenment – the harmony of the particular and the universal[14], because only in this way does the consonance of the rational will of the legislator and the will of the particular legal subject with the objective legality of the world seem to be possible.

The logical-systematic deduction and compatibilisation of legal decisions and the codification on which they draw aim at the integration of legal practice[15] and at the same time they presuppose the regularity of the "life-world". Historically, they are constituted by the break with the fragmented local practices of the law.

In German *public* law of the late 19th century, the dogma of the closed and complete character of the legal system was not widely accepted[16]. Its dominance was restricted to those parts of the law where the judge was competent in the final evaluation and decision of a legal conflict. Especially in constitutional law gaps are closed by power relations, this is the well-

12 v. Savigny, *loc. cit.* (Fn. 8), p. 294.

13 P. Laband, *Das Staatsrecht des Deutschen Reiches*, 5th ed., Tübingen, 1911, Introduction, p. X.

14 R. Wiehl, *La rationalité du singulier*, in "Critique", 1988, pp. 531, 544.

15 Cf. J. Esser, *loc. cit.* (Fn. 1), p. 66; Ph. Foriers, *Les lacunes du droit*, in "Etudes de logique juridique", 1972, p. 57ss.

16 G. Jellinek, *Allgemeine Staatslehre*, 3rd reprint, Kronberg, 1976, pp. 356, 359.

known "normative force of the fact"[17]. In a paradoxical way, pure facticity appears as a norm producing power, whereas, on the other hand, the new norm won by analogy is regarded as a form of self-explanation of the legal system. The normative creativity of the political system is openly admitted, whereas the creativity of analogy is not totally denied but the breadth of the fluctuations of new variations of norm hypotheses is, at the same time, restricted by the reference to the norm as "attractor".

The comparison with the "normativity of fact" in constitutional law shows that the norm at the turn of the century is not only oriented at the maintenance of a state of equilibrium – which does not seem to have existed in politics –, but gives structure to the form of self-thematisation of experience, as well[18].

2. THE ANALOGY BETWEEN NORM, EXPERIENCE AND CREATIVITY

The creativity of analogy is bound to the continuity of experience, which refers fluctuations in real life to an equilibrium model which, in the end, will buffer order from chaos, whereas constitutional law which underlies more and greater fluctuations draws only in a lesser sense on analogy as a method of integrating the new into the continuity of the existing system.

The relationship between normativity and facticity appears also in the French doctrine. The revolutionary tradition accepts the possibility of gaps within the legal system – Gény himself accentuated the creative character of analogy –, but this is – according to the doctrine – due to the aim of simplifying the law by way of codification. The guiding principles inherent in the legal system are supposed to be appropriate for the punctual closing of appearing gaps[19].

The predominance of the logical-deductive method is responsible for the neglect of the one creative step within analogical reasoning which leads to

17 Jellinek, *loc. cit.* (Fn. 16), pp. 356, 359.

18 R. Cooper, *Organization/Disorganization*, in "Social Science Information", 1986, pp. 299, 300.

19 Foriers, *loc. cit.* (Fn. 15).

the development of the new special legal hypothesis. On the contrary, the dominant opinion puts the accent on the test of the "fit" of this new hypothesis into the existing system constructed in a logical-systematic method. This test proceeds from a deductive-retrospective view. But apparently, in order to be able to deduce from one relation (case/norm) to another relation (case/analogical norm), one must have been "surprised" by a "referring side-view"[20]. Analogy at first formulates a "broadening hypothesis"[21] which does not accept the failure of the subsumption of the new/other case under the norm. This particular step within analogical reasoning neither has the character of the analysis of facts nor is it to be regarded as subsumption under legal concepts[22] but, it tries to understand the "sense of a new situation in analogy with the intuition of the sense of a different situation"[23].

With Peirce[24], the intermediate position of analogy between induction and deduction could be characterised by the concept of "abduction". Induction as well as deduction explicate a pre-existing general relationship between elements, they do not seem to add new elements. Analogy, on the contrary, is based on an inductive step, the comparison of a normal case with a special one, which is followed by an "abduction" in Peirce's sense: it makes possible a new kind of reasoning which leads to an innovative representation[25], which it owes to an "unconscious perception of relationships

20 A. Eschbach, *Karl Bühlers Zeichenbegriff und seine Beziehung zu Wittgensteins Spätphilosophie*, in "Zeitschrift für Semiotik", 1984, pp. 397, 405; cf. also D. H. Helman, *Situation Semantics and Models of Analogy*, in "Phil. Studies", 49 (1986), pp. 231, 237.

21 Eschbach, *loc. cit.* (Fn. 20), p. 405.

22 Eschbach, *loc. cit.* (Fn. 20), p. 405.

23 K. Bühler, *Das Gestaltprinzip im Leben des Menschen und der Tiere*, Bern/Stuttgart, 1960, p. 88.

24 Cf. Ch. S. Peirce, *Collected Papers*, vol. 2, Cambridge/Mass. 1974, p. 297; see also Th. A. Sebeok/J. Umiker-Sebeok, *"Du kennst meine Methode"*, Frankfurt 1984, p. 38; Th. A. Goudge, *The Thought of Ch. S. Peirce*, New York, 1950, p. 205.

25 Peirce, *loc. cit.* (Fn. 24); Sebeok/Umiker-Sebeok, *loc. cit.* (Fn. 24), p. 38.

between aspects of the world"[26]. This is – in legal reasoning – the normative hypothesis that the new case should be treated in a manner *similar* to an established rule. And it is only in the third step that the case is subsumed under the new norm and the produced normative result is reviewed as following from the application of a (new) norm (deduction).

The first two steps of analogical reasoning are characterised by situative and not conceptual understanding of legal norms. The complexity of analogy is more or less eliminated when putting the accent on its deductive component, by means of which it seems to be reintegrated into a logical-syntactical application of the norms.

The special norm constructed from a special fact/case is after all applied just as the general norm is applied to a normal case. Analogy in this perspective is regarded as an explicit innovative, creative procedure of raising hypotheses which – in the classical legal science – is itself subsumed under the logical-syntactical structure and, at the same time, is domesticated in this way[27]. Nevertheless, analogy signals a moment of invention, based on the understanding of the concrete situation, which resists the logical-syntactical paradigm of deduction[28].

At the same time, it opens the perspective on the dependence of the legal system on a presupposed model of knowledge: the new codifications have broken with the fragmentary particularities of tradition, in which custom and customary law had fused, and they have widened the spectre of possibilities, but not without demanding the re-construction of the unity of the particular and the general in a new model of linear equilibrium.

One could call this a model of parametric rationality inasmuch as the multiplicity of possible fluctuations does not exclude the return to a state of equilibrium.

This model of rationality comprises the cognitive and the normative component of the legal system: as the particular fluctuation of the normal does not undermine the equilibrium, the creation of a new particular legal

[26] Goudge, *loc. cit.* (Fn. 24), p. 205; Helman, *loc. cit.* (Fn. 20), p. 235.

[27] Cf. Perelman/Olbrechts-Tyteca, *loc. cit.* (Fn. 5), p. 534; N. MacCormick, *Legal Reasoning and Legal Theory*, Oxford, 1978, p. 186.

[28] Perelman/Olbrechts-Tyteca, *loc. cit.* (Fn. 5), p. 531.

hypothesis by way of analogy with an existing norm cannot shutter the deductive construction model of "rule application", because the norm still functions as the "attractor" within the fluctuations of possible normative hypotheses beyond the limits of extensive interpretation.

Only in this way, by presupposing the continuity of experience *and* the maintenance of the pyramidically structured order of law is the domestication of the situative-productive momentum of the analogy imaginable. Putting the accent on the deductive step within the trias of induction, abduction and deduction means a confirmation of the relationship of correspondence between experience and legal system: the new is but an additional variant of the possibilities already codified.

This construction cannot be reduced to a merely ideological assumption; in a constructivist perspective on models of rationality one must acknowledge that they do not just "correspond" to the given world "outside". Instead, these models (re-)produce "versions of the world"[29] which *organise* the "viability" of knowledge and the normative system[30]. Within a rationality model pertaining at the conservation of the continuity and coherence of experience in spite of the fluctuations of possible variants of "reality", it is consequent to organise invention as a variation of the given and to keep the search strategies which are part of the analogical reasoning separated from deduction, i.e. the application of norms – just as within traditional epistemology the context of discovery is separated from the context of justification[31]. For the search of analogies presupposes, on the one hand, the failure of subsumption of a case under a law but, on the other hand, the search process itself is structured by the logical-deductive character of the legal system and the assumed continuity of experience: the new situation is, from the beginning, constituted as an additional variant to the normal case, it cannot initiate the search for a fundamentally new solution. It lies "beside" the normal case: the process of "wandering" of the legal view from facts to norms and back is a vertically structured process which over-determines the relation of the case and the possibly relevant norm

29 Goodman, *Weisen der Welterzeugung*, Frankfurt, 1984, p. 125.

30 See E. v. Glasersfeld, *Wissen, Sprache und Wirklichkeit*, Braunschweig, Wiesbaden, 1987.

31 Cf. K. R. Popper, *Logik der Forschung*, 4th ed., Tübingen, 1971.

hypothesis[32]. The search fails at first and is then supplemented by a "side-view" at possibly similar cases and the solutions established for them.

This momentum of invention, the widening of the perspective[33], loosens the basic structure of the pyramidical order of the legal system, but it reproduces at the same time the layering of the particular and the universal. This is why the search for the new, which is made possible by way of analogy, is not itself organised in a systematic strategic way. The emergence of sense implied in and created by the network of situations and action fields forming a kind of connection and reference constraints[34] is subsumed as a relationship of similarity under the knowledge model which is inscribed into the codification: the "referring view"[35], which is stirred by the surprise of the new, is guided by a similar case already established.

This is why the assumption that the analogy is oriented on the principle of equivalence must be supplemented by the hint that at stake is not only the normatively equal treatment of equal cases[36] but also the orientation of the knowledge model on the (re-)construction of typical cases.

3. THE DEVELOPMENT OF METHODS IN THE "LABORATORY" OF WEIMAR

In the "laboratory" of Weimar the classical logical-syntactical paradigm of rule application comes under attack from different directions. The turbulent legislation of the period of crisis, the beginning of the interventionist policy and similar phenomena have severed the relationship between deductivism and the continuity of experience. The integrative potential of the

32 Cf. K. Engisch, *Einführung in das juristische Denken*, 7th ed., Stuttgart, 1977, p. 79ss.

33 Cf. Goudge, *loc. cit.* (Fn. 24), p. 205; Eschbach, *loc. cit.* (Fn. 20), 405; Bühler, *loc. cit.* (Fn. 23), p. 88.

34 Cf. M. Polanyi, *Tacit Knowledge*, Garden City/N.Y., 1966.

35 Cf. Eschbach, *loc. cit.* (Fn. 20), p. 416.

36 Canaris, *loc. cit.* (Fn. 2), p. 27.

"Institute"[37], the stable segmentation of the layers of the legal system are undermined by special norms and rules. This development raises the need for new stabilising structures for multiplied fluctuations and the widened spectre of possibilities.

The judiciary more and more tries to integrate the "Institute" into constitutional norms in order to be able to refer to a new positive layer of the legal system limiting the legislation in a direct way, a proof that they no longer appear to be self-evident and beyond doubt.

Another conception searches for a new "culture-scientific method" ("geisteswissenschaftliche Methode") as a way of revival of stabilising and maintaining a new version of continuity more open to the changing necessities of a modernised society[38]. Interpretation of law in this perspective takes on a teleological function of "integration", a task the judiciary is confronted with, especially because the legislator is no longer able to maintain the unity of the legal system as he was in former times.

Interestingly, the methodically reflected legal positivism changes too: it supplements the weakened reciprocal reinforcement of experience and the logical-systematic pyramidical structures of the law by a revival of formal methods of the legitimation of the binding force of law, especially by reformulating the paradigm of rule application. The incompleteness of the legal system is now acknowledged, because the legislator "has to reckon with cases which he did not and could not anticipate; his general norms

37 Cf. C. Schmitt, *Verfassungslehre*, München, 1928, p. 170ss.

38 R. Smend, *Staatsrechtliche Abhandlungen*, 2nd. ed., Berlin, 1968, pp. 136ss., 148ss., 198ss.

can regulate nothing but average cases"[39]. The theory of possible gaps within a system aiming in principle at completeness is rejected. Kelsen advocates a theory of the legislative function of the judge which is to replace the traditional "ideology of norm application".

Even more important is the method of "free law" ("Freirechtsschule"): it not only rejects the deductive paradigm superimposing itself on a continuous flow of events the creative force of which traditionally has been denied[40]. This new tendency regards social situations and relationships not only as an amorphous mass of events gaining form only by explicit normative rules[41]. A legal decision cannot be gained from deduction but only from the consensus about presupposed axioms, theses and principles[42].

It is not the logical-systematic deduction from existing rules, from norms separated from the life-world, which can justify a decision but only the usefulness of the result. "Interest oriented jurisdiction" ("Interessenjurisprudenz") challenges "Begriffsjurisprudenz". The momentum of invention which in the classical perspective of analogy is finally hidden under the deductive component of the procedure comes to the fore in the plea for the necessity of a "pre-understanding of just treatment of the case" ("Vorverständnis")[43]. In this view – as in other cultural sciences – a hermeneutical turn appears in the process of the application of the law: the problems of understanding are no longer solved by the analysis of the text and its logical-systematic deep structure[44]. The norm itself is seen as a project, which leaves behind its starting point – the legislator and his intentions on sense

39 H. Kelsen, *Reine Rechtslehre*, reprint, Aalen, 1985, p. 104.

40 Cf. only Esser, *loc. cit.* (Fn. 1), p. 67.

41 P. Ricoeur, *l'Action du texte*, vol. 2, Paris, 1986, p. 104.

42 Esser, *loc. cit.* (Fn. 1), p. 67.

43 J. Esser, *Juristisches Argumentieren im Wandel des Rechtsfindungskonzepts unseres Jahrhunderts*, Heidelberg, 1979, p. 29.

44 Ricoeur, *loc. cit.* (Fn. 41), p. 103; H. G. Gadamer, *Text und Interpretation*, in "Ph. Forget" (ed.), *Text und Interpretation*, München, 1984, pp. 24, 25.

–[45], because by its linguistic character it is, rather, structured as "being-in-the-world" and therefore it can no longer be referred to a subject occupying the centre of rationality constituting the objective universality transcending the flow of the particular events[46].

Language is regarded as having a "dialogical character"; the separation of subject and object becomes precarious because the subject is mediated and refers to the world through language. In a different perspective on the same phenomenon, Wittgenstein holds that reflection on language must turn to its use, to the "forms of life"[47]. Therewith an autonomous situative rationality which is not mediated by the logical rule structure is taken into account.

During the Weimar Republic, no unitary paradigm giving structure to legal reasoning could develop. But, within our context, we can presume that the legal system produced a lot of innovations which were introduced by way of classical flexible forms such as analogy but, apart from that – and these were new forms of change – were made possible by open reference to constitutional principles (private property, equality etc.) and, above all, to general clauses such as the principle of mutual loyalty ("Treu und Glauben"). Legal practice charged itself with tasks of "weighing" and balancing of values beyond classical methods of analogous reasoning or extensive interpretation, without being able to develop a new stable rationality of decisions.

4. EVALUATION OF THE QUANTITATIVE IMPORTANCE OF ANALOGY IN THE JURISDICTION OF THE REICHSGERICHT

The quantitative development of the recourse to analogy in the civil law jurisdiction of the Reichsgericht – leaving aside the positive or negative result – is significant, even if the reliability of the data is not beyond doubt: I

45 Gadamer, *loc. cit.* (Fn. 44), p. 29.

46 Gadamer, *loc. cit.* (Fn. 44), p. 29.

47 H. Parret, *Regularities, Rules, and Strategies*, in "J. of Pragmatics", 1984, p. 569ss.

refer to the index published for every ten volumes of the official collection of decisions of the court. The register contains a special catchword "analogy". (The distinction between analogy and extensive interpretation might not always be precise). But even with a certain reservation one can ascertain that from 1871 to 1917 the number of cases of analogy fluctuates between zero (once) and twenty; on the average, an analogy is considered nine times in every ten volumes.

From the last year of the first world war (1917) until 1933 the number of cases of analogy rises: in the first ten volumes of this period, the number increases from zero and five in the previous period to 37 and twice 56; after this the number goes down to 28 and 24 cases, numbers which still remain significantly above the previous average level.

This rise is due to the interventionist legislation mentioned above; the increased number of special norms raised the question of a possible analogy more often than the previous type of general norms.

The development is even more interesting if one considers that, in the same period, the jurisdiction has established new ways of control of norms with reference to the constitution and general principles of the positive law. These new procedures largely replace the analogy as a limited "broadening hypothesis" by the open reference to higher layers of the legal system.

The increase of both forms of innovative flexibility going beyond the application of norms in a strict sense can be explained by the fact that the new jurisdictional tendencies have developed in a fragmentary way which did not leave enough time for methodological and dogmatic stability. This was due to the heterogeneous tendencies of the Weimar discussion. But this constellation leads – far beyond the particular decisions controlling laws with reference to a super-legality – to a disruptive destabilisation of the pyramidical order of the law and as a consequence – given the lack of a new paradigm of legal reasoning – this precarious state favoured the frequency of reference to the classical method of innovation, analogy.

The decline of confidence in the auto-reproductive force of the logical-syntactic paradigm, accompanying the multiplicity of the heterogeneous interventionist legislation, permeated the "vertical perspective" and simplified the search for starting points of "broadening hypotheses".

In administrative law, analogy played almost no role at all: this is due to the fact that traditional administrative law was mainly police law and in the liberal state analogies – as within penal law – aiming at the legitimation of new charges imposed on citizens were considered illegitimate[48]. Therefore, the concept of "analogy" is only rarely to be found in the index of the Prussian Superior Administrative Court: only four times within the first 50 volumes of its decisions; and the number did not increase in the Weimar Republic.

5. THE DEVELOPMENT OF THE PARADIGM OF "CONCRETISATION" OF LAW IN THE FEDERAL REPUBLIC

In the Federal Republic, after a short period of revival of the natural law, which was intended to control and supplement the inherent rationality of positive law – discredited by the Nazi government –, a new method developed in the 1960s and 1970s turning back to a number of innovations of the Weimar time, which now could be and were integrated into a relatively consistent paradigm[49] structuring the perception and construction of legal problems.

A complete analysis of this new paradigm cannot be given in this context[50].

For, concerning our context, it is important to put the accent on the pluralistic and situative character of the new model. This means primarily that the assumption of the logical-syntactical order of the legal system and the comprehension of legal practice as deductive rule-application and, ultimately, the presupposition of a system of legal rules which is not itself transformed by its own application are given up.

In jurisdiction and methodological literature, the concept of legal "interpretation" itself – which always referred to the task of finding *one*

48 Cf. A. Gern, *Analogie im Verwaltungsrecht*, in "Die Öffentliche Verwaltung", 1985, p. 558ss.

49 For the concept of "paradigm" see A. Aarnio, *Paradigms in Legal Dogmatics*, in A. Peczenik/L. Lindhal/B.v. Roermund (eds.), "Theory of Legal Science", Dordrecht, 1984, p. 25 ss.; J. M. Broekman, *Change of Paradigm in the Law*, in A. Peczenik et al., "loc. cit.", p. 131ss.

50 Cf. K. H. Ladeur, *Konsensstrategien Staat Verfassungsinterpretation?*, in "Der Staat",1982, p. 391ss.

identical meaning of the one textual unity – is more and more replaced by the situative concept of "concretisation" of law[51]. Concretisation is equivalent to a revival of the rhetorical components of the law; the unequivocal character of the logical-systematic autonomy and identity of law is denied and instead the complex dynamic-relational time-dependent process-character of the changing network of situative legal constraints and options is accentuated. This method gives up the fixed starting point of deduction and regards the subject as implied in his world[52]: the subject, in this perspective, does not simply use the (legal) language, but is also used by it[53]. Understanding takes on a strategic character[54]; it can only open perspectives on a horizon of meanings underlying change within time and allowing for different situative stand points[55].

The continuity of experience as the knowledge basis of a hierarchically structured legal order is challenged by the assumption that in a changing society there can be no continuous, equally-distributed and transparence-guaranteeing experience: knowledge must become strategic, perspectical and plural. Understanding presupposes always a process of construction of "consensual domains"[56] between subjects which takes on the productive-dynamic character of a search for "viability".

For the concretisation of law, this means that the judge who applies the law is no longer strictly separated from the litigants: these become, rather,

51 Cf. K. Hesse, *Einführung in das Verfassungsrecht der Bundesrepublik Deutschland*, 16th ed., Heidelberg, 1988, Nr. 60; F. Müller, *Strukturierende Rechtslehre*, Berlin 1984; Canaris, *loc. cit.* (Fn. 2); W. Höfling, *Offene Grundrechtsinterpretation*, Berlin, 1987.

52 S. Borutti, *Pragmatics and its discontents*, in "J. of Pragmatics", 1984, pp. 437, 441.

53 Cf. generally U. Eco, *Semiotica e filosofia del linguaggio*, Milano, 1984, p. 51ss.

54 Parret, *loc. cit.* (Fn. 46), p. 589.

55 Parret, *loc. cit.* (Fn. 46), p. 589.

56 H. Maturana, *Biology of Language: Epistemology of Reality*, in G.A. Miller/E. Lenneberg (eds.), "Psychology and Biology of Language and Thought", New York, 1978, p. 41.

partners in discourse[57]. This process of change is dependent on the fact that the legal system more and more deals with organised subjects who plan their actions in a long-term strategic perspective with reference to others and, in this way, undermine the model of the linear equilibrium which itself remains beyond the influence of the particular acts.

Strategic acts not only apply rules but, they try to change them by their own "moves". The importance of legal procedure for the self-definition of specific interests and domains is broadened considerably. This is also valid for the participation of the citizens in the process of the definition of the public interest which can only be self-constructed by procedure and cannot be ascertained by the administration alone; the same is valid for the opening of "windows" of the legal system by which the self-definition of certain domains of action is built in the process of the definition of legal concepts[58] (e.g. art, bargaining systems in industrial relations, broadcasting etc.).

In this manner, "openness" to strategic processes of self-transformation of knowledge and action domains which are no longer defined by stable unitary and continuous substantial experience is not only acknowledged but actively organised. The same is valid for legislation. It is more and more obliged to organise processes of knowledge creation and evaluation to be integrated into the normative procedure when parliament sees itself confronted by regulation problems of complex dynamic action fields. (This obligation is legitimated by a broadened concept of constitutional liberties). The new conception goes so far as to formulate the commitment (of the legislator) to "correct" a norm according to new and better knowledge[59].

This transformation has been made possible by the immediate applicability of constitutional law, i.e. judicial control of constitutionality as ex-

57 Esser, *loc. cit.* (Fn. 1), p. 70; cf. also P. Häberle, *Die "offene Gesellschaft" der Verfassungsinterpreten*, in: "Juristenzeitung", 1975, p. 297ss.

58 For constitutional law see Höfling, *loc. cit.* (Fn. 51); for administrative law see E. Schmidt-Assmann, in P. Lerche/id./W. Schmitt Glaeser, "Verfahren als staats- und verwaltungsrechtliche Kategorie", Heidelberg, 1984.

59 Cf. only *Decisions of the Bundesverfassungsgericht* vol. 50, 290, 355; J. Cupei, *Umweltverträglichkeitsprüfung bei der Vorbereitung von Rechts- und Verwaltungsvorschriften*, in "Zeitschrift f. Gesetzgebung", 1988, p. 46ss.

tended to the legislature. Legal norms and their application are more and more permeated by constitutional values. "Interpretation of constitutional law is concretisation. Especially that which is not yet (!) evident as content of the constitution, is to be ascertained with reference to the 'realities' which are to be structured"[60]. Concretisation cannot be abstracted from the pre-understanding of the interpreter and the concrete problem at issue[61]. Pre-understanding makes it possible for the interpreter "to look at the norm with certain expectations ... and to reach at a project, which then needs deeper penetration for proof, correction and revision, until finally the unity of sense is constituted as the result of the continual approach of the ever revised projects to the 'issue' "[62].

This quotation demonstrates the important evolutionary step legal practice has taken from the 19th century to today (the above quotation is taken from a textbook on constitutional law and not from a book on methodology). But, on the other hand, it makes visible the limits of the transformation, as well – which shall be looked at later on.

For our problem it is important to note that the unity of the legal order – a postulate which in the past stood on a par with that of its "completeness" [63] – can no longer be presupposed, because its support, the completeness postulate was no longer evident either.

But, the principle of unity is not dropped altogether, it is, rather, reformulated: legal order no longer preserves a substantial "inner coherence" which confirms itself by application, but, the process of unity-*formation* reproduces a new version of coherence, not that of the legal norms alone, but that of a compatibility of norm *and* situation: the latter creates its own multiple rationality of reference potentials rising within the network of sit-

60 Hesse, *loc. cit.* (Fn. 51), no. p. 60s.

61 Cf. J. Esser, *Vorverständnis und Methodenwahl in der Rechtsfindung*, Kronberg, 1972; cf. also H. G. Gadamer, *Wahrheit und Methode*, 2nd ed., Tübingen, 1965.

62 Hesse, *loc. cit.* (Fn. 51), no. 62; cf. also the critique of E. W. Bockenförde, *Die Methoden der Verfassungsinterpretation*, in "Neue Juristische Wochenschrift", 1976, p. 2089 ss.; cf. also B. Schlink, *Bemerkungen zum Stand der Methodendiskussion in der Verfassungsrechtswissenschaft*, in "Der Staat" 1980, p. 73ss.

63 v. Savigny, *loc. cit.* (Fn. 8), p. 290.

uations. It is this situative networking which is called the "nature of matter" (Natur der Sache) by Arthur Kaufmann[64]. It is a sort of catalyst between the legal norm and the multiplicity of life-contexts[65].

The necessity to keep norm and situation compatible has replaced the presupposed harmony of the particular and the universal and has transformed it into procedural forms. The universality which was implicit in experience is no longer integrated into a hierarchical order of layers, but it rather proceeds from a horizontal "texture". "The concrete universal which is at stake in the historical process, lies 'sidewards' and rises out of a succession, a concatenation, an entanglement and a partial overlapping of manners of interpretation and rule systems. We do not find it when looking 'upwards', for a hierarchy; there we find at best abstract universals as necessary but not sufficing conditions"[66]. Waldenfels at this point refers to Merleau-Ponty's concept of the "universel-latéral", which does not come from "above" as a general scheme under which the differences are to be subsumed[67].

In legal methodology and in practice, the accepted openness of the legal order dependent on "concretisation" refers after all to a new version of the "unity of sense"[68]: the closed logical-syntactical language of law acknowledges the autonomy of "matter" and transcends itself into an argumentative rationality of *discourse*. Certain legal problems are left open inasmuch as they must be *structured* by "plural argumentation and concretisation". A

64 Kaufmann, *loc. cit.* (Fn. 7).

65 Cf. the overview in M. Pavčnik, *Argumentierte Rechtsentscheidung statt Ideologie der "Rechtsanwendung"*, in "Archiv für Rechts- und Sozialphilosophie", 1988, pp. 154, 162.

66 B. Waldenfels, *In den Netzen der Lebenswelt*, Frankfurt, 1985, p. 48.

67 M. Merleau-Ponty, *Signes*, Paris, 1960, p. 150.

68 E. D. Hirsch.

kind of organised relationship of divergencies is established[69], a model orientated on the reproduction of consensus replaces the old linear equilibrium model – which supposed fluctuations to be cancelled in a stable state of order – by a plural system making possible continuity within processes of change[70], induced by the creative task of the judiciary[71].

Considering and evaluating the fundamental change outlined – which, of course, did not come about without contradiction – it could be valuable to repeat the test done above, i.e. to consider the importance of analogy within this new evolutionary step of introducing flexibility and innovation into jurisdiction. Let us, therefore, look again at the index of the Federal Court decisions on matter of civil law. Of course, the reservation as for the correct classification of the cases must be here repeated. But the evaluation of the cases is so significant that the problem of the reliability of the indexes can be disregarded. In the first 10 volumes (1951-52), 12 cases of (considered) analogy are enumerated. In the following period (vol. 11-90), the number varies between zero and two cases in every ten volumes. This means: in the beginning – in absolute numbers – a small but relatively high number of analogies can be registered. But the intensive practice of jurisdictional and methodical innovation apparently does not correspond – unlike the evolution during the Weimar Republic – to a rise in the importance of the analogy.

The same phenomenon can be registered in the jurisdiction of the Federal Constitutional Court: in the first ten volumes, eight cases of (considered) analogy (including cases of extensive interpretation) are enumerated. In the following indexes, one finds only between none and three cases. It is worth mentioning that especially during periods of judicial activism in the '60s and '70s no cases at all can be found[72]. The same evolution can be observed

69 Höfling, *loc. cit.* (Fn. 51), p. 80.

70 Canaris, *loc. cit.* (Fn. 1), p. 22; see also J. Esser, *Grundsatz und Norm in der richterlichen Rechtsfortbildung des Privatrechts*, Tübingen, 3. Aufl., 1974.

71 Cf. *Bundesverfassungsgericht*, Dec. 34, p. 34.

72 Cf. F. Hase/K. H. Ladeur, *Verfassungsgerichtsbarkeit und politisches System*, Frankfurt/New York, 1980; see also R. Wiethölter, *Zum Fortbildungsrecht der*

in the jurisdiction of the Federal Administrative Court: in the indexes of the first 70 volumes of decisions, three cases are registered. Partially this is due to the above-mentioned restriction of analogy in traditional police law. But the rise of the interventionist (planning) state has, of course, lessened the importance of this principle, and yet the increase in methodical and substantive innovation which can be observed in administrative law, too, apparently did not lead to the increased importance of analogical reasoning. (One reason for this development is possibly to be found in the fact that the Federal Administrative Court appears to be less sensitive to problems of methodology; but this cannot be the main reason. The Federal Constitutional Court by now has taken over the leading role in the process of evolution of public law, because administrative law is more and more permeated by constitutional principles)[73].

This empirical test can be summarised as follows: increasing flexibility and innovation of the jurisdiction in civil, administrative and constitutional law does not correspond to a rise in analogical reasoning. On the contrary, the number of decisions referring to analogy has even fallen behind that of the period before World War I. This does not mean that analogy has totally disappeared from the practice of the judiciary, it still, presumably, plays its role in the practice of the lower courts. But it can be generalised that its contribution to the restructuring and flexibilisation of the legal system in the Federal Republic is negligible. This is probably due to the fact that analogy is a procedure of *punctual*, exceptional loosening of the rigid deductivism of the classical legal model whereas the introduction of more explicit methods of "concretisation" introducing more openness to innovation in legal methods seems to leave little room for analogy.

(richterlichen) Rechtsfortbildung, in "Kritische Vierteljahresschrift für Gesetzgebung und Rechtswissenschaft", 1988, p. 1ss.

73 Gern, *loc. cit.* (Fn. 48).

6. ON THE RELATIONSHIP OF UNITY AND MULTIPLICITY WITHIN THE NEW PARADIGM OF "CONCRETISATION" OF LAW

The influential methodological analysis by J. Esser "Pre-understanding and Choice of Methods in Jurisdiction" ("Vorverständnis und Methodenwahl in der Rechtsfindung")[74] is quite characteristic of the space left for analogy in the new doctrinal conception: the specificity of the new tendency is seen – just as in K. Hesse – in the assumption that the legal hypothesis is no longer regarded as a logical calculus: according to him, "the judgement of the applicant of norms has a greater scope of evaluation which the technical legal system and conventional ordinary language leave open to the comparisons intended" by analogy[75]. The ordering model of the law should be understood prospectively from the telos and not retrospectively from the standpoint of a "closed systems of signs". Analogy, in this sense, presents itself as a "mode of evaluation for cases which from pre-understanding and pre-evaluating deserve equal evaluation"[76].

It is a method of "heuristic" reference which in analogical judgement only finds its formal expression. "Thinking by analogy remains ... problem thinking which starts from the known case and by a topical approach to particular evaluations regarded as relevant turns over to re-constructed solutions"[77]. The analogical process of "association of concrete factual findings" is revealed as "jurisdictional law-making"whose teleological commitments to a legal order seen as proactive, and no longer as only retrospective norm setting confirms itself in the "search for points of reference, criteria and possibilities of comparison"[78].

74 Esser, *loc. cit.* (Fn. 61), p. 34.

75 Esser, *loc. cit.* (Fn. 61), p. 34.

76 Esser, *loc. cit.* (Fn. 61), p. 110; MacCormick, *loc. cit.* (Fn. 27), p. 186; for the Italian discussion see A. Giuliani, *Le raisonnement par analogie*, in: "Rapports nationaux au Congrès international de droit comparé", Budapest, 1978, p. 81ss.

77 Esser, *loc. cit.* (Fn. 61), p. 185; id., *loc. cit.* (Fn. 70), p. 231.

78 Esser, *loc. cit.* (Fn. 61), p. 185; id., *loc. cit.* (Fn. 70), p. 253.

As the norm does not contain a detailed design of solutions, but has to be "steered at its target", the process of compatibilisation of the demands of the ordering model and of the situative rationality with its surplus of possible references to new situations is open to evaluation and, as a consequence, analogy appears at first sight as a particular version but not as an exception to the rule.

But the new "evaluative jurisdiction" is – as mentioned above – still orientated on the "unity of language understanding of the applier of the norm"[79]. In contrast to earlier conceptions of logical closure of the legal system, its homogeneity can no longer be pre-supposed as the unity of the particular and the universal but it has to be reproduced. This is an aspect which is still more definite in Ch. Perelman's conception of the change from the "logic of truth" to the "logic of acceptability"[80].

Legal argumentation has a logical character only in a broader sense insofar as the multiple arguments are structured by certain preconditions, a constellation which cannot be identified with the development of unbound consideration of plausibility. For a feedback process is establishing itself between the preconditions of the law (and their pre-understanding) and the "post-understanding" brought about by argumentation.

But, after all, the "judgement of the rule applier"[81] takes on the function of decentralisation of the "inner relationships of the legal system"[82]. The opening of the system remains limited: the aim is relatively fixed, only the ways of its implementation and realisation seem to be unstructured: the situation itself is ascribed a rationality which is to be kept compatible with that of the aim.

In the end, this new methodological version stays within the domain of negative feedbacks as conceived by the model of the "first cybernetics" (H.v. Foerster), which does not question the aim but, rather, adapts the process of

79 Esser, *loc. cit.* (Fn. 61), p. 34.

80 Ch. Perelman, *Logique juridique, nouvelle rhétorique*, 2nd. ed., Brussels, 1979, p. 175ss.; G. Timsit, *Thèmes et systèmes de droit*, Paris, 1986, p. 110ss.

81 Esser, *loc. cit.* (Fn. 61), p. 34.

82 v. Savigny, *loc. cit.* (Fn. 8), pp. 290, 294.

implementation to the reactions of the environment. For this problem again analogy is a proper test case: it is said to be a "way of relationing in case of evident equivalence of normative problems", a momentum of surprise which, by way of "pre-understanding and pre-evaluation", is adapted to the unity of the aim[83].

It still starts from "evidence", which is equivalent to the linearity of legal reasoning. The correspondence of the particular and the universal is now *processed* by the feedback, which itself is mediated by the horizontal-situative rationality of the substratum of regulation; this catalyst function is Arthur Kaufmann's "nature of matter" (Natur der Sache). But it is precisely this "materiality" of the "nature of matter" which is no longer beyond doubt. The process of mediating the legal text and the facts of life does not lead out of the linguistic nature of the experience of norm and world[84]: the situation and the situative rationality present themselves as a context or better: co-text[85] of the legal text, whose meaning remains preliminary because of its dependence on its "viability" within certain forms of life. The "nature of matter" does not create a new "material" unity of the particular and the universal. It stands for a moment of order within a play of differences[86], whose reverse side, the moment of creativity, of "disorder" which cannot be eliminated[87], it suppresses.

In my view, this is due to the fact that the whole form of life, to which the new paradigm is committed is determined by groups and organisations. Therewith a "pluralistic" momentum is introduced and, at the same time, it is limited by the rule of the game. These are establishing the process of re-

83 Esser, *loc. cit.* (Fn. 61), p. 110.

84 For "topical" argumentation theory see Th. Viehweg, *Topik und Jurisprudenz*, Munich, 1953.

85 Parret, *loc. cit.* (Fn. 46).

86 Cf. J. F. Lyotard, *Le différend*, Paris, 1983; J. W. Murphy, *Deconstruction, Discourse and Liberation*, in "Social Science Information", 1987, pp. 417, 421.

87 I. Prigogine/I. Stengers, *Order out of Chaos*, London, 1984.

production of unity by "institutionalising schemes and gestalten"[88] inscribed into the form of life which secure an acceptable construction of the multiple "reality" and its collective dissemination. The linguistic patterns just because of their attachment to certain practices appear to be "natural" and "material", i.e. to be part of "Natur der Sache".

Analogy remains an exception – now – to the new paradigm institutionalising more flexibility and variability. The moment of heterogeneity, the auto-correction, which is proper to it – and which in the classical legal science is seen as a phenomenon of deviation of the particular and the universal – now is thematicised as a problem of broadened perception. It is not the objective deviation, the failure of the legislator, which has led to a "gap" within the normative structure, which makes a problem. But, rather, to the judge's "pre-understanding" and "pre-evaluation" problems appear to be equivalent which the legislator has apparently differentiated. Here a restriction of the procedure of topical argumentation must be considered, for Esser does not accept treating the law as one topos among others. This would question the *unity* of the linguistic understanding. As the new method opens itself to the evaluation of the judge within the process committed to the realization of the normative goal and as it no longer trusts the self-explication of the legal text within a hierarchically structured legal order, it must still be attached to the steering effect of the pre-understanding and the "consensus" of norm and decision – and this means analogy remains in the end an exception.

This reflection allows for a look back at the analysis of the role of analogy in the jurisdiction of the Weimar Republic. The greater frequency of the reference to analogy is merely a symptom of the lack of integration of the legal system, of the increasing heterogeneity of concurring norms and values. The belief in the hierarchical order of the legal system had broken away, but, at the same time, the new procedural mediation of norm and facts of life, by way of the restructuring effects of the "nature of matter", was not able to bring stability because of the lack of the integrative potential of social forces. This is why unsystematic-punctual procedure of ana-

88 C. Castoriadis, *Merleau-Ponty und die Last des ontologischen Erbes*, in A. Métraux/B. Waldenfels (eds.), "Leibhaftige Vernunft. Spuren von Merleau-Pontys Denken", München, 1986, pp. 111, 122.

logical reasoning had a greater importance in previous epochs of legal history.

7. A NEW EVOLUTIONARY STEP TOWARDS A "TRANSVERSAL RATIONALITY"?

Has analogy exhausted its potential or is it confined to a marginal role of making possible and, at the same time, limiting the oscillation of innovation at the margins of the existing order?

The still-existing irritating momentum of analogy consisted and continues to exist in the "surprising" confrontation with a conflict: something does not conform to experience and the classification scheme defined by law (the older paradigm) or it does not conform to teleological pre-understanding of the project of a legal order. And the new is not allowed to question the existing order or – in the recent perspective – the order to be created and this is why it is re-integrated and subsumed by the broadening of its rules.

The self-description attributed to the legal system – which serves the perception of relevances in the decision process – in both methodological versions is, after all, dominated by the expectation of continuity and equilibrium. The phenomenon which is to be processed by analogical reasoning asks for a self-correction of the rule by intervention of a meta-rule of a higher order (a legal principle) or – as seen by the new paradigm – the teleological pre-understanding meets with an evident self-contradiction because the goal has been formulated too narrowly and a phenomenon to be evaluated equally has been overseen. The "side-look"[89], the referring perspective, the momentum of abduction emerging from the interplay of the particular and the universal and the posterior control by deduction confronts the system which is orientated on continuous homogeneity with unregulated creativity – which was totally suppressed under the previous paradigm and still now is suffocated by the reference to the "self-evident" necessity of self-correction of the legal system. The criterion of "self-evidence" im-

89 Eschbach, *loc. cit.* (Fn. 20).

plies a homogeneity of the standards of law[90] and bars the access to the morphogenesis of the law as a process of self-organisation of the fields of experience, actions and language which are not integrated by fixed principles[91].

The selectivity of the structuring perspective which – seen from a constructivist point of view-underlies the classical and the new paradigm, is, on the one hand, – and this is its legitimation basis – necessary for the perception of differences made possible by a "cut"[92] into the flow of events (a "distinction"), and, on the other hand, especially because of the insight into the constructed character of systems of order, selectivity is only imaginable as the product of a provisional model among other possible models[93]. For – and this could be opposed to the new paradigm as well –: "The totalising perspective as well as the perspective from above miss the proper emergence of the change of order, they miss also the reflection of the conflict rising from the clash of heterogeneous orders and which is not settled by some fundamental order"[94]. The assumption of harmony between the particular and the universal – hidden behind the old as well as the new paradigm –, the assumption of a smooth order in which "the particular only gets its right insofar as it is compatible with something else and fits into the whole" is severed under the simultaneity of the heterogenous and the multiple[95].

An order based on selection and, therewith, exclusion cannot be done away with, but the confrontation with uncertainty and the multiplicity of relationing possibilities and the transformation of the self-description underlying the legal system imposes the necessity of a greater openness to inno-

90 R. Schürmann, *Legislation and Transgression*, in "Man and World ", 1984, p. 361ss.

91 Waldenfels, *loc. cit.* (Fn. 66), p. 58.

92 Cf. G. Spencer Brown, *Laws of Form*, London, 1969.

93 G. F. Lanzara, *Il problema della generatività dei sistemi sociali complessi*, in A. Ardigò/G. Mazzoli (eds.), "Intelligenzia artificiale", Milano, 1986, pp. 175, 192.

94 B. Waldenfels, *Ordnung im Zwielicht*, Frankfurt, 1987, p. 157.

95 Waldenfels, *loc. cit.* (Fn. 94), p. 191.

vation, the excluded "other" of disorder and the emergence of self-organisation of new order.

This means the legal system would not only – as did the model of the "first cybernetic"– have to consider the reaction-potential of the situations to be regulated by way of a *procedural* teleological order of concretisation, but it would have to institutionalise a broader permeability for momentums of self-transformation of the goals themselves, especially by accepting heterogenity[96]. This means the legal system can no longer orient itself on a pre-existing "layer" of legal principles guaranteeing wholeness and integration, but it must turn over to the possibility and necessity of building models which construct and reconstruct themselves from the "dialogue with uncertainty"[97]. The consequences to be drawn from this assumption cannot be outlined in detail here. For the context of our subject it means, above all, that the irritation stirred by the new, the "other" of disorder, is not to be filtered through the threshold of evidence – defined by the expectations of the "normal" –, but should be processed proactively in *search* strategies.

The accentuating of the element of creative "transversal" abduction which hitherto remained hidden between the inductive component and that vertical (deductive) reintegration through the limitation of the "side-look" to that which is "self-evident" can, once freed, open the view to other possibilities which are implied in a situation and which, simultaneously, are reflected as references[98].

The accent on "evidence" raises the threshold of attention to the new and, therewith, tries to preserve the coherence of the legal order and, at the same time, blocks the necessary creation of sensibility and permeability to learning processes by restricting the perception of variety and self-organised transversal non-evident transformation of values and by barring the coexis-

96 E. Morin, *La Méthode 3. La connaissance de la connaissance*, vol. 1, Paris, 1986, p. 61.

97 Morin, *loc. cit.* (Fn. 96), p. 62.

98 F. Inciarte, *Eindeutigkeit und Variation*, Freiburg/Munich, 1973, pp. 80, 126.

tence of a plurality of values[99].

This assumption does not imply a general postulate of morphogenesis of "order out of chaos"[100]. But, in many social fields characterised by complexity (culture, planning, telecommunication, environment, high technology etc.), the creation of variety must be generated by procedural search strategies, which submit order *and* creativity to a conflictual, heterogeneous relationship, probing the multiplicity of alternatives appearing with the particular "moves" of the game for new possibilities of order[101].

The accent is then shifted from the deductive perspective on the unity, eliminating that which does not fit into the teleological pre-understanding, to a "laterally" proceeding creative operation with relationing possibilities[102], created by the co-evolution of the legal system. The institutional component built into the legal perception takes on a character which comes into "play"[103] and is decentred therewith[104].

The multiplicity, the possibility of provocation by the "other", the surprise, would no longer be filtered away by strict supposition of order and evident goals but would, rather, be accepted by a rationality conceived as "transversal", a rationality living from the entanglement of legal texts and the co-texts they are inscribed by the situation. Analogous reasoning as a form of "transversal rationality" functions as a potential of transcending of

99 Cf. also H. Willke, in M. Glasgow/id. (eds.), *Dezentrale Gesellschaftssteuerung*, Pfaffenweiler, 1988, p. 24.

100 Prigogine/Stengers, *loc. cit.* (Fn. 87).

101 M. Zeleny, *Integrated Knowledge Management*, in "Human Systems Management", 1987, p. 59ss.

102 Waldenfels, *loc. cit.* (Fn. 94), p. 209.

103 Schürmann, *loc. cit.* (Fn. 90), p. 362; S. Benhabib, *Kritik des 'post modernen' Wissens. Eine Auseinandersetzung mit J.F. Lyotard*, in A. Huyssen/K. Scherpe (eds.), "Postmoderne. Zeichen eines kulturellen Wandels", Reinbek, 1986, pp. 103, 109.

104 J. Culler, *On Deconstruction*, London, etc. 1983, pp. 139s., 251.

closed rationalities[105]. It "passes over from one configuration of rationality to another, it articulates differences, ties relations and organises conflict and change. Its proceeding is horizontal and transitive..."[106]. It assumes unity only as a procedural form of a productive working out of differences without ever being able to hope for the transcending of the incommensurability of existing order and existing disorder as a potential source of a new and different order[107]. Order can no longer develop a hierarchical system or even be concretised from a prospective unitary goal, it remains inserted into a field of "oscillation between irregularity, deregulation and re-regulation"[108].

This model certainly needs dogmatic differentiation. But a first step can be resumed inasmuch as this new tendency does not comprise the whole system – there are still domains left which can be perceived from the previous perspectives, i.e. whose permeability to different possibilities can remain limited. But in the above-mentioned action fields the necessity of the orientation of the law on an extended potential of self-reflection and self-transformation accompanying the multiplication of options is felt most vitally. The "substrate" confronting the law in the new action fields is, rather, a complex of possibilities of network formation and relationing than a constant or even continuously changing reality. Within the action fields corresponding to the older paradigms, analogy can continue to function in the classical manner or in the more flexible version of the paradigm of concretisation of law can create limited possibilities of variation. But in those domains which can only be approached from a procedurally operating "transversal rationality", analogical reasoning which would not let the projected order bar its "referring look", would search actively for *abductive* relationing which would not be superseded by deductive reintegration[109] of the legal order but which, on the contrary, provokes experimental law conceived

105 W. Welsch, *Unsere postmoderne Moderne*, Weinheim, 1987, p. 296.

106 Welsch, *loc. cit.* (Fn. 105), p. 296.

107 Welsch, *loc. cit.* (Fn. 105), p. 296.

108 Waldenfels, *loc. cit.* (Fn. 66), p. 90.

109 Esser, *loc. cit.* (Fn. 61), p. 110.

as self-revising in a continuous manner. In this view, law can only function as a constructivist model which does not try to subsume the one and only reality, but creates more "realities"[110] and always keeps the question of justice open insofar as it ascertains the permeability of the legal order to new values[111].

110 G. J. B. Probst, *Management als Konstruktion von Wirklichkeiten – die Konsequenz der 'Verantwortung'*, in: Delfin VII (1986), pp. 60, 62.

111 J. P. Arnason, *Praxis und Interpretation*, Frankfurt, 1988, p. 296.

ANALOGY AS LEGAL REASONING
The hermeneutic foundation of the analogical procedure*

GIUSEPPE ZACCARIA

1. LEGAL UNDERSTANDING AS ANALOGICAL UNDERSTANDING

When in 1965 there appeared among the publications of the Karlsruhe Society for Legal Studies Arthur Kaufmann's article *Analogie und "Natur der Sache" : Zugleich ein Beitrag zur Lehre vom Typus*[1], response to the theses and arguments set out in it was considerable. What the German jurist was maintaining was that by its nature every application of law, every *Rechtsfindung*, consists not in a conclusion of formal-logical type identifiable as simple subsumption, but in a process of analogical type[2]. What caused astonishment in many jurists, not to say a gut reaction of rejection, was probably one very specific aspect of the problem: Kaufmann ended up dis-

* Report presented to the International Workshop "Analogy in legal science", held at the European University Institute, Florence, 10-11 October 1988.

1 Heidelberg, Decker und Müller, 1982 (2nd revised edition). There is an English translation of Kaufmann's paper by I.Tammelo, *Analogy and "The Nature of Things" ; A Contribution to the Theory of Types*, in "Journal of the Indian Law Institute", 8, 1966, p. 358-401. Among the main reviews of this important article, see I. and L. Tammelo, in "ARSP", 52, 1966, p. 148ff.; Klekatsky, in "Juristische Blätter", 1966, p. 486; T. Mayer-Maly, in "Juristenzeitung", 1967, p. 685ff. An interesting collection of responses to his article is supplied by Kaufmann himself in the *Nachwort* to the 2nd edition of the work, p. 60ff.

2 *Analogie und "Natur der Sache"*, *op. cit.*, p. 18ff., 37ff., 61.

puting the prevailing methodological opinion that there is a qualitative difference between interpretation and analogy, so that they can be separated from each other and distinguished; even if as is generally admitted it is not always easy to draw an exact boundary between the two operations. In fact, the legitimate demand to specify what this qualitative criterion is, which underlies and justifies the essential difference between extensive teleological interpretation and the search for the law of analogical type, is destined in the main to remain disappointed.

Kaufmann's lucid theses dropped like a large heavy stone spreading ever-widening ripples across the smooth surface of methodology and *Rechtslehre* in Germany: law – this is the main argument – is the correspondence between *is* and *ought*, between legal norm and the case in point[3]. It is only when *Sein* and *Sollen*, a specific life relationship and one or more norms, are brought into correspondence that law can be made concrete, that law becomes actual. This correspondence between *is* and *ought* means, however, that the knowledge, application and securing of law are based on a fundamentally analogical basis[4].

Familiar in the logic and methodology of the sciences, but also a widely used form of argumentation in the legal sphere where it counts among the

3 *Analogie und "Natur der Sache"*, *op. cit.*, p. 18ff., 37ff., 61.

4 Kaufmann's thesis is explicitly accepted by J. Hruschka, *Das Verstehen von Rechtstexten*, Munich, Beck, 1972, p. 102, Italian trans. by R. de Giorgi, Naples, Edizioni Scientifiche Italiane, 1983,p. 98; by F. Haft, *Generalklauseln und unbestimmte Begriffe im Strafrecht*, in "Juristische Schulung", 1975, p. 477ff., Strafrecht Allg. T., Munich, Beck, 1980, p. 37, and by W. Hassemer, *Einführung in die Grundlagen des Strafrechts*, Munich, Beck, 1981, p. 255. But the analogical nature of the procedure of applying and finding the law is also recognized, though with different accents, by M. Diesselhorst, *Die Natur der Sache als außergesetzliche Rechtsquelle*, Tübingen, Mohr, 1968, p. 223ff.; J. Esser, *Vorverständnis und Methodenwahl in der Rechtsfindung. Rationalitätsgrundlagen richterlicher Entscheidungspraxis*, Frankfurt a. M., Athenaeum, 1972 (2nd ed.), pp. 32ff., 183ff., Italian trans. by S. Patti and G. Zaccaria, Naples, Edizioni Scientifiche Italiane, 1983, pp. 28ff., 179ff.; W. Fikentscher, Methoden des Rechts in vergleichender Darstellung, Tübingen, Mohr, vol. III, 1076, p. 311ff.; L. Reisinger, *Zur Struktur der Analogie im Rechtsdenken, in Argumentation und Hermeneutik in der Jurisprudenz*, edited by W. Krawietz, K. Opalek, A. Peczenik, A. Schramm, in "Rechtstheorie", Beih. 1, Berlin, Duncker und Humblot, 1979, p. 271ff.; C. and O. Weinberger, *Logik, Semantik, Hermeneutik*, Munich, Beck, 1979, p. 166ff.; K. Larenz, *Methodenlehre der Rechtswissenschaft*, Berlin, Heidelberg, New York, Tokyo, Springer, 1983 (5th ed.), pp. 365ff.

tools that constitute the proper object of study for legal logic, reasoning by analogy has rather conspicuous classical antecedents: it was analysed by Aristotle in the *Prior Analytics* of his *Organon*, but there is no doubt that the very concept of "analogy" is extremely ancient, arising, it might be said, with man himself. One of the earliest and clearest images of the analogical model can in fact be found in verses 26 and 27 of *Genesis* Chapter 1: "And God said 'Let us make man in our image, after our likeness' ". But the translation risks losing sight of the true meaning of the original wording: *selem* (image) indicates the statue, or something plastically similar to the reality to be depicted, while *demut* (likeness) is instead an abstraction indicating a less exact, direct resemblance. Man is therefore similar, analogous, to God, and at the same time something very similar to God, but also something not fully identified with God[5].

In the broader context of knowledge, reasoning by analogy, as has always been recognized with classic simplicity in philosophical speculation, undoubtedly represents the dynamic, driving factor of all epistemological or research procedure, the internal, constitutively operating law of all concrete thought: while for Hegel it was the "Identität der Identität und Nichtidentität"[6], for Heidegger analogy is "Zusammengehörigkeit von Identität und Differenz", while for Mach it is the *Leitmotiv* of scientific research[7]. The speculative significance of analogy is, in short, in its bringing to light the structure of being as such and in its relationship with totality: the use of the word analogy refers immediately to diversity, but at the same time to a relationship, a relation; it involves, as the very etymology of the word says, a diversity that is necessarily led back to a point of reference, a centre: *analogos* means nothing other than according to the *logos*, corresponding to *logos*.

But if it is true that law regarded as a system is not only a unity of norms but also a logical, unitary connection of elements, a whole made up

5 Cf. G. F. Ravasi, *Il libro della Genesi*/1, Bologna, Dehoniane, 1988, p. 114.

6 G. W. F. Hegel, *Sämtliche Werke*, edited by H. Glockner, Stuttgart, 1927-1939, I, p. 31ff., IV, pp. 508ff., 525ff.

7 E. Mach, *Die Ähnlichkeit und die Analogie als Leitmotiv der Forschung*, in "Ann. der Naturphilosophie", 1902.

of elements and of the relations and correspondences that unite them, then what has just been said about knowledge in general – namely that all knowledge aimed at broadening our understanding is always and necessarily analogical – must needs apply to legal knowledge too. All knowledge of law, all *Rechtsfindung*, every subsumptive conclusion, possesses an essentially analogical structure. By making its moves and being applied where there is no longer unambiguousness and full identity, interpretation is always located in the field of the analogical[8]; it allows one to perceive how much identity there is in difference, how much coherence and unitarity emerges from the fragmentariness of the manifold. The fact that the content of the legal imperative is not definable outside of the confrontation with specific examples of application (which specify its dimensions, limits and underlying criteria) is, perhaps, most immediately and easily recognizable in the legal systems of common law, in which the characteristics of the imperative "are derived through analogical comparisons with specific situations of conflict from previous decisions, and transferred through analogical thought to the dispute in the given case"[9]. But recourse to analogical thought comes about, though perhaps less evidently, also in the case where

[8] A. Kaufmann, *Analogie und "Natur der Sache"*, *op. cit.*, pp. 4-5.

[9] Esser, *Vorverständnis und Methodenwahl, op. cit.*, p. 33, Italian trans. op. cit., p. 28. On the use of analogy in the tradition of the common-law system, see J. Stone, *Legal System and Lawyer's Reasoning*, Sydney, Maitland, 1968, p. 312ff.; R. Rinaldi, Is *Analogy a Decision Process in English Law?*, in *Le raisonnement juridique*. Actes du Congrès mondial de philosophie du droit et de philosophie sociale, edited by H. Hubien, Brussels, Bruylant, 1971, pp. 363-374; D. Lloyd, *Introduction to Jursiprudence*, London, 1969, Stevens and Sons, p. 384; J. R. Murray, *The Role of Analogy in Legal Reasoning*, in "UCLA Law Review", 1982, pp. 833-871; M. P. Golding, *The Logical Force of Arguments by Analogy in Common Law Reasoning*, in "Reason in Law", Proceedings of the Conference held in Bologna, 12-15 December 1984, vol. 3, edited by C. Faralli and E. Pattaro, Milan, Giuffrè, 1988, pp. 273-279; but also the classic G. Hammond, *Legal and Political Hermeneutics*, 1880 (3rd ed.), p. 278ff.; J. Austin, *Excursus on Analogy*, in "Lectures on Jurisprudence", New York, Burt Franklin, 1970, p. 249ff.; B. Cardozo, *Selected Writings*, ed. M. E. Hall, New York, Fallon, 1947, p. 108ff.; E. H. Levi, *An Introduction to Legal Reasoning*, Chicago and London, 1949, p. 4ff. For a comparative survey of the major conceptions of reasoning by analogy in the various national legal systems, cf. L. Legaz Lacambra, *Le raisonnement par analogie comme méthode d'interprétation et d'application du droit dans les différents systèmes nationaux*, in "General reports to the 10th International Congress of Comparative Law", Budapest, Akadémiai Kiadò, 1981, pp. 73-90.

the judge has to describe and judge, on the basis of a legal norm, a definite situation of fact within an order of closed type: in this case, in fact, "on the basis of the norm, a palette of presumable cases of application must be derived, with which the actual one can be confronted". Thus, "the constitution of a common level of judgement for the concepts of the system, utilized in a legislative case in point, with the determining concepts of common spoken language or of a technical commercial language, for judgement of the situation of fact, is possible only in the form of an analogical relationship"[10]. Not only do we see the uninterrupted emergence of ever-new specific situations, but even the apparently similar situations are never so in every detail. Experience, and hence also legal experience, is full of analogies and differences. The unity of the system is not achieved by sacrificing the differences, but by bringing them back to the unity of the normative discipline: outside of a hermeneutic use of analogy, the consideration of law would take the shape of a datum always identical to itself and expressed once and for all, in a way that necessarily rules out any possibility of subsequent enrichment.

Still more exactly, we may say that *Rechtsfindung* is the progressive construction of the relationship of correspondence between the normative datum, formulated in the legal facts of a case, and the concrete datum, through a procedure establishing their resemblance, equating them[11]. Naturally, since there is never on one side the *genus* abstractly hypothesized by the norm and perfectly corresponding *ab initio* with the *species*, represented by the specific situation offered by experience, while on the other no actual circumstance, no case, can be said to be perfectly equal to another, complete and total equation is not even attempted by the interpreter, and cannot come about[12]. Every particular case is distinguished from every other particular

10 Esser, *Vorverständnis und Methodenwahl, op. cit.*, p. 33; Italian trans., *op. cit.*, p. 28.

11 More broadly, on these aspects of the procedure of identifying the law, see our article *L'ermeneutica, in Interpretazione e decisione. Diritto ed economia*, Atti del XVI Congresso Nazionale di Filosofia del diritto, edited by F. Gentile, Milan, Giuffrè, 1989; esp. p. 67ff.

12 For a different opinion see V. Peschka, *Typus und Analogie im Recht*, in "ARSP", LXVI, 1980 p. 85, for whom the relationship between norm and case in application is not

case. Looked at properly, in the interpreter's operation of subsumption it is not so much the material facts that are subsumed – how indeed could they be? – as the declaration that the characteristics contained in the legal description are present also in the specific fact that is the object of judgement. More than an assessment of total identity, subsumption concerns an assessment of substantial analogy between actual events that have to be disciplined and circumstances of fact that can be brought within the minor premise of the interpretive syllogism. Between specific cases, all that is possible is a degree of coincidence that is sufficient for the interpreter to establish correspondence.

The assertion that the two polarities of Sollen and Sein, while remaining distinct, come increasingly closer together to the point of meeting in the procedure of Rechtsverwirklichung[13] certainly does not mean "liquefying" the objectivity of the content of the norm by reducing it to an interpretive process and thereby orienting the decision exclusively towards the individual case[14]. Indeed there remains, in all its relevance, the need for a legal description of the fact which can undoubtedly not be derived "automatically" from the specific situation alone. But it is just as clear that the establishment of the normative content of a specific situation, just like clarification of the contents actually contained in a norm, cannot come about through separate, isolated acts, but only in a reciprocal procedure of gradual approach and adjustment[15], which at the point of the actual legal decision arrives definitively at the adaequatio: a procedure which, as is the very nature of our understanding, is fundamentally, but productively, circu-

a relationship of resemblance but of identity, even though this identity is understood in a highly dialectical fashion.

13 For a criticism of this sort of description of legal proceeding see M. Kriele, *Theorie der Rechtsgewinnung entwickelt am Problem der Verfassungsinterpretation*, Berlin, Duncker und Humblot, 1976 (2nd ed.), p. 205.

14 Unlike F. Haft, *Falldenken statt Normdenken: Einige Bemerkungen und "Normempfehlungen" zur juristischen Sprachverwendung*, in "Der öffentliche Sprachgebrauch", vol. III, p. 153ff.

15 On this see A. Kaufmann, *Analogie und "Natur der Sache"*, *op. cit.*, p. 70.

lar[16] . Let us now shift our attention to analogical reasoning as such. In analogical interpretation, regarded as an extra-textual means of interpreting law founded upon reasoning by analogy and aimed at making the legal system complete in the event that it presents a lacuna[17], it is undoubtedly the interpreter that has the task of considering whether two situations may have the same legal value for the purpose of treating their resemblance as relevant, just as in the case of Rechtsfindung mentioned above it was for the interpreter himself to carry out the operation of bringing the legal statement into correspondence with the actuality of the case presented by experience.

The time is ripe, then, to bring up a first question: what is there in common in the procedures of analogical interpretation in the strict sense and the "normal" *Rechtsfindung* of the jurist? We can say that in both cases it is only after the "preparation of the premises" (which consists in setting up a resemblance between two legal cases, that is in supplying a pre-assessment of the appropriateness of the correspondence between the normative datum and the datum from the life-world) that analogical reason can act with the "logical status" of a syllogism. Before subsumption, the norm and the

16 A. Kaufmann, *Über den Zirkelschluss in der Rechstfindung*, in "Beiträge zur juristischen Hermeneutik", Cologne, Berlin, Bonn, Munich, Carl Heymanns, 1984, pp. 65-77.

17 For a first approach, among the vast literature see, N. Bobbio, *L'analogia nella logica del diritto*, Turin, Istituto Giuridico, 1938; U. Klug, *Juristische Logik*, Berlin, Springer, 1951, p. 98ff. (4th ed. 1982); L. Caiani, entry *Analogia*, in "Enciclopedia del Diritto", II, Milan, 1958, pp. 349-378; H. Bartholomeyczik, *Die Kunst der Gesetzesauslegung. Eine wissenschaftliche Hilfe zur praktischen Rechtsanwendung*, Frankfurt a. M., Kommentator GMBH, 1960 (2nd ed.); T. Heller, *Logik und Axiologie der analogen Rechtsanwendung*, Berlin, De Gruyter, 1961; E. Garcia Maynez, *Die Argumente a simili ad simile, a maiori ad minus und a minori ad maius*, in "ARSP", Beih. 41, 1965, pp. 115-135; N. Amato, *Logica simbolica e diritto*, Milan, Giuffrè, 1969, p. 392ff.; I. Tammelo, *Outlines of Modern Legal Logic*, Wiesbaden, Steiner, 1969, p. 129ff.; G. Lazzaro, *Argomenti dei giudici*, Turin, s. e., 1970; R. Alexy, *Theorie der juristichen Argumentation. Die Theorie des rationalen Diskurses als Theorie der juristischen Begründung*, Frankfurt a. M., Suhrkamp, 1978, p. 343ff.; G. Tarello, *L'interpretazione della legge*, Milan, Giuffrè, 1980, pp. 350-355; L. Gianformaggio, *L'analogia giuridica*, in, "Studi Senesi" XCVII, 1985, pp. 430-451 and in "Digesto" IV ed., vol. I, Turin, Utet, 1987, pp. 320-329; M. Atienza, *Sobre la analogia en el Derecho. Ensayo de analisis de un razionamento juridico*, Madrid, Civitas, 1986; *Idem, Algunas Tesis sobre la analogia en el Derecho*, in "Doxa. Cuadernos de Filosofia del Derecho" no. 2, 1985, pp. 223-229: *Idem, L'analogie en droit*, in "Revue interdisciplinaire d'études juridiques", 1988, 21, pp. 33-56.

specific case in the one operation and legally similar situations in the other must be made capable of subsumption[18]: both in legal interpretation and in argument from analogy, the core of the procedure is in fact in the value judgement that concerns the relationship running between the norm and the fact on the one hand, and equality of the legal value of the two cases compared on the other[19].

Accordingly, from an analogical viewpoint in a very broad sense, in the sense from which the general methodological need for recourse to analogy emerges, every interpretation of law, just like every finding that extends our knowledge in every sphere, whether theoretical or practical, of human life (from biology to anatomy, from epistemology to economics to theology) may legitimately be termed analogous.

2. ANALOGY AS AN EXCEPTIONAL HERMENEUTIC MEANS

If the typical and normal interpretive procedure which brings a factual circumstance into correspondence with a norm does not constitute a specific method for solving the problem of lacunae[20], the traditional *analogia*

18 K. Engisch, *Logische Studien zur Gesetzesanwendung*, Heidelberg, Winter, 1963 (3rd ed.), p. 26 speaks of "equation of the actual case to be judged with the cases indubitably intended by the legal description" and defines this as the "actual subsumption". Again from Engisch on analogy, see also *Einführung in das juristische Denken,* Stuttgart, Kohlhammer, 1977 (7th ed.), p. 146ff.; Italian trans. by A. Baratta and F. Giuffrida Repaci, Milan, Giuffrè, 1970, p. 230ff.

19 This latter aspect, that there necessarily is assessment at the basis of analogy, is convincingly stressed by Heller, *Logik und Axiologie der analogen Rechtsanwendung, op. cit.*, p. 93ff.; G. Kalinowski, *Introduction à la logique juridique*, Paris, Librairie générale de droit et de jurisprudence, 1972, Italian trans. by M. Corsale, Milan, Giuffrè, 1971, p. 232; Englisch, *Einführung, op. cit.*, p. 256, Italian trans., *op. cit.*, p. 236; R. Zippelius, *Rechtsphilosophische Aspekte der Rechtsfindung*, in "Juristenzeitung" 31 (1976), p. 153.

20 On this classic problem of theory of law, from among the endless bibliography see at least: E. Ehrlich, *Über Lücken im Recht*, in "Juristische Blätter", 1888, p. 447ff.; E. Zitelmann, *Lücken im Recht*, Leipzig, 1903; D. Donati, *Il problema delle lacune dell'ordinamento giuridico,* Milan, 1910; G. Brunetti, *Sul valore del problema delle*

legis[21] instead represents, as is well known, an atypical, subsidiary means, in a certain sense exceptional, whereby the rule given in the law for a case A is transferred to a case B not governed by the law but judged by the interpreter to be similar to A. Even though the distinction between *analogia legis* and *analogia iuris* was defined by legal thought only in relatively recent times[22], the substantive procedure aimed at filling in lacunae by recourse to analogical argument is undoubtedly much older. It is perhaps appropriate to recall that Roman lawyers already knew and widely used anal-

lacune, in "Scritti giuridici vari", I, Turin, 1915, pp. 34-45; *Il senso del problema delle lacune dell'ordinamento giuridico*, in "Scritti giuridici vari", III, Turin, 1920, pp. 1-29; W. Burckhardt, *Die Lücken des Gesetzes und die Gesetzesauslegung*, Bern 1925; S. Romano, *Osservazioni sulla completezza dell'ordinamento statale*, Modena, 1925; and *idem*, *Lo Stato moderno e la sua crisi. Saggi di diritto costituzionale*, pp. 171-185; K. Engisch, *Der Begriff der Rechtslücke. Eine analytische Studie zu Wilhelm Sauers Methodenlehre, in Festschrift für W. Sauer zu seinem 70. Geburtstag*, Berlin 1949 pp. 85-102; T. Ascarelli, *Il problema delle lacune e l'art. 3 disp. prelim. c. c. (1865) nel diritto privato*, in "Studi di diritto comparato e in tema di interpretazione", Milan, Giuffrè, 1953, pp. 209-243; Anna Ravà, *Il problema delle lacune dell'ordinamento giuridico e della legislazione canonica*, Milan, Giuffrè, 1954; K. Larenz, *Wegweiser zu richterlicher Rechtsschöpfung, in Festschrift für Arthur Nikisch*, Tübingen, 1958, p. 275 ff; A. G. Conte, *Saggio sulla completezza degli ordinamenti giuridici*, Turin, Giappichelli, 1962; C. W. Canaris, *Die Feststellung von Lücken im Gesetz. Eine methodologische Studie*, Berlin, Duncker und Humblot, 1964; J. Esser, *Grundsatz und Norm in der richterlichen Fortbildung des Privatrechts*, Tübingen, Mohr, 1974 (3rd ed.) 4 p. 179ff. See also, as well as Bobbio's entry *Lacune del diritto*, in "Novissimo Digesto Italiano", vol. IX, Torino, Utet, 1963 (with P. Comanducci's notes *Sulle lacune: note in margine a Bobbio*, in "L'analisi del ragionamento giuridico", ed. P. Comanducci and R. Guastini, vol. II, Turin, Giappichelli, 1989 pp. 207-213), the 1966 and 1967 years of "Logique et Analyse", as well as *Etudes de logique juridique*, ed. C. Perelman, Brussels, Bruylant, 1966 and 1967, and the collective volume *Le problème des lacunes en droit*, ed. C. Perelman, Brussels, Bruylant 1968.

21 On this hermeneutic method cf. A. Peczenik, *Analogia Legis, Analogy from Statutes in Continental Law*, in "Le raisonnement juridique", pp. 329-336. The existence of a clear distinction as regards both structure and outcome between *analogia legis* and *analogia iuris* is maintained by Bobbio, *L'analogia nella logica del diritto, op. cit.*, p. 152ff., while it is instead played down by A. Baratta, *Note in tema di analogia giuridica*, in "Studi in onore di Emilio Betti", Milan, Giuffrè, 1961, p. 577ff. and more recently by N. MacCormick, *Legal Reasoning and Legal Theory*, Oxford, Oxford University Press, 1978, pp. 153ff. and 186. On the concept of "normative coherence" in MacCormick, cf. our *Ermeneutica e comprensione narrativa*, in "Materiali per una storia della cultura giuridica", XVIII, 1988, p. 503ff.

22 Cf. Baratta, *Note in tema di analogia giuridica*, *op. cit.*, pp. 571ff., 590ff.

ogy as an interpretive method[23], while the glossators and commentators distinguished in the sphere of interpretation between "comprehensio legis" and "extensio legis": referring in the first case to the interpretation of words and the legislator's intent, in the second to procedures for supplementing the law. The *argumentum a similibus ad similia* can be seen as the typical example of the type of argumentation later termed analogy[24]. Analogy has, then, always represented an essential aspect of the jurist's practical wisdom, identifying a major part of his task of setting up analogical comparisons between different cases and identifying the decisive aspects of an equal or differentiated legal assessment; among the various types of interpretation – as Piovani appositely notes[25] – the analogical one by its very nature induces untrammelled confidence in the omniscient foresight of legislation.

It is certainly well-founded to note that today, with the technique of contemporary legislation preferentially developing through general clauses and standards, the case where specific situations do not have at least some aspect of foresight in norms is becoming increasingly rare; and that recourse to analogy as a way of filling lacunae is becoming increasingly infrequent, while the provision of forms of analogical explanation seems to be ever more frequent. But it might also be noted in a partly opposite direction that the so-called "regulatory lacunae"[26] regularly produced by the emergence of

23 Cf. A. Steinwenter, *Prolegomena zu einer Geschichte der Analogie*, in "Festschrift für F. Schulz", Weimar, Boelhaus, 1951, II, p. 344ff. On the history of legal analogy see also Bobbio, *L'analogia nella logica del diritto, op. cit.*, pp. 7-78, and the entry *Analogia*, in "Nov. Dig. It. ", I, Turin, Utet, 1968, p. 602ff.; P. Mortari, *Premessa storica,* under the entry *Analogia* in "Enclic. del dir. ", II, Milan, Giuffrè, 1958, p. 344ff.; A. Giuliani, *Le raisonnement par analogie*, in "Rapports Nationaux Italiens au Xe Congrès International de Droit Comparé Budapest 1978", Milan, Giuffrè, 1978, pp. 80-94.

24 On this cf. B. Brugi, *Per la storia della giurisprudenza italiana*, Turin, Nuovi saggi, 1921, p. 42ff.; Baratta, *Note in tema di analogia, op. cit.*, p. 571ff.; V. Villa, *Evoluzione e nuovi orientamenti del procedimento per analogia,* in F. Viola, V. Villa, M. Urso, *L'interpretazione e applicazione del diritto tra scienza e politica*, Palermo, Celup, 1974, p. 139ff.

25 *Linee di una filosofia del diritto*, Padua, Cedam, 1964 (2nd ed.), p. 156.

26 On this point see Larenz, *Methodenlehre der Rechtswissenschaft, op. cit.*, p. 357ff.; Zitelmann, *Lücken im Recht, op. cit.*, p. 27ff., speaks instead of "not real lacunae".

new economic and technological processes[27] (from the telephone to the computer, from atmospheric pollution to organ transplants to artificial insemination) necessarily tend to multiply and expand in periods of rapid social and technological change. This is so, and this must be said though it is not possible to dwell on it, even though it is not always licit to confuse the legislator's inaction or indecision in offering legislative discipline for a particular subject with a real "lacuna" in the law.

In fact, in the classical conception of the legal system, typical of the most rigorous positive-law theories, analogy constituted a specific means of filling the extremely rare and in any case exceptional lacunae of an order understood as being complete or at least as completable by purely logical means: the common opinion was that the logical development of norms would allow any legal question that could be imagined and presented to be solved, so that the judge, thanks to a merely cognitive activity plus application of the law, could always solve a case brought to judgement by strictly syllogistic reasoning[28]. The fundamental point to bear in mind is, then, that in the cultural context in which logical positivism was largely dominant, all jurists agreed with no trouble or excessive problems on the unity, coherence and completeness of the system, that is, in a series of characteristics which in the contradictory societies of the present day have largely got lost. The exceptional case has become the rule: the means whereby the system goes about completing itself have been largely changed and considerably extended. Today, the old analogy of traditional jurisprudence, as an expedient allowing the completeness of the legal system to be conceived, is really dead, in the sense that by being transformed into a general form of integration of the law it inevitably tends to lose the specific relevance at one time attributed to it, in theoretical terms too, as the solution to one of the

[27] W. Fikentscher, *Die Verwendung von Analogie und allgemeinen Rechtsprinzipien in der Rechtsprechung*, in "La sentenza in Europa. Metodo, tecnica e stile". Atti del convegno internazionale per l'inaugurazione della nuova sede della Facoltà di Giurisprudenza di Ferrara (10-12 October 1985) Padua, Cedam, 1988, pp. 94-95, Italian trans. by C. Mayr, pp. 538-539.

[28] A similar conception based on the logical perfection and completeness of the system is, for instance, emblematically offered in a classic of legal positivism, K. Bergbohm, *Jurisprudenz und Rechtsphilosophie*, vol. 1, 1892, esp. p. 367ff.; he speaks of the "logische Expansionskraft" of positive law and of its "innere Fruchtbarkeit".

fundamental problems of any legal system, that of innovation in the system while maintaining its structure. Lacking the assumption, the coherence of the system, its role as intermediate link, and as such non-compromising, between the mechanical interpretation of law and the feared free creation by judges, tends to become restricted. The broad "relativization" of the legal text brought about in the interpretive technique of our case law in fact allows greater hermeneutic possibilities than those offered by traditional analogical procedures, while broad judicial recourse, failing specific provisions, to general principles, even though it does not seem truly essential, is in fact probably dictated by the objective of increasing the acceptability of an analogical application. In essence this procedure, which has been defined as "disguised analogy", involves appealing to analogy in a chiefly rhetorical and apodeictic fashion, which makes verification of judicial motivations and conclusions problematic[29].

But if we now raise the problem which bears upon us on more than others at the moment, of differentiating the normal procedure of seeking the law, as an analogical procedure, from *analogical argument* as an argument that can produce new norms, we may say that in the former case the generic existence of lacunae that emerges at the moment of application depends on the constitutive impossibility for the legal norm to completely provide for the specific case to which it must be adapted; whereas in the latter the *specific* presence of a lacuna depends on the absence of a positive legal rule able to describe directly a case that the judge has to decide: and analogy serves for just this filling of the lacunae present in the law[30]. In the former case one or more norms exist; in the latter no specific norm exists (and it is then produced through analogical reasoning). In the first case, the point was to compare a norm with a factual circumstance; in the latter to compare two

[29] On relativization of the legal text and the crisis of the principle of "clear text", see A. Giuliani, *L'applicazione della legge*, Rimini, Maggioli, 1983, p. 61ff.; on appeal by judges to forms of "disguised analogy" see G. Lazzaro, *Argomenti dei giudici, op. cit.*, p. 20ff.

[30] The impossibility of separating analogy from the problem of lacunae is well shown by Canaris, *Die Feststellung von Lücken im Gesetz, op. cit.*, and stressed by Fikentscher, *Die Verwendung von Analogie, op. cit.*, pp. 530-531. For Heller, *Logik und Axiologie der analogen Rechtsanwendung, op. cit.*, pp. 75, 82ff., 86ff., analogy does not serve solely, in the legal sphere, to fill up lacunae in the law.

similar actual circumstances in order perhaps to extend to the one assessed as not disciplined by law the same legal consequence as for the one that is disciplined. We have accordingly to do, as we can see, with rather big differences. But these differences, important as they certainly are, do not prevent us from recognizing, as Luigi Caiani very well saw[31], the problematic nature of a qualitative distinction, that is, one regarding the logical structure of the two procedures, between normal and general activity of making the law specific, and individual analogical completion. While it remains that the degree of *extensio* applied by the interpreter is very different in the two cases, and that *analogia iuris* lacks the "precedent" of a normative "datum" that offers the judge a binding solution, it is not impossible from the viewpoint of the fundamental unity of the application of law to reinterpret analogical completion through interpretation as a particular, specific aspect of a broader analogical understanding. The common factor to the two different forms of analogy is in fact that in each case we have to do not exclusively with operations of a formal logical nature, but also with procedures of evaluative thought. In short, every analogy requires – as we have already mentioned – a value judgement, an assessment of the *ratio* of the norm and of the teleology inherent in it[32].

3. RESEMBLANCE BETWEEN CASE IN POINT AND PRINCIPLE OF JUSTICE AS PROPORTION

In the specific case of *analogia legis*, or single analogy, the argument

[31] Entry, *Analogia, op. cit.*, pp. 350ff., 353ff., 360.

[32] This point, more or less generally admitted by German legal scholarship, is also recognized by an author free from suspicion of sympathies for axiology, namely Canaris, *De la manière de constater et de combler les lacunes de la loi en droit allemand*, in, "Etudes de logique juridique", edited by C. Perelman, Brussels, Bruylant, 1966, p. 19ff.; and it is particularly stressed by Baratta, *Note in tema di analogia giuridica, op. cit.*, p. 585, and Heller, *Logik und Axiologie der analogen Rechtsanwendung, op. cit.*, pp. 55, 78ff., 82ff., 109ff.

clearly pivots, as many authors recognize[33], round the concept of resemblance between two cases. Analogy is nothing other than statement of a resemblance (between the case regulated by the law and the unregulated case). But if analogy is the *means* through which the judge finds the existence of lacuna in the system, the *criterion* thanks to which he fills it is instead given by the principle of legal equality, which dictates that different cases with the same essential features[34] are to be disciplined using the same treatment. The foundation of analogy is the principle of universalisability[35], which is constitutive both for the practical discourse in general and more specifically for the legal one, that is, the assumption of equality, a question that always has to be raised in specific terms. Analogy, as Larenz correctly points out[36], is not a logical deductive procedure, but an equal evaluation of circumstances of fact regarded as legally similar.

In turn, in the case of *analogia iuris*[37], application of a legal provision outwith the case explicitly provided for implicitly involves application of a

33 On resemblance as the keystone of argument from analogy see Bobbio, *L'analogia nella logica, op. cit.*, pp. 88-90; Engisch, *Einführung in das juristische Denken*, p. 147, Italian trans., op. cit., p. 232; Canaris, *De la manière de constater et de combler les lacunes, op. cit.*, p. 28; U. Klug, *Juristiche Logik, op. cit.*, pp. 122-123, speaks of area of similarity (*Ähnlichkeitskreis*), in order to base the criterion of logical validity of analogy on the *calculus of relations* of modern logic. On Klug's theses see J. Horovitz, *Ulrich Klug's Legal Logic. A Critical Account*, in "Etudes de logique juridique", *op. cit.*, pp. 78-144, but also M. Atienza, *Sobre la analogia en el Derecho, op. cit.*, p. 71ff.

34 On this point see Canaris, *De la manière de constater et de combler les lacunes, op. cit.*, p. 28.

35 Cf. Alexy, *Theorie der juristischen Argumentation, op. cit.*, p. 344; Zippelius, *Rechtsphilosophische Aspekte der Rechstfindung, op. cit.*, p. 153.

36 *Methodenlehre der Rechtswissenschaft, op. cit.*,p. 132. On similar positions see Esser, *Vorverständnis und Methodenwahl, op. cit.*, p. 110, Italian trans. *op. cit.*, p. 106, for whom "analogy is relevant for jurists not as a working method of logic, but as a *modus* for assessing cases which, on the basis of prior understanding and prior assessment, seem to merit an equal judgement...It...is...an attempt, in the presence of manifestly equal validity, to link questions of legal discipline which on the basis of prior understanding merit corresponding treatment."

37 On the distinction but also the close methodological relationship between analogy and general principles, see Fikentscher, *Die Verwendung von Analogie, op. cit.*, p. 83ff., Italian trans. *op. cit.*, p. 529ff.

general principle the existence of which is testified to by the particular provisions. Neither operation, consisting in the last analysis of setting up a proportion among four factors brought together in pairs (respectively, two cases, one contemplated by the law and the other not, and two legal effects, one already given and the other to be found), can in the field of legal interpretation attain the logical stringency characteristic of mathematics, or in other words operate, as Aristotle would have wished, like a proportion of geometrical type (a : b = c : d). Instead they are operations which, while not able to reach the certainty to which Bobbio tied legal analogy[38], can lay claim to the convincingness of a procedure not purely logical in nature[39] but also metalogical and axiological, and therefore capable of interpretations that may even differ (which, as we shall immediately see, plainly does not mean arbitrary).

At this point there arises, and it is a widespread and recurrent objection, the accusation against analogical thinking of being unscientific because of its insufficient precision. But while it is certainly indisputable that scientific language must aim above all at formal logical clarity and at exactness of language, it too can not completely do without a dimension of metaphoric, intentional type, having to do with the logically transcendental meaning of language[40]. How much progress would science have had to forego had it been strictly limited solely to logically rigorous conclusions? Anyone claiming to eliminate all recourse whatever to analogy and

38 Bobbio, *L'analogia nella logica, op. cit.* On Bobbio's theses see G. Conte, *Ricerche in tema di interpretazione analogica*, Pavia, 1957; R. Guastini, *Completezza e analogia. Studi sulla teoria generale del diritto italiana del primo Novecento*, in "Materiali per una storia della cultura giuridica", VI (1976), p. 569ff.; M. Atienza, *L'analogie en droit, op. cit.*, p. 36ff.

39 The exclusively logical nature of argument from analogy is disputed, though from different positions, by T. Heller, *Logik und Axiologie der analogen, op. cit.*; Amato, *Logica simbolica e dirittto, op. cit.*; Tammelo, *Outlines of Modern Legal Logic, op. cit.*; Kalinowski, *Introduzione alla logica giuridica, op. cit.*; Tarello, *L'interpretazione della legge, op. cit.*, p. 354; Gianformaggio, *L'analogia giuridica, op. cit.*, p. 440ff.

40 A. Kaufmann, *Analogie und "Natur der Sache", op. cit.*, p. 73. On the factors common to the procedure of legal interpretation and the procedures operating in scientific enquiry, see our *Positivismo ed ermeneutica nell'epistemologia giuridica contemporanea*, in "Riv. trim. dir. proc. civ. ", XL, 1986, p. 937ff., 946ff.

metaphor in scientific language would gravely impoverish its creativity and innovative capacity: sometimes they allow clearer definitions than abstract thought can guarantee[41].

In the intellectual procedure adopted for interpretation, argument by analogy operates like a rule of legal production which has an effect of normative invention, through the finding and formulating of a new norm that extends the normative description of a subject or a class of subjects in the given statement to include subjects or classes of subjects not strictly and literally covered by it, but "similar"[42]. But while the core of analogical argument consists in the creation of a new norm that describes in the same way acts which though different are similar to those described by another norm already in existence, it is nevertheless undeniable that a decisive act of interpretation interwoven from logical elements but also teleological evaluative ones, *precedes* and *follows* this creation of a new norm: it precedes it at the starting point of the argument itself, when the interpreter decides not to include the "similar" acts in the class of acts provided for by the norm already in being, in order subsequently to establish whether it is a case of an *analogia legis* or of an *analogia iuris*: it follows it when he proceeds to establish an inclusive relationship between the newly produced norm and the acts in need of legal description[43]. A particularly decisive aspect is the hermeneutic pre-selection of the features of coincidence on the one hand and of distinction on the other, brought about in the mind of the jurist making the comparison. The logical scheme of the analogy rests ultimately on a principle of justice, more specifically distributive justice: the one that to

41 For a reassessment of the cognitive value of analogy and metaphor see Perelman, *Analogie et métaphore en science, poésie et philosophie*, in "Revue intern. de Philos. ", 1969, p. 3ff. On analogy and metaphor in science see B. M. Hesse, *Modelli e analogie nella scienza*, Milan, Feltrinelli, 1980; S. Petruccioli, *Atomi metafore paradossi. Niels Bohr e la costruzione di una nuova fisica*, Rome-Naples, 1988; and earlier E. Mach, *Die Ähnlichkeit und die Analogie als Leitmotiv der Forschung, op. cit.*

42 See Tarello, *L'interpretazione della legge, op. cit.*, p. 351 and similarly Fikentscher, *Die Verwendung von Analogie, op. cit.*, p. 99, Italian trans. *op. cit*, p. 542. Bobbio too speaks of analogy as production of a new norm; see the entry *Analogia, op. cit.*, p. 605.

43 For a partly different opinion see N. Amato, *Logica simbolica e diritto, op. cit.*, p. 395, for whom analogical argument "rather than being logical, uses logic, and rather than being interpretive, is part of a different aspect: the creation or elaboration of law".

similar cases there should correspond identical legal effects[44]. The model of legal analogy is very ancient, rooted specifically in the Aristotelian conception of analogy, understood even in more recent interpretations as analogy of proportionality and not of attribution[45]. Proportion – says Aristotle in the *Nicomachean Ethics*[46] – is fundamentally an equity of relationships, and hence presupposes at least four terms: similarly, there is no sense in speaking of analogy as proceeding from a single norm; instead it comes from a rational context which links legal relationships among themselves "harmoniously"[47]. Today, when one of the major assumptions of analogy, the coherence of the legal system, has been largely dissolved, great difficulty is emerging in continuing to treat the instrument of analogy in accordance with its ancient technical significance. This does not mean that analogy as a form of argumentation has become superfluous: the relationship of analogical resemblance, the aim of treating different cases as if they were equal, continues to represent an important factor that jurists can still take as

44 R. Dworkin, *Taking Right Seriously*, London, Duckworth, 1981, (3rd ed.), Italian trans. by F. Oriana, Bologna, Il Mulino, 1982, pp. 209-216.

45 Aristotle, *Nicomachean Ethics I*, 4, 1096 b. V. 6, 1131 a, Italian trans. by A. Plebe, Bari, Laterza, 1957, pp. 11ff.; *Metaphysics VIII*, 2, 1043 a, 2-7, Italian trans. by G. Reale, vol. II, Naples, Loffredo, 1978, p. 6. On the Pythagorean model of mathematical proportions cf. P. Grenet, *Les origines de l'analogie philosophique dans les dialogues de Platon*, Paris, Boivin, 1948, p. 10ff. On the Aristotelian conception of analogy of proportionality, see: P. Aubenque, *Les origines de la doctrine de l'analogie de l'être*, in "Les Etudes Philosophiques", 103 (1978), pp. 3-12; E. Berti, *L'analogia dell'essere nella traduzione aristotelico-tomistica*, in AA. VV., *Metafore dell'invisibile*, Brescia, Morcelliana, 1984, pp. 13-33; *idem, L'Analogia in Aristotele. Interpretazioni recenti e possibili sviluppi*, in AA. VV., "Origini e sviluppi dell'analogia da Parmenide a S. Tommaso", ed. G. Casetta, Vallombrosa-Roma, ed. Vallombrosa, 1987, pp. 94-115; C. Rutten, L'analogie chez Aristote, in "Revue de philosophie ancienne", 1983, pp. 31-48. There is effective emphasis on how analogy in law is basically proportionality in Gianformaggio, *L'analogia giuridica, op. cit.* p. 441.

46 On the Aristotelian philosophy of justice see A. Giuliani, *La definizione aristotelica della giustizia. Metodo dialettico e analisi del linguaggio normativa*, Perugia, GLB Edizioni Universitarie, 1985, as well as the fine work by E. Opocher, *Analisi dell'idea della giustizia*, Milan, Giuffrè, 1977, p. 33ff.

47 Thus F. Gény, *Méthodes d'interprétation et sources en droit privé positif*, Paris, Sirey, 1919 (2nd ed.), p. 118ff.

a guide in moving over the stratified, disconnected terrain of present-day systems.

On the other hand, recourse to the parameter of equality of relationships in the case of analogy does not at all constitute an *unicum* within the legal system: we can in fact note that a principle of justice as proportion among causes, or pieces of human conduct, and legal effects lies at the basis not only of the analogical schema but also of all arguments, such as systematic interpretation, which can be reduced to coherence of content among differing norms[48]. Accordingly analogy, as Donati already clearly saw[49], represents the meeting of a fundamental ethical need for justice, and may be regarded as one aspect in a greater problem of the relationships between justice as certainty and justice as equity: at the root of it is the principle of equality, which dictates similar treatment, or the identity of legal consequences for two cases of the same value. The decisive question in any case is what features are to be regarded as essential for the purpose of treating in the same way two different cases, and what distinctive features ought instead to lead to different treatment: analogy is thus revealed as a mere case of the principle of equal treatment. As a legal proceeding, it thus finds its justification in the precept inherent in the very idea of law of treating in the same way that which is equal (or more specifically that which is similar: otherwise there would be identity rather than analogy of situations)[50].

It should be noted more specifically that the principle of equality may operate not only in a *positive* sense but also in a *negative* sense, that is, when the interpreter finds that legally differing circumstances of fact ought to be given different treatment. What is nevertheless required in order to be able to treat similar situations in the same way, or to treat differing situations differently, is that the principle of equality, which underlies analogy, not be merely assertable as an ideal of justice and hence as an ethical principle, but also be proved to exist on the terrain of positive law. The decisive

[48] Cf. G. Lazzaro, *L'interpretazione sistematica della legge*, Turin, Giappichelli, 1965.

[49] *Il problema delle lacune, op. cit.*, p. 234ff.

[50] On this point see Canaris, *De la manière de constater et de combler les lacunes, op. cit.*, p. 27. On extension of the principle of equality in criminal law see M. Danti-Juan, *L'égalité en droit pénal*, Poitiers, Cujas, 1988.

point is that the judge clearly separate his subjective criticism of the law, his "feeling" of the law, from the objective content of the system. Accordingly it remains clear that in this way the problem is shifted entirely onto the plane of interpretation, which is necessary in order to establish whether the case in point is contemplated by the law or not, and also to identify the common feature that governs both the case provided for and the one not provided for by the norm, and finally to decide when there is or when there is not "resemblance" between two legal situations regarded as similar.

The aware, experienced judge, accustomed to coping with the solution of cases brought before him under the primacy of the law, may certainly anticipate through his pre-understanding the outcome of the procedure of *Rechtsfindung*, or intuitively note the presence of a lacuna in the system, which will need to be filled by recourse to analogical argument, that is, by extending to the case not explicitly provided for the same discipline as laid down by a norm that contemplates a similar case. But these anticipatory judgements of his, being mainly psychological, are not, properly considered, decisive. What is instead truly decisive is a complex methodological procedure which, in addition to elements of formal logic, includes a teleological evaluation that brings in the *ratio* of the norm under consideration[51]; with the certainly not irrelevant clarification that this evaluation by the interpreter must not be purely subjective but has to take the shape of specification in the given case of the evaluation intrinsic in the whole legal system[52].

4. ANALOGY IN CRIMINAL LAW

On the view, hermeneutic in the broad sense, we decided above to adopt, on which analogical cognition plays a part in every interpretation of law, it also becomes easier to solve the difficulty, neither slight nor insuperable, of accepting forms of analogical thought in the area of law which just because

[51] That similarity exists when the two cases have the same *ratio legis* is the dominant thesis of legal scholars: on this cf. Bobbio, *Il positivismo giuridico, Turin*, Giappichelli, 1979, p. 257ff.; *idem*, entry *Analogia*, *op. cit.*, p. 603.

[52] In this connection see, Canaris, *De la manière de constater et de combler les lacunes*, *op. cit.*, p. 32.

of its different, special nature tends to circumscribe recourse to analogical extension. We intend, it will be clear, to refer to criminal law, where there is particular stress on the principle of the liberal Enlightenment expressed in the aphorism *nullum crimen, nulla poena sine lege*[53], where the legislation of many countries explicitly lays down a prohibition of analogy. Thus, the Italian Article 14 of the Provisions on law in general, taken together with Article 1 of the Penal Code ("No-one may be punished for an act not explicitly specified as an offence by law, nor with penalties not laid down thereby") and with Article 25 (2) of the Constitution ("No-one may be punished except in virtue of a law that entered into force before the act committed"), provides that "the criminal laws and those making exceptions from general rules or other laws shall not apply outside the cases and the times contemplated by them". It is true that it would not seem possible to assert the existence of a necessary correlation between a prohibition of analogy in criminal law and systems of a liberal democratic type – in many countries of indubitable liberal democratic traditions, from Britain to the Scandinavian countries, no such prohibition exists[54]; but it is also true that, particularly in criminal law where the principles of the certainty and incontrovertibility of law prevail over those of equity and the renewal of the legal system, analogy represents a crucial sore point of a legality whose logic operates so as to restrict the possibilities of extending penal norms.

What meaning can one, then, attribute to this prohibition on analogy, while remaining within the general framework of an interpretive procedure that we have acknowledged, in however broad a sense, to be necessarily ana-

[53] On this principle, in its historical, theoretical and legal aspects, see, as well as the entries by G. Vassali in "Noviss. dig. it., XI, 1965, p. 498ff. and G. Marini, in "Encicl. Dir. ", XXVIII, 1978, pp. 950-961, G. Grünwald, *Bedeutung und Begründung des Satzes "nulla poena sine lege"*, in "Zeitschrift für die gesamte Strafrechtswissenschaft", 76, 1964, pp. 1-18; G. Grasso, *Il principio "Nullum crimen sine lege" nella Costituzione italiana*, Milan, Giuffrè, 1972; H. L. Schreiber, *Gesetz und Richter. Zur geschichtlichen Entwicklung des Satzes nullum crimen, nulla poena sine lege*, Frankfurt a. M., Metzner, 1976; B. Schünemann, *Nulla poena sine lege? Rechtstheoretische und verfassungsrechtliche Implikationen der Rechtsgewinnung im Strafrecht*, Berlin, De Gruyter, 1978.

[54] This observation is from F. Mantovani, *Diritto penale. Parte generale*, Padua, Cedam, 1979, pp. 103-104.

logical, while still not abandoning the indefeasible requirement not to accept undue extensions of the criminal liability of subjects?

It is needful firstly to establish the error committed by those who regard analogy as *per se* arbitrary, as well as the ingenuousness of those who through the mere prohibition of analogy feel that they have a hermeneutic recourse available that can guarantee a completely precise, unambiguous finding of law. The reason is very simple: the ban on analogy too, like the very principle of legality, remains always within the interpretive procedure, and as such must in turn be interpreted[55]. All attempts by legislators to prescribe the interpretations of their own legislative imperatives are constantly destined to fail, as has appositely been noted, since the instruction to comply with the literal terms of the law in fact itself constitutes an interpretive criterion, in a restricted sense, of the law[56]. The interpretation of the ban on analogy is not forbidden and cannot be: it is, therefore, one of those prohibitions that by being inaccurately defined and in turn in need of interpretation rarely secure the effect desired by the legislator.

It may with good foundation be averred that the attempt to set up and maintain a distinction between extensive interpretation and analogy is based essentially on reasons of a meta-legal or political/ideological nature, more than on effective and convincing theoretical reasons.

It has indeed been authoritatively asserted[57] that the criterion for distinguishing between extensive interpretation and analogy as such consists in the fact that while in the first case the content of an *existing* legal norm is extended to cases not provided for, in the second it is instead a *new* legal norm that is produced, which includes both the regulated case and the similar case in need of regulation. It seems, however, hard to dispute the observation that the borderline between the two cases is in practice much more

[55] On this point, with various positions, see W. Hassemer, *Einführung in die Grundlagen des Strafrechts, op. cit.*, p. 256; K. Larenz, *Methodenlehre der Rechtswissenschaft, op. cit.*, p. 238; Gianformaggio, *L'analogia giuridica, op. cit.*, p. 450.

[56] Very effective on this is V. Frosini, *Prolegomeni all'interpretazione giuridica*, in "Nomos. Le attualità nel diritto", 1988, no. 1, p. 39.

[57] M. S. Giannini, *L'analogia giuridica*, in "Jus", 1941, p. 519ff.; whose thesis is shared by Bobbio, entry *Analogia, op. cit.*, p. 605.

unstable and fluctuating than theory suggests, and that it is not always easy to recognize in practice[58] when there is extensive interpretation, which is permissible, and when instead there is analogy proper, which is prohibited.

A typical, exemplary case, much discussed in criminal doctrine and case law – but there are parallel problems in civil doctrine and case law too – concerns the responsibility of *de facto* administrators in running a firm: in other words, whether the criminal norms in the event of company offences and those to do with bankruptcy involve not only those who are "formally" administrators (or also agents, liquidators or managing directors) but also those who *de facto* perform the functions concerned. On the one hand, a broad, authoritative approach in the literature asserts that for purposes of criminal responsibility the *de facto* administrator should be equated with the *de iure* administrator[59]; on the other hand another part of the literature, it too, however, rather authoritative, argues in the opposite direction, asserting that in the absence of the formal title of administrator, it is possible to

[58] As well as Bobbio himself, entry on *Analogia, op. cit.*, p. 605, and *Ancora intorno alla distinzione tra interpretazione estensiva e analogia* in "Giur. It. ", 1968, I,I, p. 695, this is recognized by Engisch, *Einführung in das juristische Denken, op. cit.*, p. 150, Italian trans. *op. cit.*, p. 238 and Hassemer, *Einführung in die Grundlagen des Strafrechts, op. cit.*, p. 254. More radically, W. Sax, *Das strafrechtliche "Analogieverbot"*, Göttingen, Vandenhoek und Ruprecht, 1953, denies any differentiation between extensive interpretation and analogical interpretation. On this subject see also Z. Ziembinski, *"Analogia legis" et interprétation extensive*, in "La logique juridique", Paris, Pedone, 1967.

[59] Among those who assert this line are M. Punzo, *La bancarotta impropria e gli altri reati previsti dalla legge fallimentare*, Padua, Cedam, 1957, p. 18; T. Ascarelli, *Ancora in tema di imprenditore occulto*, in "Riv. soc. ", 1958, p. 1174; Antolisei, *Manuale di diritto penale. Leggi complementari. I reati fallimentari e sociali*, Milan, Giuffrè, 1959, p. 109ff.; G. Zuccalà, *Il delitto di false communicazioni sociali*, Padua, Cedam, 1964, p. 33; Conti and Bruti Liberati, *Esercizio di fatto dei poteri di amministrazione e responsibilità penali nell'ambito delle società irregolari*, in, "Il diritto penale delle società commerciali", Milan, Giuffrè, 1971, p. 119ff.; A. Traversi, *Responsabilità penali d'impresa*, Padua, Cedam, p. 154ff. On the topic see also A. Borgioli, *Amministratori di fatto e direttori generali*, in "Giur. Comm. ", 1975, I, p. 593ff. (esp. p. 608ff.); *idem*, *L'amministratore "di fatto" non fallisce, ibid.*, 1978, II p. 595ff.; M. Cassottana, *La responsibilità degli amministratori nel fallimento di s. p. a.*, Milan, Giuffrè, 1984; F. Galgano, *La società per azioni, Trattato Galgano, vol. VII*, Padua, Cedam, 1984, p. 270ff.; F. Bonelli, *Gli amministratori di società per azioni*, Milan, Giuffrè, 1985, p. 253ff.

speak of exercise of the office only in a manifestly improper sense[60]. In the first case an interpretation sometimes extensive in nature (involving total equation of the *de facto* administrator with the *de iure* one or with legitimately installed agents), sometimes analogical, is applied to a constitutive element of the criminal offence, such as the qualification of being an administrator, thereby extending the range of subjects on whom company obligations bear. In the second case the possibility is ruled out of having recourse inevitably and in all cases to analogical supplementation, even if it is accepted cautiously for individual areas of the discipline in accordance with the specific position of the administrator, which may be diverse in legal terms[61]. The border between extensive interpretation and analogical supplementation is thus, in this case too, rather unstable and fluid; looked at closely, either of the solutions just proposed to the responsibility of *de facto* administrators brings with it a more or less broad range of problems that at least in part are clarified and simplified if the question is considered in the way appropriate to it, consisting in an eminently hermeneutical option, a clarification of what the norm states, rather than in an extensive interpretation or analogical creation of a new norm. Thus, for instance, in the case of Article 223 of the law on bankruptcy or of Articles 2621-2642 of the Italian Civil Code the point is to ask who are the "administrators" within the meaning of those Articles rather than analogically to extend to "de facto" administrators the discipline laid down for "de iure" administrators.

It nevertheless remains true that the passage from the stage of recognizing the normative meaning, that is from the merely declarative interpretation of what is stated by the norm, to the phase of adapting the norm to the specific case – or to the supplementary interpretation of the system – far from appearing as a crude factor of breach, represents a gradual, essentially homogeneous transition. As may also be said of the traditional adage *in*

60 C. Pedrazzi, *Gestione d'impresa e responsabilità penali*, in "Riv. soc. ", 1962, p. 220ff. From the same author, still on the theme of penal responsibility of administrators, see *Profili problematici del diritto penale d'impresa*, in "Riv. trim. dir. pen. econ. ", I, 1988, no. 1, p. 134ff.

61 Pedrazzi, *Gestione d'impresa e responsibilità penali*, *op. cit.*, p. 247.

claris non fit interpretatio[62], at the basis of some versions of the ban on analogy in criminal law is probably the illusion of being able to do without the work of the interpreter or at any rate of limiting his function to a merely declarative one: "true clarity is always subsequent, not prior, to interpretive activity."

Instead, the difficulty or indeed impossibility of distinguishing extensive interpretation and analogy with respect to particular norms is often due to a formulation of the elements of the criminal offence that is not in conformity with the principle of exhaustiveness[63]. It is true that the most authoritative research on the *Analogieverbot*, from Sax to Heller initially and to a now extremely widespread opinion among German criminalists later[64], has

62 On this maxim cf. C. Perelman, *L'interprétation juridique*, in "Arch. phil. dr. ", XVII, 1972, p. 30; E. Fazzalari, *Introduzione alla giurisprudenza*, Padua, Cedam, 1984, p. 38 f; P. Perlingieri, *L'interpretazione della legge come sistematica ed assiologica. Il broccardo "In claris non fit interpretatio", il ruolo dell'art. 12 disp. prel. Codice civile e la nuova scuola dell'esegesi*, in, "Rassegna di diritto civile", 1985, pp. 990-1017; Frosini, *Prolegomena all'interpretazione giuridica, op. cit.*, p. 39ff.

63 Thus Mantovani, *Diritto penale, op. cit.*, p. 105.

64 W. Sax, *Das strafrechtliche "Analogieverbot", op. cit.*; Heller, *Logik und Axiologie der analogen Rechtsanwendung, op. cit.*; Engisch, Methoden der Strafrechtswissenschaft, in "Enzyklopädie der geisteswissenschaftlichen Arbeitsmethoden", 1972, p. 66; E. Schmidhäuser, *Strafrecht. Allg. T.*, Tübingen, Mohr, 1975 (2nd ed.), p. 111; J. M. Prieter, *Zum Analogieverbot im Strafrecht*, in, "Juristische Methodenlehre und analytische Philosophie", edited by H. J. Koch, Frankfurt a. M., Athenaeum, 1976, p. 162; H. H. Jeschek, *Lehrbuch des Strafrechts. Allg. T.*, Berlin, Duncker und Humblot, 1978 (3rd ed.), p. 106; P. Bockelmann, *Strafrecht Allg. T.*, Munich, Beck, 1979, (3rd ed.), p. 17; W. Naucke, *Strafrecht. Eine Einführung*, Frankfurt a. M., Metzner, 1980 (3rd ed.), p. 79; and, by the same author, from a historical viewpoint, *Die Aufhebung des strafrechtlichen Analogieverbots 1935*, in *NS-Recht in historischer Perspektive*, Munich-Vienna, Oldenbourg, 1981, p. 71ff.; G. Stratenwerth, *Strafrecht Allg. T., I*, Munich, Heymann, 1981, p. 41. On the ban on analogy, in the vast quantity of Italian literature see G. Bellavista, *L'interpretazione della legge penale*, Rome, Lib. Ulpiano, 1936; G. Delitala, *Analogia in "bonam partem"*, in "Riv. it. di dir. pen. ", VIII,, 1936, pp. 605-612; Bobbio, *L'analogia e il diritto penale*, in "Riv. pen. " 1938, p. 526,ff.; G. Vassalli, *Limiti del divieto d'analogia in materia penale*, Milan, Giuffrè, 1949, (and by the same author see the entry *Analogia del diritto penale*, in "Nov. Dig. it. ", I, Turin, Utet, 1968 pp. 607-611); A. Schönke, *Intepretazione, analogia e consuetudine nel diritto penale*, Italian trans. by C. Pedrazzi, in "Riv. it. di dir. pen., II, N. S., 1949, pp. 511-525; G. Roncagli, *Analogia e consuetudine in generale e nel diritto penale*, Milan, Giuffrè, 1949;

definitively demonstrated that this prohibition cannot be respected in absolute fashion in the criminal law. It remains instead possible to conceive of it as an interpretive criterion of restrictive type, like a border which, in ethical terms[65], by way of guaranteeing the *favor libertatis*, may very well be maintained even within a conception of law that understands *Rechtsfindung* as reasoning based on analogical models. A border which, chiefly because of its great practical political importance, still has reason to exist, being linked with the liberal democratic conquest of the rule of law, setting precise limits, in guarantee of the individual freedom of the subject, on any extensive type of interpretation of elements of criminal offences. Then the ban on analogy reduces, from a theoretical viewpoint, to pointing out that the punishable act must previously be described in a legal norm in sufficiently determinate form, and is understood as a prohibition on violating the guarantee function vis-à-vis the culprit with an "impermissibly extended"[66] extensive interpretation. Noting that the border between extensive interpretation and analogy is extremely precarious and accordingly that *even* extensive interpretation is analogy, compels the judge still more to furnish a specific justification for every extension of the criminal law to the disadvantage of the culprit, without taking refuge in the comfortable assertion that this is "only" interpretation[67]. Up to the point of remaining bound by the principle of legal civilization that liberty is to be regarded as the rule and the penalty instead as the exception, it is politically appropriate for the accusation that a judge has infringed the ban on analogy by applying an extended meaning of the criminal norm against the person concerned to remain a grave reproach, which still weighs heavily in our legal and political cul-

M. Boscarelli, *Analogia e interpretazione estensiva nel diritto penale*, Palermo, Priulla, 1955.

65 That the ban on extension in criminal law constitutes an "equitative principle" more than a "norm of good law" is asserted also by Bobbio, *L'analogia nella logica del diritto*, *op. cit*., p. 179.

66 Hassemer, *Tatbestand und Typus, op. cit*., p. 165.

67 On this point see Hassemer, *Tatbestand und Typus, op. cit*., p. 164; A. Kaufmann, *Analogie und "Natur der Sache"*, *op. cit*., p. 68.

ture[68]. Much will obviously depend on the broader or narrower room left by the legislator to case law[69], that is, by the techniques of drafting legislative documents, by the criteria adopted by the legislator in formulating the elements of the incriminating penal norms and above all by his effort at clearly fixing the meanings of words and his refraining from using vague, emotional or elastic elements, which would lead to indeterminacy in the precept and unpredictability, even in degree, of the statutory response to the wrongful act. Tying oneself to the principle of determinacy and exhaustivity of the elements of the offence[70] implies careful protection of the system of procedural guarantees, which obviously turns round the charging of the accused with a precise, clearly identified accusation. On the other hand, the well-foundedness of the principle of "recognizability" by the actor of the

68 After the degenerative factors that laws and practices of emergency have introduced in the past decade into the criminal system, the conviction has spread that the criminal law ought to brake the "inflationary" impulse and regain its function as means of exceptional intervention to protect essential legal interests. In this connection see D. Pulitano, *Supplenza giudiziaria e poteri dello Stato*, in "Quad. Cost. ", 1983, p. 93ff., and the collective volumes *Diritto premiale e sistema penale*, Milano, Giuffrè, 1983, and *Funzioni e limiti del diritto penale. Alternative di tutela*, edited by M. de Acutis and G. Palombarini, Padua, Cedam, 1984, with important articles by F. Bricola, F. Galgano, E. Gallo, E. Rosini.

69 On this point see U. Scarpelli, *Introduzione all'analisi delle argomentazioni giudiziarie*, in "Il foro italiano", XCV, 1970, vol. 63, then in *Diritto e analisi del linguaggio*, edited by U. Scarpelli, Milan, Comunità, 1976, pp. 414-415. On the problems of legislative technique see G. Floridia, *Scomposizione e rappresentazione grafica degli enunciati normativi fra teoria dell'interpretazione e tecnica del drafting legislativo*, in "Materiali per una storia della cultura giuridica", XV, 1985, pp. 493-495; *Modelli di legislatore e scienza della legislazione. L'educazione giuridica*, edited by A. Giuliani and N. Picardi, V, Edizioni Scientifiche Italiane, Naples, 1987; *Normative europee sulla tecnica legislativa*, edited by R. Pagano, intro. by R. Pagano and V. Frosini, Rome, Servizio informazione della Camera dei Deputati, 1988; *Lezioni di tecnica legislativa*, edited by S. Bartole, Padua, Cedam, 1988. On the relationships between technique and interpretation with particular respect to formulation of the elements of an offence see also Palazzo, *Tecnica legislativa e formulazione della fattispecie penale in una recente circolare della Presidenza del Consiglio dei Ministri*, in "Cass. pen. ", 1987, p. 231ff.

70 Concerning this see F. Bricola, *La discrezionalità nel diritto penale*, Milan, Giuffrè, 1965, p. 229 ff; B. Petrocelli, *Appunti sul principio di legalità nel diritto penale*, in "Saggi di diritto penale", Padua, Cedam, 1965, p. 191ff.; F. Palazzo, *Il principio di determinatezza nel diritto penale*, Padua, Cedam, 1979.

contents of the penal norms and the need to bear in mind in shaping the substantive law also the conditions of actual application of the norms are today amply recognized by the recent, but already "historic" verdict of 23 March 1988, No.364, in which the Constitutional Court declared the partial unconstitutionality of Article 5 of the Penal Code in force[71]. While it is thus undeniable that clarity and exhaustivity of the elements of an offence present an ideal and a guideline for legislative policy to pursue, and cannot be renounced, the impossibility nevertheless remains of securing absolute determinacy in the elements of an offence, even in the penal sphere, so that no obligation of exhaustivity will ever be capable of entirely eliminating an irreducible margin of discretion in the interpretive act. The concept of determinacy of the elements of an offence is itself indeterminate, and the possible literal meaning of the words that may serve as a boundary on penal interpretation is still a hermeneutic construction which is executed in accordance with an axiological principle and in a fundamentally analogical structure[72]. This does not alter the fact that the crucial problem, though perhaps not easily soluble, may then become that of setting the degree of determinacy that the elements of the criminal offence have to have in order to satisfy the principle of exhaustivity.

71 On this important judgment, apart from the immediate positive assessments by G. Neppi Modona, *L'ignoranza non è reato...*, in "La Repubblica", 6. 4. 1988; F. Stella, *Italiano più libero. Ignorare la legge adesso è un diritto*, in "Corriere della sera", 6. 4. 1988 and U. Scarpelli, *Ignorantia legis excusat*, in "Mondo economico", 18. 4. 1988, see also the critical annotations by G. Fiandaca, *Principio di colpevolezza ed ignoranza scusabile della legge penale: "prima lettura della sentenza, no. 364/88, in "Foro it. "*, 1988, I. p. 1385 ff; F. C. Palazzo, *Ignorantia legis: vecchi limiti ed orizzonti nuovi della colpevolezza*, in "Riv. it. dir. proc. pen, 1988, no. 3, pp. 920-962; P. Patrono, *Problematiche attuali dell'errore nel diritto penale dell'economia*, in "Riv. trim. dir. pen. econ. ", I, 1988, no. 1, pp. 87-124; L. Pegoraro, *Linguaggio e certezza della legge nella giurisprudenza della Corte Costituzionale*, Milan, Giuffrè, 1988, p. 19ff.; D. Pulitano, *Una sentenza storica che restaura il principio di colpevolezza*, in "Riv. it. dir. proc. pen", 1988, no. 2, pp. 686-730; L. Stortoni, *L'introduzione nel sistema penale dell'errore scusabile di diritto: significati e prospettive*, in "Riv. it. dir. proc. pen", XXXI, 1988, no. 4, pp. 1313-1350; G. Vassalli, *L'inevitabilità dell'ignoranza della legge penale come causa generale di esclusione della colpevolezza*, in "Giur. cost. ", XXXIII, 1988, no. 1, pp. 3-15.

72 Hassemer, *Tatbestand und Typus, op. cit.*, p. 161; Larenz, "Fall-Norm-Typus. Eine rechtslogische Studie", in *Rationalität-Phänomenalität-Individualität. Festgabe für Hermann und Marie Glockner*, edited by W. Ritzel, Bonn, 1966, p. 151ff.

A great deal of attention will then have to be paid to not confusing the ban on analogy in criminal law with the principle *nullum crimen, nulla poena sine lege*. It is one thing to maintain that the type of the criminally wrongful act must not remain indeterminate, and must be established on the basis of the legal elements of the offence[73]. It is quite another thing to state that even the ban on analogy, like every type of criminal wrongful act, must necessarily be subjected to a hermeneutic activity aimed at distinguishing, specifically on the basis of a linguistic-hermeneutic construction referred to the norm, the limits of permissible interpretation and the limits of impermissible interpretation. It is certainly possible, in short, to be among the supporters of an application, even a strict one, of the principle *nullum crimen, nulla poena sine lege*[74], while stressing that there is no appreciable qualitative difference between extensive interpretation and analogy, just as a rigid boundary between extensive interpretation of a teleological nature and *Rechtsfindung* developed in accordance with analogical models can be upheld only on paper. In other words, the guarantee function of the *favor libertatis*, an advantage best not renounced in a democratic society, is something different and logically distinct from the Enlightenment illusion of an absolute completeness of legislation, which appears vitiated by a clear excess of trust in the superiority of the legislative power over the judiciary.

The true danger for legal certainty is not in recognizing a situation of a necessary room for interpretation, which cannot be removed even in systems marked by the most rigorous legality, but in thinking of establishing this certainty in an entirely aprioristic fashion and of being able magically to constitute it beforehand outside the actual process of interpretation and

73 The fact that *nullum crimen sine lege* has nothing to do with analogical interpretation is stressed by Bobbio, *L'analogia nella logica del diritto, op. cit.*, pp. 171ff., 193 ff; on Bobbio's theoretical approach see the critical annotations, which we do not always agree with, by Guastini, *Completezza e analogia, op. cit.*, p. 587ff.

74 Thus e. g. A. Kaufmann, *Analogie und "Natur der Sache", op. cit.*, p. 69. Among those who uphold rigorous application of the principle are H. L. Schreiber, *Gesetz und Richter, op. cit.*, p. 232ff.; B. Schünemann, *Nulla poena sine lege?, op. cit.*; Lenckner, *Wertausfüllungsbedürftige Begriffe im Strafrecht und der Satz "nullum crimen sine lege"*, in "Juristische Schulung", 1968, pp. 249ff., 304ff.

decision within which it is necessary to reach, not absolute certainty, which is unattainable, but, in practice, *the greatest possible certainty*.

MILKING THE METER
On analogy, universalisability and world views

CEES W. MARIS

1. ANALOGICAL REASONING

During the year 1918 the Dutch dentist A.M.M. regularly fed his instruments with electric energy, supplied by the municipal electricity company, after having disconnected the electricity meter. In 1920 he was given a three month's prison sentence for theft. The dentist appealed against this conviction to the Dutch Supreme Court. He argued that the lawcourt had violated art. 310 of the penal code, which states: "He who takes away any property that belongs completely or partly to someone else, with the purpose of appropriating it illegally, will, being guilty of theft, be punished with imprisonment for a maximum of four years [...]". Obviously the text of this law dated from a time – 1881 – that no legislator had ever thought of the possibility of stealing something immaterial like energy. The dentist pleaded, firstly that electricity cannot be subsumed under "property", because this word in its Dutch language context refers to tangible objects, and secondly that milking the electricity meter falls outside the meaning of "to take away", which also refers to something tangible. The Supreme Court however rejected his arguments. It decided that milking the meter is similar to "take away" in its relevant respects; just as electricity is to "tangible property" (in contrast to either mental inventions like copyrights or other rights, that need specific protection laws) (Supreme Court, May 23rd 1921, N. J. [Dutch court reports] 1921, 564).

This judgement on the theft of electricity is a classical example of analogical legal reasoning. What tips the scale in a juridical decision like this is the question, whether a case that is not covered by the law, should nevertheless be treated equally to covered cases, because it is similar in its relevant respects. The same problem concerning the illegal appropriation of electric energy has arisen in many European legal systems, but has been resolved in different ways (see section 2).

In this paper I shall discuss a specific thesis on analogical reasoning, that professor Nerhot has propounded in his introductory remarks to the conference "Analogie en science juridique": that this kind of reasoning "représente toujours *la valeur unitaire et rationelle d'une législation*, unité et rationalité où nous trouvons les origines et la justification de ce qu'on l'appelle les principes généraux du droit" (represents the unity and rationality of a legal system, that constitutes the source and the justification of the general principles of law).

Now prof. Nerhot's thesis is open to different interpretations. One can understand "unity" and "rationality" in the narrow, purely formal sense of internal *consistency*. In this interpretation it is sufficient that the body of particular positive laws and jurisprudence can be constructed as derivable from one or more central principles, regardless of what they materially prescribe or forbid. These basic legal principles then constitute the central *ratio iuris* of the system, that can serve as a guideline for the determination of juridically relevant criteria, by which the similarities of two cases in analogical reasoning can be judged. In this interpretation, the *content* of these basic legal principles (and thus of the system as a whole) in its turn does not necessarily have to be justifiable or rational in a broader, more substantive sense. This means that a similar justification is binding only for those who already take an internal view on the positive legal system in question and accept its validity. This kind of justification is of little value, because it lacks any guarantee that it will be acceptable outside the group that happens to hold juridical power, and that decides what is juridically relevant.

According to a second interpretation, prof. Nerhot's thesis could refer to a rational justification of the legal system in a more substantive sense, as universally binding for everyone. In this paper, I shall comment on the rational quality of analogical reasoning in both interpretations.

But first I would like to make some preliminary remarks, which all share the same feature: I shall be using "analogy" in a broad sense. Firstly, I shall consider legal analogy within the broader frame of reference of a general ethic. Secondly, I understand "analogy" in accordance with current juridical usage in the broad sense of similarity or resemblance of the properties of different cases. This usage diverges from the more specific and technical use of "analogy" in traditional philosophy, which in the field of legal reasoning has been propagated *inter alia* by Perelman. In his *La Rhétorique Nouvelle* Perelman reserves the concept "analogy" for the similarity of structure or functions of two separate *domains*, formally stated as a : b = c : d. The interpretation of this formula leads to comparisons such as: old age relates to life, as evening relates to day (ARISTOTLE, *The Poetics*, 1457 b). That is to say, the passing of a day functions as a *metaphor* for the passing of life. Poets make use of such *metaphors* by fusing domains in phrases like "the evening of life" or "milking the meter". Furthermore, in metaphorical comparisons by analogy such as "an individual relates to the state, as a hand relates to the whole organism", relations or functions of the first domain (that of biological organisms) serve as a frame of reference for relations or functions in the second domain (that of the state).

As to law, Perelman concludes that "analogy" can only apply to a comparison between two different systems of positive law, in contrast to a comparison between two cases within the same legal system, and in contrast to a comparison between two cases from different systems of positive law which are considered as derived from one and the same system of natural law (*La Rhétorique Nouvelle*, p. 503). Unlike Perelman, I shall use "analogy" both as referring to the comparison of similar cases within one positive legal system, as well as to testing these against a natural law or a general ethic.

I conceive analogical reasoning as a specific application of the *universalisability principle*, which demands that similar cases should be treated equally. In order to evaluate to what extent analogical reasoning implies the rationality of the legal system as a whole, I shall discuss the working of the universalisability principle in varying fields of application of gradually increasing extension. I start from its most limited and local use, the comparison of an uncovered case with just one law, then gradually extend its range to analogical reasoning on the basis of a systematic interpretation of the whole of positive law, concluding with an analysis of the general application of the universalisability principle in ethics, conceived as a frame of reference for the substantive rationality of law. In contrast to prof. Nerhot, I shall arrive at a sceptical conclusion.

For the sake of brevity, I shall limit my explicit argument to the continental European legal systems based on written laws. But most of it can be applied analogically to the jurisprudential legal systems of Anglo-Saxon countries.

2. EXTENSIVE INTERPRETATION, ANALOGICAL REASONING AND THE UNIVERSALISABILITY PRINCIPLE

In the electricity judgement, a case that is not explicitly covered by law is nevertheless treated in the same way as a case of legal theft, because it is considered as similar in its relevant respects. Now according to prof. Nerhot's thesis, analogical reasoning like this represents the rational unity of the legal system. In order to discuss this thesis, a further analysis is first needed of the structure of analogical argumentation.

Analogical reasoning is a specific application of the *universalisability principle*, which demands that equal or similar cases should be treated equally. In jurisprudence and in ethics the principle of universalisability is often equated with the principle of formal justice or equality, which has the same content. However, this principle as such does not give much hold, because of its purely formal character. It does not give any material criteria as to *which* cases are to be considered as similar. In the empirical world, cases that are completely unequivocal are extremely rare, if they exist at all. As far as they exist, they must be treated identically according to the universalisability principle, but here no analogical reasoning is needed. But mostly the application of the universalisability principle is less simple, because the cases under consideration are equal in some respects, but different in other respects. Then the question arises, whether one should abstract from the differences (analogical reasoning), or, inversely, from the similarities (a contrario reasoning)? Therefore, analogical reasoning shares its main problem with the universalisability principle: which aspects of the cases under consideration are to be considered as *relevant*?

In jurisprudence, what is to be considered as relevant is determined by the juridical point of view, the *ratio iuris*. Thus, the next problem would be to determine what the *ratio iuris* is.

According to "legism", the nineteenth century theory that written laws are the exclusive source of law and that the judge should confine himself to a strict application of the letter of the law, the literal legal text settles this matter. This view excludes analogical reasoning, because a case not explicitly covered by the law is for that very reason considered as juridically different in its relevant respects from a covered case.

But today it is generally realized that a law always needs interpretation. Of every law, there will be a hard core of cases about which there exists a general consensus that they come under its head. But inevitably there will also be more peripherical cases. Then the judge will have to decide whether or not these are similar in their relevant respects. To determine the question of juridical relevancy, he must interpret the facts of the case as well as the text of the law, using the well known methods of juridical interpretation: grammatical, historical, systematical or teleological. He applies *extensive interpretation* if he decides that a borderline case does indeed come under the law.

A further departure from the "legistic" literal application of the law presents itself when the judge is confronted with a case which definitely is not covered by the law in question, but of which it nevertheless can be argued that it should be treated in a similar way. Usually it is said that the judge now stops *interpreting*, and starts *reasoning* analogically, in order to fill up gaps in the law.

Generally, two kinds of analogical reasoning are distinguished, "*analogia legis*" and "*analogia iuris*". In reasoning by *analogia legis* the judge compares an uncovered case with cases covered by just one law, as in the electricity judgement. In the electricity case, the Dutch Supreme Court judged that electricity can be compared to tangible property: although the presence of electricity can only be established in relation to a material object, it can be generated, accumulated, transferred and stored by human action in the same way as something material. Furthermore, electricity also represents a certain value, because its generation entails expenses, and because its producer is able to use it himself, or to convey it for profit. Because of these similarities, the stealing of electricity should be equated to the stealing of material objects.

In reasoning by *analogia iuris*, the judge treats the uncovered case similarly to cases covered by a *number* of different laws, because these are said to cohere so systematically, that they can be seen as tacitly implying a common general principle which also applies to the uncovered case. This kind of reasoning played an important role in the judgement of the Dutch Supreme Court on a case concerning "unjustified enrichment" (H.R. 30-1-1959, N. J. 1959, no. 548). A building firm had built a number of houses on a piece of ground, as the fulfilment of a contract with Hubertus te Poel, who claimed to be the landowner. Once the building was completed, Hubertus was found to be insolvent. Moreover, the ground appeared to be owned, not by Hubertus, but by Hubertus' brother Heinrich, Hubertus only being his tenant. This implied that Heinrich also had become the owner of the newly built houses. Now the building firm tried to get its losses compensated by a legal action against Heinrich te Poel, on the grounds of "unjustified enrichment". The problem of this was however, that Dutch civil law did not know a general action based on "unjustified enrichment". Only in a number of specific cases, it explicitly recognized an action like this, each exactly circumscribed by a particular law. The case in question was not one of them. Nevertheless, the building firm argued that from the systematic coherence of these specific laws it followed, that a general principle to reimburse unjustified enrichment was tacitly implied in the system of Dutch law. This principle should also be applied to the case concerned. The Law Court agreed with this argument. The Court of Appeal however overturned this judgement, because art. 1269 of the Dutch civil code only recognizes obligations that either are a result of contractual relationships, or of written law. By a contrario reasoning this court judged therefore that Dutch law does not recognize any unwritten principle as a source of obligation. Against this, the Supreme Court decided that this was too narrow an interpretation of the words "from written law" of art. 1269: The meaning of this phrase is not limited to explicit legal determinations, but can also refer to implicit rules that fit into the system of the law. Subsequently, the Supreme Court took an intermediate position between the Law Court and the Court of Appeal. It decided that in the case of unjustified enrichment, Dutch law does not without further qualifications imply a general action, *inter alia* because otherwise obligations could arise for someone who gets a profit thrust upon him against his will. Nevertheless, depending on the circumstances, the judge may in some uncovered cases in this field decide these obligations exist if this fits into the system of the law and links with the explicitly covered cases. But as to this specific case, the Supreme Court decided that the explicit laws pointed in the opposite direction: Art. 1603 of the Civil Code stated that a landowner was not obliged to compensate for the enrichments that are a consequence of improvements made by his tenants (for these are thrust upon him). Reasoning by *analogia legis* the Supreme Court extended this to the uncovered case under consideration, where the enrichment was provided by a contractual partner of the tenant.

Extensive interpretation, reasoning by *analogia legis* and reasoning by *analogia iuris* do not differ fundamentally. This appears in the first place from the repeated occurrence of disagreement as to whether a certain juridical judgement is to be considered as extensive interpretation or as reasoning by *analogia legis*. The electricity case for instance is conceived by most jurists as an example of the latter, but others maintain that it is just a matter of extensive interpretation. Illustrative of this disagreement are the diverging reactions to the problem of the theft of electricity in different European countries. In all these countries analogical reasoning in penal law is forbidden, because of the extra need for legal certainty in this field. On the ground of this prohibition, in Germany and Switzerland it was decided that the stealing of electricity could *not* be subsumed under the existing law. The German Reichsgericht based this decision on the consideration that even physicists do not know the real nature of electric energy; this scientific uncertainty also prevented the legal decision that electricity could be conceived of as a "mobile material object", in which interpretation there would have been no need for analogical reasoning. The theft of electricity could then have been subsumed under the existing law by extensive interpretation. But because this was judged impossible, and because analogical reasoning was not permitted, a new specific law against the theft of electricity had to be made. In contrast, in France and Holland the illegal appropriation of energy has been brought under the existing law, notwithstanding the analogy prohibition. Here apparently the judge rather conceived of his judgement as extensive interpretation rather than as analogical reasoning. These divergent reactions illustrate that extensive interpretation and analogical reasoning show a close family resemblance, because there is a sliding scale from hard core cases, via borderline cases, to analogous cases.

In the second place, these three kinds of juridical argument are closely akin because their argumentation is structured in the same way. They are all specific applications of the universalisability principle: hard cases are treated equally to cases that are clearly covered by the law, because they are judged similar in their relevant respects. Furthermore, in extensive interpretation and in reasoning per *analogiam legis* and iuris, the way by which the judge determines what should count as juridically relevant is identical. In extensive interpretation and in reasoning by *analogia legis* he does implicitly what he does explicitly in the case of *analogia iuris*: These three forms of argumentation are all based on the construction of an underlying principle, which is considered as the *ratio iuris* in question. In the electricity case too the judge has implicitly constructed a more general underlying principle. In this case the Dutch Supreme Court stated that the purpose of art. 310 of the penal code is to protect property. In this way, it invoked as an underlying principle that property should be protected by law, which implied the criteria of relevancy by which it was decided that the illegal appropriation of electricity resembled a hard core theft in its relevant aspects.

To summarize, extensive interpretation, reasoning by *analogia legis* and reasoning by *analogia iuris* are all specific applications of the universalisability principle, which demands that similar cases should be treated alike. The question as to whether the cases concerned are similar in their *relevant* aspects is answered by ex- or implicitly constructing an underlying principle which constitutes the *ratio iuris* of the laws involved. So, all three ways of juridical argumentation are concerned with determining relations of analogy in a broad sense.

Their difference lies mostly in their degree of relative locality within the whole of positive law. In the case of *analogia iuris*, the underlying principle is derived from various places in positive law. Analogia legis is more local: the underlying principle originates from one law only. Extensive interpretation is even more local: it just extends the field of operation of one law to a borderline case, which lies very close to the hard-core case. These variances in locality are mainly of importance only to the research strategy in the heuristic phase. In the context of justification however, the rational reconstruction of the argumentation is principally similar. The next burning question is exactly how rational such a reconstruction is. In other words, what is the rational quality of the *ratio iuris* thus constructed?

3. ANALOGICAL REASONING AND RATIONALITY

So, in analogical reasoning several cases are unified under the head of one juridical principle. This is probably one of the main reasons why prof. Nerhot maintains that this way of argumentation is possible only if positive law as a whole is conceived as a unified, rational system, based on some fundamental legal principles.

However, the above analysis of Dutch jurisdiction shows that this is not necessarily so. The unity that is presupposed can be of a very local nature. Prof. Nerhot is surely right in that *some* system must be presupposed in positive law, if the choice between analogical or a contrario reasoning is not to be completely arbitrary. But this does not without further presuppositions imply the extreme opposite: the supposition that positive law as a whole constitutes a rational system with a central *ratio iuris*. To decide the electricity case by analogical reasoning, by constructing an underlying principle in the way mentioned above, it would for instance suffice if only that part of penal law which protects the citizen's belongings forms a more or less coherent whole. Reasoning by *analogia iuris* is less local, because it presupposes the coherence of various, though related, places in the law, but still need not rest on basic principles which supposedly lie at the basis of the whole system.

Only in specific legal theories is the unity and rationality of the system *as a whole* a necessary presupposition of analogical reasoning. Prof. Nerhot's thesis would for instance be supported in a Dworkinian or a natural law conception of law, but not in the views of legal positivism or the critical legal studies movement.

Legal positivism, that equates law with what the legal authorities recognize as such, would subscribe to the conclusion of my analysis of positive jurisprudence in section 2, that analogical reasoning only presupposes a local legal unity. So, in the positivist conception of law, analogy as such is not enough to represent the unity and rationality of the complete legal system, nor of any fundamental legal principles.

Furthermore, as far as a rational unity is presupposed, according to legal positivism this would only be a formal rationality in the sense of consistency. In this legal theory, the application of the universalisability principle leads to an extension of the applicability of the existing laws and jurisprudence. In this way consistency in a relatively larger field of application of positive law will be achieved. But the material quality of this extended systematicness will depend entirely on the quality of the already existing positive laws. According to legal positivism this depends in its turn entirely on what the legal authorities choose to legislate. There is no guarantee at all that such laws will pass the test of a substantive rationality. Extension of the legislation on theft to the stealing of electricity may for example produce unity in a larger sphere of application of the penal code. But whether this can be justified as rational in a substantive sense depends on the contents of other parts of the legal system in question. If for instance social goods are distributed very unequally, under certain circumstances illegal appropriation of electricity by the underprivileged could be defended as pre-eminently rational. In that case, analogical application of the law may increase consistency, but at the same time run contrary to a substantive rationality.

In short, according to legal positivism, analogical reasoning is related to a rationality and unity which is rather deficient in two ways. Firstly, a very local unity will do. Secondly, it will yield a mere formal rationality.

According to the view on law of the *Critical Legal Studies Movement*, the latter deficiency is even worse. This movement views positive law as an incoherent set of prescriptions, that are the expressions of conflicting social interests. Therefore, it conceives any attempt to construct law as a unified consistent system as an irrational political judgement, in which the judge takes sides with one of the interested parties. In the theory of the critical legal studies movement, such an attempt to legal unity necessarily implies a substantive irrationality.

Only in other non-positivistic theories of law may this two-fold deficient rationality be overcome, notably in a Dworkinian conception, or in natural law theory.

4. DWORKIN'S SUPER ANALOGIA IURIS

Dworkin conceives positive law in accordance with prof. Nerhot's thesis as a coherent rational whole, based on one or more central substantive legal principles. These principles constitute the core of the legal system, although they need not be formulated explicitly. According to Dworkin, they are inherent in the legal system, because they are tacitly presupposed in the particular positive laws. The judge can find them by formulating that set of moral principles, which best justifies as much as possible of the totality of the explicitly given laws and jurisprudence. Against legal positivism and the critical legal studies movement, Dworkin contends that at this point law has a necessary connection with morality. He maintains that law's central principle is that of equality: that everybody has a right to equal respect and concern. Once found, the judge can use these underlying principles as a guideline to reach a solution in cases that are not or not clearly covered by the law. So, Dworkin's fundamental principles serve as the central *ratio iuris* of the whole system, which prevents arbitrary decisions in hard cases. As to analogical reasoning, they can determine which aspects in a case are juridically relevant.

Thus, according to Dworkin, analogy problems should be decided by what can be labelled as reasoning by "*super analogia iuris*": The judge should construct underlying principles that are implied in the systematic coherence of *all* positive laws, and use these to determine criteria of relevancy for the application of the universalisability principle and analogical reasoning. In other words, Dworkin extends the way of argumentation inherent in extensive interpretation and analogical reasoning to positive law as a whole. In this way, analogical reasoning loses its local character. It derives its ratio from a set of principles that unify the complete legal system.

So, prof. Nerhot's thesis seems to fit perfectly into a Dworkinian conception of law. Firstly, law as a whole is conceived as a rational unity in a formal sense. Secondly, it is based on some substantive central principles, such as that of the equal value of all men. Analogical reasoning, as a specific application of the universalisability principle, represents this system, because what is relevant can be determined from the viewpoint of the *ratio iuris* of the system as a whole, as embodied in its basic principles.

On taking a closer, critical look, however, only the first point is satisfactorily guaranteed by Dworkin's theory. Dworkin's method of reasoning by *super analogia iuris* will indeed result in a consistent hierarchical system, consisting of some fundamental principles, from which the multitude of particular laws can be derived and thus justified. But this does not at all guarantee that these principles, as for their *content*, are capable of serving as a justification of the claim to general obedience to the legal system in question. This is so, because the content of these legal principles is to be derived from the combined content of the particular positive laws and juridical decisions – this is what makes them *legal*, instead of mere moral principles. Therefore, from the moral point of view Dworkin's fundamental principles can be no better than the positive legal system as a whole. This in its turn depends on what the juridical officials in fact decide.

For instance, Dworkin's method of interpretation does not necessarily in all legal systems lead to the universal principle that all human beings are to be treated as equals. In the United States it could very well result in a substantive principle of equality. But when applied to South African law or classical Roman law, the very same method will lead to a fundamental principle of *in*equality: it is this principle that best justifies positive laws which prescribe racism and slavery.

So, Dworkinian fundamental principles are contingent on whatever those in power posit as law, and can therefore only serve as a justification to those participants in the legal system in question, who already have accepted it as obligatory. In other words, Dworkin's method leads at most to a purely *formal* rationality of the law. And in an immoral legal system, all that more systematicness may lead to is a more efficient immorality.

Now Dworkin tries to avoid this pitfall by stating that the interpretation of a work of art or of a social practice always takes place within the horizon of social expectations as to what the purpose of the object under consideration is and should be. Interpretation therefore is "a narrative story that makes of these practices the best that can be." (*Law's Empire*, p. vii). Legal interpretation is not merely a passive mirroring of the material the interpreter finds, but a creative construction in which he emphasizes those parts of the positive law that he values most. After having thus constructed a set of central justifying legal principles, he can next criticise other parts of positive law that fail these standards. Through this view on interpretation, Dworkin may be able to partly avoid the conclusion drawn above: interpretation may lead to a moral improvement of the existing legal system.

However, this is not sufficient to save Dworkin's case. For according to Dworkin, this way of interpretation does not give the interpreter very much freedom to deviate from positive law. Although his rational reconstruction need not cover all parts of the legal system under interpretation, it must at least accommodate a sufficient part, lest it becomes the invention of a completely new legal practice (*Law's Empire*, p. 66). So, reducing the South African legal system to the principle of equal respect and concern would be too Herculean a task.

Furthermore, interpreters who are participants of the South African legal system, such as its judges, will not even strive for a reform towards racial equality. On the contrary, they will consider the effective maintenance of Apartheid as the main purpose of their legal system. Thus, they will as readily affirm a central principle of inequality as the best justification of *their* legal system, as Dworkin propagates equality as the core of his legal culture.

Dworkin indeed recognizes the relative value of his interpretative legal theory: "Interpretative theories are by their nature addressed to a particular legal culture, generally the culture to which their authors belong. Unless these theories are deeply sceptical, they will treat that legal system as a flourishing example of law, one that calls for and rewards the interpretative attitude". (*Law's Empire*, p. 102). Therefore, such theories will not always be suitable for foreign legal practices, based on completely different ideologies (*Law's Empire*, p. 103).

This relativity is illustrated by Dworkin's discussion of the interpretation of immoral legal systems, such as Nazi-German law. Dworkin disagrees with the natural law view, that such a system lacks the character of law. He considers the Nazi system as one of the historically developed realizations of the same general practices and institutions, from which his own legal practice has also developed (*Law's Empire*, p. 103). Nevertheless, a justificatory interpretation of the Nazi law, which in Dworkin's view must "consist of an argument why a practice of that general shape is worth pursuing" (*Law's Empire*, p. 66), will meet with great difficulties. It will result in the sceptical conclusion that a justificatory interpretation is impossible here, because this practice does not serve any good purpose (*Law's Empire*, p. 79, 105). Obviously, Dworkin's interpretative theory does not easily agree with this foreign legal practice. In Dworkin's view, another possibility could be to interpret only the non-ideological part of Nazi-law, such as its contract law. Finally, Dworkin also admits the possibility of an interpretation, not of how the Nazi judge should have decided according to the ideology of the interpreter, but of how this judge would have decided *in fact*. The interpreter then has to imagine himself in the shoes of a Nazi judge, who sees the national socialist regime as the most flourishing example of what law should be.

However, Dworkin should have drawn more radical conclusions from his relativism. He only discusses the difficulties that a participant of Dworkin's own legal culture meets, when he tries to interpret a foreign culture which he abhors. But Dworkin's starting-point was that interpretative theories can only be developed meaningfully from an *internal* point of view within the legal system in question, by a participant who subscribes to its ideological purpose (*Law's Empire*, p. 64). His theory on interpretation is based on a phenomenological analysis of the way judges generally argue: they implicitly refer to the basic principles inherent in *their* legal system. Therefore, if one takes Dworkin's conception of interpretation seriously, interpretation from an external ideological point of view does not even make sense. It will not result in a *legal* interpretation at all, but only in a dogmatic moral condemnation. So Dworkin should have concluded straightaway that Nazi law is as its *participants* materially interpret it: as based upon racist principles.

In other words, Dworkin should make a distinction between the methodical and the material parts of his interpretative theory. The methodical part is applicable to every legal system that is characterized by adjudication based on legal principles (in contrast to adjudication as a lordly right, as in feudal cultures), even if ideologically it deviates from Dworkin's egalitarian ideology. But this part only guarantees a formal rationality, i.e. consistency. In contrast, the material part is more specifically connected with the ideological purposes that particular legal cultures attach to their legal systems. Dworkin's interpretation of the legal system of the United States could result in an equality principle, but the majority of the historical and foreign legal cultures may have a fundamental inequality at their basis. And because Dworkin conceives these different legal cultures as the products of historical traditions, his theory cannot guarantee a substantive rationality of any of these diverging legal systems.

5. NATURAL LAW THEORY AND NATURAL CRITERIA OF RELEVANCY

This may be different in traditional *Natural Law* theory, which identifies the core of law with some *universal* moral principles. This theory claims that nature implies a set of substantive principles, that guarantee and justify the rationality of a legal system. These natural principles constitute an *a priori* and universal *ratio iuris*, which serves as an objective test to the positive law system. They can also be used to determine what is relevant for a comparison of two cases.

The grounds for these pretensions of traditional natural law theory lie in an essentialistic world view, such as the metaphysics of Aristotle and Thomas Aquinas. According to this metaphysical ontology reality consists of a rational unity, ordered in "natural classes", each characterized by some essential properties. This natural order of classes is also binding for the legal categories to be posited by the legislator, as a guarantee against the arbitrary power which legal positivism would allow him. This metaphysical world view makes it possible to discern the essential from the accidental features of a case. What is relevant is objectively given in the *ratio*, i.e. the essential nature of the case, that also constitutes a guideline for establishing the *ratio iuris*. This ontology makes it in principle possible to reason analogically or *a contrario* on the basis of objective and just discriminations.

Traditional Christian Thomistic natural law theory would for instance produce an easy answer to some analogy problems that have greatly interested Dutch lawyers recently. One of these problems concerned an unmarried father, who asked for the right to see his under-age child regularly, although art. 161 of the Dutch Civil Code stated that a legal arrangement of the right to regular intercourse between parent and child can only be adjudged by a divorce sentence, therefore only if the child is born from the marriage of the parents. Now this father had been married to the mother, but they were divorced six years before the birth of their child. Notwithstanding their divorce, the couple had continued to live together, and the father had also legally recognized his child. The children's court magistrate had decided that the father's claim was not admissible, because the child was born six years after the divorce sentence. The Supreme Court however reversed this judgement: because the cohabitation had been continued after the divorce in the same way as during marriage, this relationship should be treated as analogous to a marriage relationship (H. R., May 26th 1977, N. J. 1978, 417). But in another case, where the parents never had been married at all, the Supreme Court refused a similar claim, because admittance would deviate too much from the intention of the legislator (H. R., November 4th 1977, N. J. 1978, 418).

Another problem of family law relating to analogy problems in the field of legislation has recently been much debated. This debate concerns new legislation on adoption. It focusses on the question as to whether a homosexual relationship can be considered as similar to a heterosexual marriage – which is the standard case in adoption laws. Both adversaries and advocates appeal to art. 1 of the Dutch Constitution and to several international treatises, which prescribe that equal cases should be treated equally. But whereas the advocates plead equal treatment of the relationship of cohabiting homosexual couples because of its similarity with heterosexual marriage, adversaries defend the opposite thesis that homosexual and heterosexual relationships are fundamentally *un*equal in their relevant respects. According to the latter opinion, there is a fundamental difference in the light of child-raising. A child brought up by a homosexual couple would not be able to benefit from the normal parent-child relationship, i.e. being brought up by two heterosexual parents of different sexes. This might prevent a well balanced development of the child, and even cause an identity crisis. Supporters of homosexual adoption deny this. They appeal to recent scientific research which does not substantiate such a claim. Furthermore, in other cultures child-raising is effectuated in many different ways, for instance by groups of women, without leading to undesirable developments. The supporters also point to the fact that it is often the way of life of *married* parents that prevents a well balanced development of their child.

Thomistic natural law theory would have not much difficulty in answering these problems. It maintains that there exists a natural order, created according to a divine plan. In this order, the exclusive natural function of sex is to serve the procreation of mankind. For the upbringing of the offspring God has invented the institution of lifelong heterosexual monogamous marriage. Therefore, only sex and child-raising within the marriage institution is in accordance with natural law, and should be supported by positive law. This implies firstly that an extra-marital heterosexual relationship should be treated as dissimilar to marriage. Secondly, homosexuality and child-raising by homosexuals deviate even more from the natural essence of sexual and family life. Homosexual couples should therefore not be allowed to adopt children.

The problem with this kind of metaphysical argument is, however, that by using other metaphysical theories quite different conclusions can be reached. Platonic metaphysics for instance results in completely different views on child-raising, heterosexual marriage and homosexuality. In his *Republic* Plato maintains that the leading men and women should live in polygamous groups (V, 458). Upbringing is not the task of a married couple. On the contrary, children are in common possession. They are raised in a commune of men and women, without knowing their biological father (V, 457). According to Plato this way of upbringing prevents egoism. In *Symposium* Plato suggests that male homosexual love is superior because it is the most masculine form of love (192 b).

Because of the unprovability of all these contradictory metaphysical claims, essentialistic ontology and traditional natural law theory have lost their wide acceptance nowadays. As to their content, the world views of both Aquinas and Plato, as well as that of Aristotle, would yield results that are contrary to the now dominating equality principle, such as propagated by Dworkin. These classical philosophers defend a fundamental inequality between men and women, or between Greeks and foreigners, or between free men and slaves, because of natural differences in kind between these categories.

In the field of epistemology, essentialistic ontology is nowadays considered as an arbitrary and unprovable choice from the whole of reality. In recent linguistic philosophy for instance, the school of Wittgenstein has maintained that essential definitions are not possible, because the meaning of a word depends on its use in a specific context. General concepts cover heterogenous, though overlapping fields of meaning, loosely united by family resemblances. Moreover, concepts do not have any universal meaning, because the way one orders the world depends on the world view and the way of life of the culture in which one is raised. So, reasoning analogically is possible only within a specific context within a specific world view. And because there are no standards of rationality to be found independent of such world views, the latter constitute frames of reference that cannot in their turn be evaluated as to their rational quality. With this relativistic conclusion we are back with Dworkin, who also relates the possibility of interpretation to the internal point of view from within a particular historical way of life.

6. UNIVERSALISABILITY IN ETHICS

So, a substantive justification of decisions about relevancy in analogical reasoning appears to be problematic in any existing legal theory. Perhaps then a solution can be found outside the legal field, in a general theory of ethics which views the universalisability principle from a broader perspective.

As in natural law theory, in ethics the belief in the validity of an essentialistic world view has strongly diminished. This has resulted in a general tendency to deny the possibility of justifying any universal conception of "the good life". This in its turn has led to the replacement of traditional "broad" or "perfectionistic" ethics by a formal or procedural ethic. This modern ethic often has as its core the very same principle of universalisability, that also constitutes the basis of analogical thought in law. Such different ethical theories as that of Kant, Habermas and Hare all share this same characteristic, although in quite divergent ways.

Some authors consider the principle of universalisability as one of the fundamental characteristics of morality. M. G. Singer for instance states that its "traditional name [...] is the principle of justice" (*Generalization in ethics*, p. 46). N. Hoerster translates it as the "principle of equality", one of the fundamental principles of ethics (*Utilitaristische Ethik und Verallgemeinerung*, p. 56). Others, such as Hare, see it as a purely logical principle, which nevertheless "without assuming any antecedent moral premisses, but given that people are as they are and the world as it is, will lead them (provided that they will think morally and exercise their imaginations, and will face the facts, and take pains to understand what they are saying) to agree upon certain moral principles which are conducive to the just reconciliation of conflicting interests [...]". (*Freedom and Reason*, p. 185).

In this paragraph I shall examine whether ethical universalisability leads to any results which could serve as a frame of reference for making legal analogical thought rational in a substantive sense. As a focal point I shall consider the question whether the ethical universalisability principle can say anything about the justifiability of such contrary legal basic principles as the equality principle of the legal system of the United States, and the inequality principle of South African law. If it would appear that the universalisability principle even cannot decide this fundamental moral disagreement, it probably is not able to set any rational limits at all to the arbitrariness of positive law and in particular of analogical reasoning.

I shall concentrate on the theory of R. M. Hare, because Kant and Habermas have already integrated the substantive principle of equality of all human beings in their versions of the universalisability thesis. Kant has formulated the universalisability principle in a neutral sense in the version of his categorical imperative that commands: "Act only on that maxim through which you can at the same time will that it should become a universal law" (*Groundwork of the Metaphysics of Morals*, p. 421). But in another formulation he adds to this the substantive principle of the equal value of all human beings: "So act that you treat humanity in your own person and in the person of everyone else always at the same time as an end and never merely as means". (*Groundwork of the Metaphysics of Morals*, p. 429). This implies that everyone should respect and recognize everyone (*Groundwork of the Metaphysics of Morals p.* 427-428). This second version however presupposes an unprovable essentialistic metaphysics. Habermas also introduces a substantive equality principle by referring to an essentialistic anthropology, to which I shall return in section 6.3. Hare on the contrary only propounds a purely *logical* universalisability test. Therefore his theory has the advantage of being provisionally neutral as to a variance of competing moral claims.

6. 1. Hare's universal prescriptivism

R. M. Hare is one of the exponents of post-positivist linguistic moral philosophy. He allows for more rationality in ethics than the logical positivists, who considered only the empirically verifiable propositions of natural science as meaningful language, and declined moral language as purely subjective emotional expressions. Hare agrees with the later linguistic philosophers who reject this one-sided emphasis on cognitive language, and maintain that there are many other meaningful ways to use language. The later Wittgenstein mentions for instance commanding, acting, telling jokes etc. These all have their own sense and rules for correct word usage.

Hare analyzed the rules of moral language in *The Language of Morals* (1952) and *Freedom and Reason* (1963). As the title of the latter book indicates, Hare considers morals as partly rational and partly "free", i.e. not bound by any rules. He shares a meta-ethical non-cognitivism with the earlier positivistic linguistic philosophers: We have much more freedom in our moral statements than in our factual ones, which have to correspond with verifiable empirical phenomena. Ultimately moral views are based on subjective decisions. Contrary to the logical positivists, however, Hare does not consider moral choices as completely arbitrary. They are bound by the rules of moral language, that imply certain restrictions which guarantee a degree of rationality to moral discourse.

These rules are based on two characteristics which Hare distinguishes in the conceptual structure of moral language. Firstly moral statements have the purport of guiding or prescribing human action. Secondly they thereby refer to standards that claim universal validity. According to Hare, these characteristics have a number of consequences that form a test for the tenability of a moral statement. Hare calls this test *Universal Prescriptivism.* According to universal prescriptivism, a moral statement only obeys the rules or the "logic" of moral language if the speaker is willing to take its *universal* purport seriously. I.e., he must be willing to *prescribe* to himself the same moral standard, which he invokes in his moral prescriptions to others, in the hypothetical case that he would be in their position. This test, according to Hare, excludes certain moral claims like a racist policy.

Hare infers this test on the basis of the following analysis. He distinguishes two meaning-aspects in moral terms like "good" or "ought", a *descriptive* and a *prescriptive* or evaluative meaning. Moral statements are basically prescriptive: they are meant to give guidance to human action. If I say "charity is good", I recommend that you act charitably. In this fundamental respect moral statements are more akin to commands than to descriptive statements, in spite of their grammatical form.

Besides this prescriptive character, moral utterances also possess descriptive meaning. The speaker implicitly refers to certain properties of the thing recommended, that constitute the reason why he calls it "good". If for instance I say "it is good that you undergo this operation", I probably say this because the operation has the property of restoring health and diminishing human suffering. Hare calls this reference to good-making properties the "supervenient" character of "good". Because of this supervenient character "good" has a *universal* purport: it would be inconsistent to say of anything else with the same or similar properties (in this case: restoring human health) that it is not good. So, the speaker has implicitly formulated a universal standard of goodmaking properties of a class of cases.

In fact, not only moral words, but all descriptive words have this supervenient character. It would be as inconsistent to say "that is a table", but of something else with exactly the same properties "that is not a table", as to say that St. Francis is a good man, but deny that someone else with exactly the same properties is good. In other words, all descriptive words are universalisable: they apply to all the cases that answer to the description. Thus, according to Hare, universalisability is not a special characteristic of moral language, but of all descriptive language.

Nor is prescriptibility specific to morality. Commands are also prescriptive. Furthermore, the combination of prescriptibility and universalisability characterizes all normative judgements, including esthetical or prudential ones. What singles out *moral* judgements is their claim to override all other kinds of prescriptions.

According to Hare, in moral words the prescriptive or evaluative meaning dominates the descriptive meaning. Their main function is to prescribe, not to describe. Furthermore, the implicit normative standard which a speaker implicitly describes is not objectively given, but depends on his evaluations. Ultimately his moral views are determined by his subjective disposition. Most people will for instance call human suffering bad, but Christian martyrs and masochists who approve of it do not sin against the rules of moral language.

In other words, the moral evaluation of a case is never identical with the description of the factual properties of the case. Each speaker has the freedom to apply his own moral preferences to a given case, and to recommend these to others. This freedom discriminates moral utterances from purely descriptive statements like "the world is round", that are bound by objective facts. It constitutes the priority of the evaluative above the descriptive aspect of moral words.

Hare derives his test of universal prescriptivism from these combined descriptive and prescriptive meanings of moral words. According to his ethical non-cognitivism each moral agent has the freedom to choose his own moral standards. But once a speaker has stated a moral evaluation, his freedom is henceforth restricted by the universal purport of the descriptive part – the implicit universal standard – of his statement. The descriptive meaning of "good" demands universalisability. It implies that a speaker who predicates it to a certain action or situation, must also apply it to all actions or situations that are similar in their relevant respects. To be more specific, he must accept the consequences of universalisability: that his moral judgement about others also applies to himself, if he were in a comparable situation. So, if "Robinson Crusoe" maintains that it is good that "Friday" is a slave, the logic of the word "good" obliges him to accept that it would also be good for himself to be a slave, in the hypothetical case that he were in the same situation. And because of the prescriptive meaning of "good", he should be willing to factually act according to this prescription, and enter slavery. Given the psychological human constitution, Hare thinks it very unlikely that the speaker would accept this consequence, unless he is a "fanatic" who takes his standards so seriously that he would be willing to undergo severe hardships for the sake of his ideals. Thus, the test of universal prescriptivism will in most cases exclude moral principles that imply considerable human suffering.

In this way, Hare's universalisability criterion can to a certain extent serve as a critical test for the acceptability of moral views. It can eliminate some unacceptable principles. On the other hand, it can *not* positively justify moral principles as demanding universal adherence.

Indeed, Hare considers it as a merit of his theory that it propounds a purely formal test, which is based merely on the "logical" structure of moral words, and is compatible with a variety of different normative views. (I do not discuss here his later turn to an utilitarian ethics in *Moral Thinking* (1981)). Hare emphasizes repeatedly that someone who keeps putting forward non-universalisable moral prescriptions is not making any *moral* fault, but only a logical mistake. Universalisability and prescriptivity are characteristic of all normative judgements, not only of moral ones. Universalisability is even a property of all descriptive words. Failing the test of universal prescriptivism is therefore just a sin against logic. One is inconsistent, contradicting oneself by asserting that certain properties provide a sufficient basis for calling something "good" in one case, while denying that the same properties are sufficient in another, but similar case.

As is mentioned above, Hare does not claim that logic alone suffices to eliminate moral claims that involve severe human hardships. As the case of the idealistic "fanatic" who is immune to Hare's logical test would seem to imply, in addition a number of empirical human characteristics is also needed: a disposition to empathy with others, imagination, and an aversion to suffering. But according to Hare, as a matter of psychological fact most people have these dispositions. Fortunately, "fanatics" are very rare in reality.

6. 2. The logical universalisability principle and equality

The question that I shall consider now is, whether the universalisability principle such as Hare has developed in ethics can serve as a substantive frame of reference for legal universalisability, of which analogical reasoning is a specific application. That is, can it justify some juridical principles which should constitute the centre of a legal system? Can it restrict the arbitrariness of the legislator? And more specifically: can it decide between the contrary claims of egalitarian and elitist legal systems?

Hare claims that universal prescriptivism can at least in most cases exclude certain moral positions such as slavery, or extreme inequality, because no one would like to be on the receiving end. So his test would reject racist principles, which a Dworkinian interpretation would point out as central to the South African legal system. In other words, it would deny that these racist principles can serve as a substantive justification of South African positive laws, and in general of any criteria of relevancy for legal analogical reasoning.

However, it seems that the universalisability thesis can not even do this, without assuming a *petitio principii* by tacitly introducing a substantive moral principle, that of equality of all human beings.

Hare's universal prescriptivism demands that anybody who gives a moral judgement should be willing to place himself in the positions of all other persons involved. This, Hare claims, follows from the universal purport of moral language, which implies that moral judgements should not refer to individuals, but only to general properties (a.o. *Moral Thinking*, p. 91, 154). So the logic of moral language forbids me to award myself a privileged position for the only reason that it is *me*. Although even this can be questioned (see F. JACOBS, *Ten overstaan van allen*, p. 32 ff; H. S. SILVERSTEIN, *Universalisability and Egoism*, p. 242-264), I shall not go into this point here. But even if, for the sake of argument, this point is granted to Hare, it does not help very much. Notably, it does not prevent the formulation of an elitist theory in *general* terms, by referring, not to purely personal properties, but to properties of an exclusive class of human beings, which make them "superior", such as having an I.Q. above 140.

Hare admits that his universal prescriptivism logically leaves open the possibility of defending an elitist moral theory. But he marginalises the defenders of such positions as rare "fanatics", identifying them with hard core Nazis, striving for the ideal to eliminate all Jews. If someone adheres so strongly to such an elitist ideal that he would pass the test of universal prescriptivism, by accepting it even if he were in the position of a member of the inferior class, his moral view is logically perfect, concedes Hare. Nevertheless such idealists are labelled "fanatics", because they are willing to sacrifice no matter how many human interests to their ideals. Hare expects that, after the reflection that universal prescriptivism demands, very few fanatics will actually remain. The moral agent first has to imagine himself in the position of the persons who will suffer from his ideals, and view the consequences his proposal from the perspective of *their* interests, preferences, and needs, as if these were his own. A Nazi must for instance accept to go to the gas-chamber himself. Hare expects that very few people will then still stick to their original ideals – not on logical grounds, but as a consequence of the contingent psychological constitution of most men (*Freedom and Reason*, p. 172).

(In *Moral Thinking* Hare tries to eliminate the problem of fanaticism altogether, by translating "ideals" into a special kind of preferences, that then can be weighed against, and overruled by the preferences of the others concerned. This solution however is based on a debatable swing towards utilitarianism.)

But Hare's effort to marginalize the "fanatic" to an oddity on the ground of an appeal to psychological empathy fails. In the first place, it cannot hold because it leans on a hidden tendency to utilitarianism which brings ideals down to the level of mere preferences. This appears from Hare's expectation that from the psychological perspective normal (non-fanatical) people will give priority to the interests of as many people involved as possible above their own ideals. This may sound appealing when it concerns an evaluation of Nazi ideals against the needs of its victims. But what about the evaluation of the ideal of justice against the interests of an unjust majority? Is it also desirable to sacrifice the rights of one individual to contrary desires of the rest of the population? As a fact of moral psychology, conscience might lead many people to a preference for justice above the utilitarian optimalization of interest satisfaction. In that case "fanatics" might be less rare than Hare thinks.

My second objection is more central to my argument, because it is specifically aimed at Hare's marginalization of elitist ideals. Hare's universal prescriptivism fails in its intended elimination of elitism, because an elitist will not even arrive at the point of *psychological* empathy by changing positions with the other people involved. The *logical* part of universal prescriptivism gives the elitist sufficient reasons to refuse any empathic identification with people that he considers as inferior. As such, the universalisability principle, just like the principle of formal justice, only implies the purely formal demand that equal cases should be treated equally. It does not specify *which* cases are to be considered as equal. In other words, it lacks further material criteria of relevancy. Now all the elitist has to do is to claim that *different* kinds of human beings constitute fundamentally different cases in their relevant respects, and that therefore there is no ground for a further comparison by way of empathy.

For instance, on the grounds of an elitist theory that takes physical beauty as the fundamental criterion of relevancy for differentiation, a beauty queen can refuse to imagine herself in the position of the underpriviliged hunchback of Notre Dâme. She can just deny that he counts as a similar case in its relevant respects. Her prescription to ugly persons to keep out of sight is therefore *not* directed at herself – the other side of the coin of the universalisability thesis is that unequal cases should be treated unequally.

In other words, Hare's demand that a moral agent should imagine himself in the situation of all other people concerned rests on the presupposition of the substantive moral principle of the principal equality of all human beings. Hare explicitly admits this: "The principle [...] 'Everybody to count for one, nobody for more than one' can [...] be justified by the appeal to the demand for universalisability [...]. For what this principle means is that everyone is entitled to equal consideration, and that if it is said that two people ought to be treated differently, some difference must be cited as the ground for these different moral judgements. And this is a corollary of the requirement of universalisability" (*Freedom and Reason*, p. 118). Hare asserts here that the burden of the proof of differential treatment of human beings rests on those who propound inequality. But why should this be so, given that human beings are similar in certain respects, but dissimilar in others? Why could not an elitist return the challenge, and ask for grounds for *equal* treatment? Universalisability as such does not give any clues here, because it lacks any material criteria of relevancy. Therefore, contrary to Hare, this principle does not oblige an elitist to hypothetically identify with beings that he considers as inferior, and therefore dissimilar in the relevant respects. (For a more elaborate criticism of Hare, see MARIS, 1981.)

Of course, elitist ideals can founder on other grounds. Hare's universal prescriptivism allows the Nazi wrongly to stick to his anti-semitic ideals, if only he is fanatical enough. In the first place, if such ideals are based on completely illusory properties, they can be refuted empirically. Anti-semitic ideals can be refuted because they are based on pseudo-scientific racist theories that are easily unmasked by scientific research. In the same way Aristotle's differentiation between free men and slaves by nature does not hold. Aristotle bases his defence of slavery on a difference in kind between Greek men and foreigners, claiming that they have an unequal share in reason. Closer examination would have taught him that in reality rationality is not distributed along this line.

Secondly, one can eliminate differentiations based on criteria of relevancy, that are too absurd in the context of the world view in which they are propagated. In our culture it would for instance be absurd if a privileged treatment was given to a class of people, solely on the ground that they have six fingers on each hand.

But one should be very tolerant in one's judgements on absurdity, because of the enormous variety in world views. As already has been said, modern linguistic philosophy – that forms the starting-point of Hare's universal prescriptivism – maintains, that there is not one objective way to categorize the world. Instead, there are many different ways to order it, depending on one's point of view. Linguistic philosophers maintain that the way one orders the world depends on an interpretation, which is determined by the conceptual scheme of the culture in which one participates. The social conventions of everyday language constitute as it were a window on reality, within which we structure our knowledge. Furthermore, the world view of each culture is compounded of a pluriformity of different "language games", as Wittgenstein calls them – different symbolic expressions of our diverging relations to the world around us. Hare's "moral game" is one of them. Every language game has its own perspective that determines its own criteria of relevancy. As Wittgenstein remarks, what counts as "the same" or as "identical" depends on the use of a rule within a settled institution of language (WITTGENSTEIN, *Philosophical Investigations, I*, p. 215 ff.). Following Wittgenstein's footsteps Peter Winch has stated that "two events which count as qualitatively similar from the point of view of one rule count as different from the point of view of another" (WINCH, *The Idea of Social Science*, p. 83). In *Understanding a Primitive Society* Winch has derived a radical cultural relativism from Wittgenstein's conception of world views. Different cultures all have their own incommensurable conceptual orders, that constitute what counts as true, rational, good and so on. There is no cognizable independent reality, against which such a world view can be tested. This implies that what counts as "relevantly similar" also can vary with the world views of different cultures, and can only be evaluated from within the standards of its own culture. In old Egyptian culture for instance, a preferential treatment of six fingered people would not be absurd at all, because this was considered as characteristic of the pharaohs (in fact due to their intermarriage of brothers and sisters). Also, it is not absurd to defend a caste society in a culture with a Hindu world view, characterized by a belief in reincarnation in a new form of life according to one's merit in one's former life. And from the point of view of this elitist world view, Hare's universalisability test implies no logical reason why a Brahman should identify himself with an untouchable.

Even within one culture there can exist an enormous variance of competing perspectives, depending on different, but irrefutable world views. Within western culture it is not difficult to find world views that would emphasize the differences rather than the similarities between different kinds of human beings. If one believes that some people have a superior insight in a perfect world of ideas, it is not absurd to defend a Platonist hierarchical state.

In general, as soon as an elitist appeals to real differences that are not too absurd, his theory is irrefutable. Nietzsche for instance draws a line between the supermen on the one hand, and the grey herd of the "much too many" on the other hand. They are distinguished by real differences, such as creativity, courage, honesty, vitality and strong self-awareness. And it is not absurd to attach a high value to such characteristics.

Neither can Hare's universalisability principle refute Nietzsche's elitism. Nietzsche's superman would refuse to hypothetically change places with people of inferior status, because these represent cases that are fundamentally dissimilar in their relevant respects.

Contrary to this, Hare suggests in chapter 5 of *Moral Thinking* that all human beings are similar in one fundamental respect: in their self-consciousness of their suffering, and in their equal aversion to it. But Nietzsche would give short shrift to this criterion of moral relevancy. His Superman precisely distinguishes himself from the mass of inferior human beings by his *amor fati*, his heroical acceptance of his hardships. Therefore, they belong to incomparable catagories. "What is the ape to man? A laughing-stock or a painful embarrassment. And just so shall man be to Superman: a laughing-stock or a painful embarrassment" (NIETZSCHE, *Thus Spoke Zarathustra*, p. 41).

This considerable freedom with which one can point out similarities or differences as relevant, is a consequence of the insight that man is free to categorize the world as he likes, as distinct from Aristotelian essentialistic ontology. Modern linguistic philosophy, the source of inspiration of Hare's analysis of the moral concepts, asserts that there is not one exclusive objective way to categorize the world. Instead, there are many different ways to order it, depending on your point of view. Linguistic philosophers maintain that any world order is relative to the conceptual order of the culture in which you participate. So, the same insight that has lead to the formal ethics of Hare's universal prescriptivism, also frustrates Hare's test to work in the way wished for: it implies a lack of objective criteria as to what cases are alike, in other words which properties count as relevant to a comparison. Because human beings are similar in some, and dissimilar in other respects, one can choose either as relevant. Therefore, Hare's logical universalisability principle leaves you the freedom to maintain that different categories of human beings are dissimilar in their relevant respects. It cannot even resolve the opposition of egalitarianism versus elitism. More generally, it too is unable to guarantee a substantive rationality for analogical reasoning.

6. 3. Universalisability and inter-subjective acceptability

On the basis of a vision of man as a being that is characterized by symbolic communication, which is similar to linguistic philosophy, philosophers like Habermas and Apel have nevertheless maintained that it is possible to justify an ethic which combines universalisability and equality. Instead of Hare's claim of *logical* universalisability, i.e. of consistency of the moral judgements of one individual, they interpret the universalisability principle as a test of whether moral claims are *inter-subjectively* acceptable to all persons concerned.

According to Hare, every value judgement is supervenient to a set of factual properties of a situation or an action, that constitute the reason why the speaker attaches value to it. In his logical interpretation, the universalisability principle is directed to the individual speaker only, and demands that henceforth he shall attach the same value to everything with similar properties. Habermas and Apel add to this that such a value-claim also implies that other persons can challenge the speaker to an inter-subjective debate, in order to prove that these properties really constitute a sufficient reason for his valuation.

Apel justifies this interpretation with an appeal to a "transcendental a priori of the communication community". By this he means that the very possibility of all language usage presupposes a general consensus on interpretation criteria in a communication community – a thesis similar to that of Wittgenstein. Now according to Apel, the essence of communication is a mutual exchange of sincere arguments, not frustrated by inequalities in power. Therefore, all human beings *as* communicative persons have the obligation to strive for an ideal communication society, i.e. for a way of life based on power free argumentation. All decisions should be made by all participants, under conditions of freedom and equality. This implies a reciprocal recognition of all of its members as equal partners in the discussion about the organisation of society. In this egalitarian view, universalisability implies that only those claims count as valid, which can be inter-subjectively justified as reconcilable with the claims of all others.

Habermas shares Apel's conception of universalisability as symmetrical inter-subjectivity, but criticizes his appeal to transcendentalism. Nevertheless, Habermas' argument is also based on the view that all human communication is essentially directed towards the idea of truth or rightness, and therefore is principally open to reciprocal argumentation about what is to count as true or right.

However, this egalitarian interpretation of the universalisability principle does not hold, because it is based on an untenable essentialism: that sincere argumentation is the essence of human communication. Communication has many different functions, of which argumentation is just one. Giving misinformation is another. For by his possession of language, man is able to dissociate himself from his immediate surroundings: it is characteristic of linguistic symbols, that one can express something by them which is *not* present. Therefore, language is pre-eminently suited to be used for fiction, lies and manipulation. An observation of the neurologist Oliver Sachs teaches us that the possibility of manipulation grows with the increase of the level of abstraction. He describes in *The Man who Mistook his Wife for a Hat*, how a television speech by president Reagan produced great hilarity in a group of aphasia patients. Reagan's rhetoric lacked its usual effect, because aphasics are not able to hear words, but have compensated for this by developing an extreme sensibility to non verbal expression. And because abstract words can much more easily deceive than direct body language, these patients immediately see through the insincerity of rhetorical speech.

Often this point is countered by the argument that deception is parasitic on sincere language usage, because lying would have no effect if there did not exist a general belief in the trustworthiness of the major part of communication. However, this is only so in cultures that give high priority to the exchange of objective information. In contrast, in countries with a "shame-culture" the main usage of language is euphemistic. Its function is to save social harmony, prior to giving honest information.

Contrary to the equation of communication with a power-free exchange of arguments, Nietzsche even stated that in its very *origin* language is an expression of the power of the rulers, who coined the words in accordance with their will (NIETZSCHE, *On the Genealogy of Morals*, p. 26).

Therefore, even if it is conceded that communication is an essential characteristic of mankind, this does not imply a duty to recognize all human beings as equal argumentation partners. Apel's and Habermas' attempt to couple universalisability with equality is based on a selective conception of communication. A Nietzschean elitist would probably react to their claims that what is acceptable for all is for that reason unacceptable to him. In short, the ethical universalisability principle would allow for so many opposing moral instances that one should not expect that it can offer any substantive rationality.

7. CONCLUSION

In an attempt to evaluate the rational quality of reasoning by analogy, I have understood this way of reasoning as a special application of the universalisability principle, which demands that similar cases should be treated similarly. As to their rationality, universalizing and analogical reasoning share the same problem, that of justifying material criteria of relevancy to determine the similarity of two cases. In this paper, I have analyzed the claim to rationality of varying applications of the universalisability principle. I have started from its most local application, gradually extending its field of working to the legal system as a whole. Finally, I have discussed the most general application of the universalisability principle in ethics, in order to determine to which degree this can serve as a frame of reference to the substantive rationality of legal criteria of relevancy for analogical reasoning.

In legal argumentation, analogical reasoning can be placed on a sliding scale that ranges from very local extensive interpretation to Dworkin's reasoning by *super analogia iuris* in relation to the legal system as a whole. Extensive interpretation, reasoning by *analogia legis* and by *analogia iuris* differ mainly in their relative degree of locality within the total system. All these ways of juridical argumentation have in common that they are applications of the universalisability principle. Furthermore, they are characterized by the same argumentation structure.

If a judge decides that a case that is not (clearly) covered by a law is similar in its relevant respects to cases that are undoubtedly covered, he has implicitly constructed an underlying principle that covers both kinds of cases. In the light of this principle the cases in question are similarly relevant, and should therefore be treated equally.

In this respect, analogical reasoning can be seen as a reflection of the rational and systematic character of legal thought, as is propounded by Prof. Nerhot. However, this is only so in a restricted sense. In the first place, because of its local character, analogical reasoning as such does not necessarily presuppose the systematic coherence of the legal system as a whole. Such a presupposition would be valid only in a specific theory of law, notably that of Dworkin, who conceives juridical reasoning as a kind of argumentation by "super *analogia iuris*": in order to resolve hard cases, the judge should construct some legal principles from the systematic coherence of the whole of law. Secondly, as far as analogical reasoning does presuppose rationality, this is only of a purely formal character. Even if the judge would derive the criteria of relevancy from some fundamental central legal principles, inferred by a Dworkinian systematic interpretation of the legal system as a whole, this would only produce rationality in the sense of consistency (or coherence). Such analogical reasoning would have no necessary relation to a rationality of a more substantive kind, i.e. to some basic universal principles that are binding for all mankind. For the contents of the central legal principles are to be derived from the factually existing body of positive laws and jurisprudence, and these depend in their turn completely on the arbitrariness of those who exercise juridical power.

On the other hand, in traditional natural law theory, positive law should derive a substantial rationality from a set of objective universal legal and moral principles, that are supposed to be immanent in nature. Because according to this theory the world can be categorized in natural classes, each differentiated by its own essential properties, it would be possible to establish objectively which properties count as relevant in analogical reasoning. This view however is based on an unprovable essentialistic metaphysics, which does not find much acceptance nowadays.

For that reason, in both natural law theory and ethics, one has withdrawn to a more formal or procedural approach. Many modern ethical theories consider the same principle of universalisability, that also underlies legal analogical thinking, as the very core of ethics.

Therefore, after moving within the legal system from the most local to the most broad application of the universalisability principle, I have extended this movement to extra-legal, ethical universalisability. The question is whether this can produce a frame of reference that guarantees a substantive rationality to legal analogical reasoning. I have concentrated on the logical version of ethical universalisability, as developed by the linguistic philosopher Hare, and which is based on an analysis of moral language.

Hare claims that his "universal prescriptivism" can lead to a universal agreement upon certain moral principles. However, after a closer analysis, his ethical universalisability thesis also implies nothing more than a formal demand for consistency. It is essential that the logical universalisability principle is supported by the psychological effects of empathy with all the participants in a moral claim, in order to implement the desired eliminatory function. This, however, can only be realized after the tacit introduction of the substantive moral principle of human equality.

Contrary to traditional essentialistic metaphysics, modern linguistic philosophy, towards which Hare's ethical theory is orientated, generally maintains that what counts as "the same", or "relevant", or "rational" is determined by the world view of one's culture. As a consequence of the lack of independent standards of rationality, the relative rationality of opposing world views can not be judged. Each has its own right. This relativistic view could lead to the adoption of a (rational) consensus as a criterion for deciding normative controversies. Habermas and Apel indeed interpret the universalisability principle as a claim for the inter-subjective acceptability of all normative claims. However, such relativism also allows for intolerant or elitist world views, which deny beforehand the substantive equality principle which underlies the criterion of inter-subjective acceptability. This leads to the conclusion that it depends entirely on the point of view one takes, whether the similarities or rather dissimilarities of various kinds of people are to be conceived as relevant. Neither of these ways of interpretation is more rational than the other.

Thus modern linguistic philosophy results in an epistemological perspectivism and an ethical relativism that does not offer any universally valid points of reference to determine objective rational criteria of relevancy for analogical reasoning. On the contrary, perspectivism, when understood radically, makes *all* knowledge metaphorical or analogical. In this way, the problem of the rationality of analogy in the broad legal sense is dispersed in the problems concerning analogy in the narrow philosophical sense:

> "A word becomes a concept insofar as it simultaneously has to fit countless more or less similar cases – which means, purely and simply, cases which are never equal and thus altogether unequal. Every concept arises from the equation of unequal things [...]. What then is truth? A movable host of metaphors, metonymies and anthropomorphisms: in short, a sum of human relations which have been poetically and rhetorically intensified, transferred, and embellished, and which after long usage, seem to people to be fixed, canonical, and binding." (NIETZSCHE, *On Truth and Lies in a Non-moral Sense*, p. 83, 84).

BIBLIOGRAPHY

APEL, K. O., *Transformation der Philosophie I, II*, Frankfurt am Main, 1976

ARISTOTLE, *The Poetics*, London, 1965

DWORKIN, Ronald, *Law's Empire*, London, 1986

HABERMAS, Jürgen, *Moralbewußtsein und Kommunikatives Handeln*, Frankfurt am Main, 1983

HABERMAS, Jürgen, *Theorie des Kommunikativen Handelns*, Frankfurt am Main, 1988

HARE, R.M., *The Language of Morals*, Oxford, 1972

HARE, R.M., *Freedom and Reason*, Oxford, 1972

HARE, R.M., *Moral Thinking*, Oxford, 1981

HOERSTER, Norbert, *Utilitaristische Ethik und Verallgemeinerung*, München, 1977

JACOBS, Frans, *Ten overstaan van allen*, Amsterdam, 1985

KANT, Immanuel, *Groundwork of the Metaphysics of Morals*, New York, 1959

MARIS, C.W., *Critique of the Empiricist Explanation of Morality*, Deventer, 1981

NIETZSCHE, Friedrich, *On the Genealogy of Morals*, New York, 1969

NIETZSCHE, Friedrich, *Thus Spoke Zarathustra*, Harmondsworth, 1961

NIETZSCHE, Friedrich, *On Truth and Lies in a Non-moral Sense*, in "Philosophy and Truth (ed. Daniel Breazeale)", New Jersey, 1979

PERELMAN, CH., *La Traité de l'Argumentation*, Bruxelles, 1970

PERELMAN, CH., *The Idea of Justice and the Problem of Argument*, London, 1970

PERELMAN, CH., *The Realm of Rhetoric*, Notre Dâme, Indiana, 1982

PLATO, *Republic*, London, 1956

RICOEUR, P., *Hermeneutics and the Human Sciences*, Cambridge, 1984

RICOEUR, P., *La Metaphore vive*, Paris, 1975

SACKS, Oliver, *The Man who Mistook his Wife for a Hat*, London, 1978

SILVERSTEIN, Harry S., *Universalisability and Egoism* in "Australasian Journal of Philosophy", 46 (1968), p. 241-264

SINGER, M.G., *Generalization in Ethics*, New York, 1971

UNGER, R.M., *The Critical Legal Studies Movement*, in "Harvard Law Review", 96, 561-675

WIMMER, Reiner, *Universalisierung in der Ethik*, Frankfurt am Main, 1980

WINCH, Peter, *Understanding a Primitive Society* in P. Winch, "Ethics and Action", London, 1972

WITTGENSTEIN, Ludwig, *Philosophical Investigations*, Oxford, 1958

THE FUNCTION OF ANALOGY IN LAW: RETURN TO KANT AND WITTGENSTEIN

JACQUES LENOBLE

From the very beginning, philosophical reflection on law has been confronted with questions of legal reasoning and of the relation between judge and rule. These questions entail indeed as Gadamer pointed out[1] the issue of the role of Reason in human activity (moral, political and legal), and hence ultimately the issue of the statute of Reason.

The same relatedness explains the present renewal of philosophy of law and of reflection on the legal judgment. At the same moment that the philosophical debate on Reason takes a new flight, we perceive the development of theoretical controversies on legal reasoning. This link is even that much more explicit because the same model underlies this double renewal.

"Neokantian" criticisms essentially account for the revival of the philosophical debate in Reason[2]. K. Apel and J. Habermas are prominent representatives of the "neokantism", that at the same time counters hermeneutic philosophies of Heideggerian inspiration (which became dominant on the European continent) and also at positivist philosophies (largely domi-

[1] H. G. Gadamer, *Vérité et méthode*, French trans. by E. Sacre, Paris, Seuil, 1976, pp. 153ff. (pp. 295ff. in the second German edition "*Wahrheit und Methode*", Tübingen, J. C. B. Mohr).

[2] For a detailed presentation of this contemporary debate and its link with contemporary legal and political thought, see J. Lenoble and A. Berten, *Dire la norme, Droit-politique et langage*, vol. I, *Les paradigmes en présence*, Paris, 1989 (forthcoming).

nating in Anglo-saxon countries). Undoubtedly, this re-kindling of Kant re-interprets and also exceeds his philosophy.

Kant continued to think Reason in terms of a philosophy of conscience; but the present and post-metaphysical statute of Reason is now reconstructed in terms of a communicational Reason. The insights of the philosophy of language made this possible. Nevertheless, this movement affirms the relation between Reason and the universal, contrary to the radical criticisms of the philosophies of the deconstruction.

This relecture of Kant also conducts to a double criticism of positivism. First, in order to comply strictly with a semantic approach of the truth of theoretical discourse, positivism lacks the hermeneutic dimension of theoretical judgement and the structural kinship between theoretical Reason. Second, and correlatively, in order to restrict without justification the range of Reason to theoretical knowledge, positivism disrupts the relation between Reason and ethics that Kant tried to ground and that the horizon of universality, which is implied in the pragmatic logic of communicational Reason, helps to redefine.

It is symptomatic that the present renewal of theoretical reflection on law is structured by the same positions and the same theoretical issue. The two contemporary debates which dominate philosophy of law demonstrate this. The first debate opposes R. Dworkin to deconstructivist (Critical Legal Studies) or positivist (arising from H. Hart) approaches. The second confronts Habermas with Luhmann (systemic positivism) in their analysis of the evolution and the function of law in the Welfare-State. Even though their object differs, both debates focus on the analysis of legal reasoning. Dworkin as well as Habermas criticise the insufficiency of the positivist approaches which essentially reduce the intervention of the judge to a determinant judgement, in the meaning Kant attributed to this term in *Kritik der Urteilskraft*. Of course, this denunciation takes different forms.

Dworkin trashes the inadequacy of analytical positivism to account for the legal judgement. Confined to a legalistic approach to law (law is reduced to rules that are identified referring to the rule of recognition, which is a social convention), positivism fails even if the limits of an exclusively formalistic approach are recognised, as is the case with Hart and his successors[3]. The radical hermeneutic moment of every normative judgement is lacking. For Dworkin on the contrary Law is the interpretation of its own history that society continuously produces through its judges. Within this perspective, the judgement reveals its intrinsic ethical dimension and the similarity in the rational structure that underlies moral reasoning and legal reasoning.

The Habermas-Luhmann debate invites a different question: how to account for the changes in legal structure in reference to the evolution of social structures?[4] What type of legal rationality tends to be instaured following the recent evolutions of the Welfare-State? Beyond the points of convergence[5] that rally them, Habermas denounces Luhmann's denial of the ethical dimension that crosses this legal rationality. The modern concept of Law contains a moral dimension that the functionalist analysis does not adequately account for. Legal argumentation entails ethical evaluations. The application of legal rules presents a logical structure that is affiliated with the model of normative reasonings dealing with questions of legitimacy. For sure, Habermas defines this ethical dimension differently than the classical theories do. Material values are no longer defined *a priori* and based on reason. On the contrary, ethics is only procedural. It can be defined as the acceptance of rules of argumentation that are implied by the search for a rational consensus on what is just.

We will not develop here this double debate, which polarises contemporary legal philosophy. It shows first that the positivist approaches of legal reasoning are presently criticised either in a descriptive way or in a normative way. It shows also that these critics are in direct or indirect relation with contemporary reflection on the statute of Reason. They attempt to

3 In this sense, H. Hart and particularly N. MacCormick, his best interpreter and disciple, do some justice, though not enough in our view, to the hermeneutic aspect that is constitutive for all scientific reasoning and all practical reasoning. It is in order to stress this "ambiguity" that we have elsewhere called this legal positivism originating in Hart "hermeneutic positivism" (on this see note to work cited).

4 On this see esp. the excellent article by G. Teubner, Substantive and Reflexive Elements in Modern Law, *Law and Society Review.*, vol. 17 no. 2 (1983), pp. 239ff. and bibliography cited.

5 G. Teubner endeavours to combine the two view points (*loc. cit.*).

open up legal rationality to an ethical perspective. This new conceptualisation also forces us to rethink the relation between judge and rule. Dworkin tries to think this new relationship through his "narrativist" approach. Habermas provides a framework with his concepts of "communicational ethics" and "practical discourse on the rightness of norms of action"[6].

It is in relation to these contemporary issues that we wish to re-examine the question of analogy in legal reasoning. This question appears to be technical and of a limited scope, but constitutes an interesting challenge to help renew the conception of the relation of the judge and the rule and deepen the contemporary denunciation of positivist perspectives. Let us explain this hypothesis.

We have already pointed out that the contemporary debate puts forward the question of the relationship between law and practical Reason. The thesis developed by J. Habermas seems to us the most adequate in facing positivist and systemic perspectives. This position, which also sustains the works of R. Dworkin and R. Alexy, is double. First, the modern concept of law is "oriented towards practical Reason"[7]. This thesis affirms the relatedness between ethics and reason (cognitivist ethics-confronted with sceptical theses), and, at the same time, states that "the legal discourse is a special case of the general practical discourse"[8]. Further, if legal rationality is thus linked with ethical rationality, the latter is defined as procedural and is connected to the respect of procedural rules, implied in communicational activity. A theory of discourse or universal pragmatics can reconstruct these rules of communicational ethics.

A correct understanding of the role of analogy in law provides a philosophical justification of this double thesis.

Such an understanding will furthermore also allow us to leave behind the ambiguities that still figure in the ethical and procedural lecture of legal ra-

6 On this see esp. *Morale et communication (Moralbewußtsein und Kommunikatives Handeln)*, Frankfurt, Suhrkamp, 1983, French transl. by Chr. Bouchindhomme, Paris, Cerf, 1986, pp. 63ff. *Théorie de l'agir communicationnel (Theorie des Kommunikativen Handelns*, 3rd. ed. 1985, Frankfurt, Suhrkamp), Paris, Fayard, 1987, pp. 38ff.

7 R. Alexy, "Idée et Structure d'un système de droit rationnel", *Archives de philosophie du droit*, vol. 33, 1988, p. 38.

8 *Ibid.*, p. 33.

tionality that Habermas, Alexy and Dworkin present. We will only mention these ambiguities here in order to indicate how the approach of the function of the analogy in law provides the conceptual instruments to go beyond these ambiguities.

The first ambiguity concerns the distinction between the constatative and normative level. These three authors pretend to cover both levels, as they define the rationality of law as traversed by the argumentative model proper to practical rationality in general. Such a concept of law does not only respond to the needs of a concept of law that follows from an adequate appraisal of the exigencies of democratic Reason in the Welfare-State, but also, according to these authors, accounts for the effective functioning of the legal discourse in our actual society. We consider the adequacy of the procedural model of the "rational practical discourse" as limited to a normative perspective and not reaching the descriptive perspective. In its actual state, our law remains tied to a systemic functioning, which is the source of a dogmatism that the "argumentative" lectures of law does not sufficiently take into account. From this point of view, the systemic approaches, as developed by Luhmann, account much better for the normative closedness which continues to sustain the formalism of our legal system. This leads us to the second ambiguity.

To be sure, this lack of recognition is not the heritage of the ties our legal system carries with deductive rationality. It has long been established (we only need to refer here to the works of Ch. Perelman) that the logic of law is a logic of the reasonable; this logic is hence argumentative. Who would seriously challenge this thesis? However, it is not enough to take act of this construction of modern law in its relationship with the procedural requirements of argumentative logic to conclude that our law respects, in its functioning, the exigencies of rationality of the rational practical discourse constructed by Habermas and Alexy. This last rationality actually implies a normative openness, which means that every assertion can be made problematic. This rule, constitutive for procedural ethics[9], is partly neutralised in contemporary law by a pre-comprehension that is still at work: the pos-

[9] R. Alexy, *op. cit.*, p. 26.

tulate of rationality of the legislator[10]. This postulate does not only function as as a simple regulative idea, but also as a dogmatic preconditon. It rests upon a semantic and not a pragmatic approach of the legal system. Ultimately, it rests upon the ontological illusion of a proper meaning of legal rules. This precondition is not without effect: it partly neutralises the possibility of a pragmatic reconstruction of the meaning of the rules that are constitutive of the system from the point of view of the ideal axiological exigencies carried by the general principles of the system and supports of the search for an ideal consensus on what is just. The rationality that is proper to communicational ethics evidently does not imply that the judge and the pleading parties would renegotiate the rules that are formally posed by the competent public authorities. But it does only imply permanent reconstruction of the meaning of norms (rules and principles) when they are applied to concrete cases. The pragmatic and indefinite reconstruction which is demanded by communicational ethics and the perception of the ideal character of the search of consensus on what is just, operates in the juridical discourse by this last way. The formalistic and dogmatic approach that is related to the pre-comprehension that guides our contemporary legal hermeneutics partly seems to neutralise this exigency of an articulation of law towards the proper rationality of practical discourse. Even though this is not the place to develop upon this point, we must make two remarks. Terms of formalism and dogmatism seem more adequate with regard to our European legal systems. Does the interpretive model of R. Dworkin not correspond better with the American legal system which has always, since the American Revolution, attributed a more important place to the judge than in Europe? As recently very well demonstrated by R. Summers and P. S. Atiyah[11]. American legal reasoning is more apt to meet ethical exigencies and hence the constitutive elements of a normative openness of the legal system. On the contrary, English legal reasoning (and we expand this to

10 On this see *Dire la norme, op. cit.* and references cited, see also *Droit, Mythe et Raison* (in collaboration with F. Ost), Bruxelles, Publication des F.U.S.L. 1980 et F. Ost, et M. van de Kerckove, *Jalons pour une théorie critique du droit*, Bruxelles, publication des F.U.S.L., 1987.

11 *Form and Substance in Anglo-american law A comparative Study of Legal Reasoning, Legal Theory and Legal Institutions*, Oxford, Clarendon Press, 1987.

continental legal reasoning) is presently still often caught in the formalistic illusion that has marked the philosophy of the Enlightenment. The second remark deals with the evolution taking place in at least the continental European legal systems. This evolution is not unrelated with the present mutations in our Welfare-State[12]. An important transformation of the function of judging is taking place. The role of the judge tends to grow in our European societies. The multiplication of constitutional jurisdictions, since the end of the second world war, is an important example: the judge is the guard and the interpreter of the principles that underlie the public liberties proper to our social democracies. This transformation of the function of judging seems to indicate the evolution of our legal systems towards an appraisal of the exigencies of practical rationality, as conceived in the model of communicational ethics.

Why did we put forward these two ambiguities of contemporary approaches which, at the encounter of positivist theories, inscribe the legal reasoning in the perspective of practical Reason? The relative misunderstanding of the dogmatic pre-comprehension that continues to animate the discourse of the judge is not only an empirical fact. Without doubt, we contest the descriptive pretensions of procedural theories of practical Reason as far as the present rationality of our European legal systems is concerned. However, the remark goes even further. This misunderstanding results, according to us, from an "insufficient" construction of the logical presuppositions of an interpretation of practical reason as purely procedural. This insufficiency carries on two levels: the more fundamental level of the philosophical analysis of the statute of Reason and the particular level of the nature of the "rule" in practical reasoning (ethical and legal).

As far as the statute of Reason is concerned, we have demonstrated elsewhere[13] how much the model of universal pragmatics risks to lack, in its analysis of the discourse on which it leans, the paradoxical character that is constitutive of every enunciation. We will not develop this point further here. Let us only mention that this does not necessarily completely disqual-

[12] On this see the works cited in note 4 above.

[13] On this see J. Lenoble and A. Berten, *op. cit.*

ify the Habermasian re-interpretation of Kant based on the philosophy of language, and his critical phenomenological or positivist analysis.

However, this lack has its consequences for particular analyses, as such of normative reasoning. Even if Apel and Habermas very well grasped the purely procedural character of practical Reason and the normative openness that results from the only aim of the general consensus on what is just, they did not perceive the paradoxical character in the logical operation of the application of the rule in a normative reasoning. A correct appraisal of the role of analogy in law indeed constitutes an appropriate entry to point out this question of the paradox of the rule that Wittgenstein as the first, to our knowledge, has tried to construct. The indication of this paradox is important: it allows to deepen the argumentative model of Habermas and Alexy or the narrativist model of Dworkin, while it avoids the idealisation that these models continue to produce with respect to modern law and its dogmatic presuppositions. The implications of a correct appraisal of the role of analogy in law are therefore very important. They are at the heart of the principal contemporary questions of philosophy of law. The preceding reflections had a double purpose: to determine the importance of the question of analogy in law and to define the conclusions that we will draw from its analysis. Let us analyse now this role of the analogy which justifies in the same time the procedural approach of practical Reason (ethical and legal) and the paradoxical character of the logical operation of the application of a rule. Two propositions resume our analysis

1. The presentation of the role of analogy in law offered to us by contemporary legal theory is unsatisfactory, as demonstrated by the ambiguities that run through it. The reason for this is that the analogy is still thought as "imperfect resemblance". The correct perception of the role of analogy in legal reasoning implies a modification, a new conception of analogy. This modification is the same as, in the proper field of philosophy, Kant imposed on the concept of analogy.

2. The role played by the concept of analogy is central in Kant's thought, particularly in his analysis of practical Reason and more precisely in his analysis of judgement. As a result from the conceptual modification forwarded by Kant, the analogy must not be considered as a particular phenomenon (a rhetoric argument amongst others), but as the resort of prac-

tical judgement. This implies the rejection of a dogmatic lecture and of a sceptical lecture of practical judgement. One of the logical implications of this approach of the practical judgement is the paradoxical mechanism that sustains the judgement of application of a rule. Wittgenstein has shed light on this. Only procedural ethics succeed to integrate the results of the analysis of the practical judgement of which Kant provided the logical framework thanks to his concept of analogy. This concept of analogy is in its turn the result of the philosopher's will to take into account the radical finiteness of human Reason. Finally, this will allow us to return to the legal judgement, one simple species of practical judgement.

We will now develop these arguments.

1. At first sight, the question of analogy in law does not seem to pose many problems. Is this not one of the questions on which the theoreticians of law find consensus? Who would deny that jurists turn to analogical reasoning as a rhetoric argument? Ch. Perelman revealed that it is one of the "classical arguments of the logic of law". The judge relies upon it in order to cover the inevitable gaps in law[14]. This argument is traditionally further grounded in the rule of justice that holds that similar cases must be treated in a similar way.

However, a deeper lecture of theories of legal reasoning reveals areas of uncertainty (for not to say ambiguity) beyond this consensus. We will take only three examples.

A first trace is found with Ch. Perelman himself. Without doubt, and as already pointed out, this author has again and again demonstrated the importance of the use of the analogy argument. In his basic treatise on argumentation however[15], he adopts an analysis which seems to be contradictory. Here the analogy is not defined as an imperfect resemblance, but as an identity of relations within different domains. Herefrom the author deduces that

14 Ch. Perelman, "Raisonnement juridique et logique juridique", *Archives de philosophie du droit*, 1966, p. 6.

15 Ch. Perelman and L. Olbrechts-Tyteca, *Traité de l'argumentation – La nouvelle Rhétorique*, 1rst ed. 1949, 2nd ed. 1970, Brussels, Edition de l'U. L. B.

the use of the reasoning by analogy is exceptional in law and is only limited to "a confrontation on particular points, between positive legal systems, distinct by time, geographical space or regulated". Every time that jurists, because of the similarity of two factual situations, argue "in favour of the application of a determined rule on new cases, it is not a reasoning by analogy". In this hypothesis indeed "one affirms that one is within the same domain"[16] The same idea is further again expressed in clear terms: the conditions of legal reasoning themselves exclude the recourse to analogy. "...In law, the reasoning by analogy occupies a much more limited place than it seems. When a rule is applied to new cases, we find, by the exigencies of law, ourselves at the interior of one domain, since we can not leave, the domain that the rule assigns us"[17].

A second trace of ambiguity in the general agreement on the role of analogy in law can be found with A. Peczenik. He finds that legal dogmatics distinguish "different spheres of application of a norm: the first one is established by natural linguistic reading of the norm. The second sphere of application is determined by juristic interrogation, using many technical methods and revealing "the proper meaning" of the norm. The third sphere of application is established by other intellectual relations, exceeding the proper meaning of the norm, e.g. by frank evaluations"[18]. The reasoning by analogy, he notes, belongs to the third category as it is traditionally distinguished from the technique of extensive interpretation which remains tied with the "proper juristic meaning". Therefore the judge less frequently turns to it. This distinction is equivocal and criticisable[19], but beyond its theoret-

16 *Op. cit.* p. 503; Perelman remarks: "thus, the rehabilitation of analogy as a procedure of extensive interpretation, meeting the desire of some jurists to see in it something other than a term to disparage what the opponent is bringing forward as an example, will be brought about by giving analogy a different meaning from what we have proposed" (*ibid.*, pp. 503-504).

17 *Op. cit.*, p. 532.

18 A. Peczenik, "Analogia legis. Analogia from Statutes in Continental Law", in *Le raisonnement juridique*, Actes du Congrès Mondial de philosophie du droit et de philosophie sociale, Brussels, Bruylant, 1971, p. 329.

19 We shall quote here one of his criticisms: "The concept proper juristic meaning is unclear, since it depends on many controversial rules of interpretation, the primary

ical weakness, continues Peczenik, it serves practical purposes. In certain fields, for example criminal law, the judge does not accept the reasoning by analogy. Again, the apparent consensus of jurists seems to rest upon distinctions which are hard to elucidate on a theoretical level. The theory seems to blur the apparent clarity of the first intuition on which the consensus on the use of the argument by analogy in law is based.

Finally, we refer to Rinaldi, who contests the use of the argument by analogy in law in his article "Is analogy a decision process in English law?"[20]. It is argued that when jurists claim to turn to analogy (extend the application of a rule to similar cases) actually the decision is not grounded on the knowledge of essential identity of things. The decision more attempts to evaluate the weight of indices of similarity and difference in function of axiological criteria and based on the proper values of the social environment. The author concludes that the analogical argument in the sense of logicians is seldom used in law.

This triple observation contaminates the apparent consensus that jurists share on the use of the reasoning *a pari* in law in order to cover the lacunae in law. Where does this lead us? First, nobody can contest the use of the argument *a pari*. This rhetoric argument (one argument amongst the others) presents a double characteristic: it related to the idea of the analogy as an imperfect resemblance and the theoretical support of its use does not clarify the theory of legal reasoning. This accounts for the ambiguities in the three authors cited. To cling to the concept of the rule, it seems that the analogy in law can not be thought of otherwise than as an imperfect resemblance. This approach makes its own limits evident. Peczenik is right to reveal the insatisfaction of the classical distinctions concerning the different modes of application of a rule. It is opportune for Rinaldi to underline that, contrary to common intuition, when the argument *a pari* is used, it follows that similarity is not the basis of the judgement. Indeed, as A. Kaufmann pointed out well, "where there is an analogical conclusion, it is logically always possible to draw the conclusion "*a contrario*". What is decisive is the choice of the "*tertium comparationis*" from which angle the elements to

function of those rules is the same as the function of analogia; it consists in adapting the law to requirements of justice and 'life' in general" (*op. cit.*, p. 334).

20 In *Le raisonnement juridique, op. cit.*, pp. 363ff.

compare are considered"[21]. This is also the reason why Horovitz, contrary to Klug, mentions that "only a psychological – heuristic explanation of the concept of analogical argument is possible"[22].

So, at the same moment where the theory of law recognises the importance of reasoning by analogy in the judgement that applies the legal rule, it fails to produce a satisfactory explanation. Either it more or less defines analogy as imperfect resemblance, but then it must recognise the theoretical insufficiency of the provided explanation (Peczenik, Rinaldi); either it rigorously defines analogy as identity of relations between dissimilar realities, but then an aporie appears: in this case, indeed, there would not be analogy in law (Perelman).

We would like to advance the hypothesis that these difficulties are maybe due to an unthought taciturnity related to dogmatics which often continue to run through the way in which theory and practice of law consider on the operation of application of a rule, and more fundamentally, on the significance of a rule. According to us, this taciturnity accounts for the difficulty legal theory faces to establish a more fundamental role for analogy in legal reasoning. We think A. Kaufmann understood this central role well, as he holds that in law "every operation called subsumption is characterised by the structure of analogy". It is a pity that the following explanation remains enigmatic: this operation of analogy would consist in the establishment of the similarity of the norm and the situation by means of a teleological procedure[23]. Beyond the use of the rhetoric argument *a pari*, there is, according to us, an other dimension of analogy in law, consubstantial with every practical "ethical and legal" reasoning. This other use implies the modification of the question of analogy. This modification supposes an other redefinition of the concept, like Perelman proposed himself. But contrary to Perelman, this other definition does not lead to the exclusion of

21 In "Analogie und Natur der Sache", p. 25, quoted by H. A. Schwarz Liebermann von Wahlendorf, *Réflexions sur la nature des choses et la logique du droit*, Paris, Mouton 1973, p. 188 no. 29.

22 J. Horovitz, "Ulrich Klug's Legal Logic – a Critical Account", in *Etudes de logique juridique*, 1966, p. 111.

23 *Op. cit*, pp. 188-189, no. 30.

analogy in law. To be able to think this other role, we need to return to Kant. This author presented a theory of analogy in practical reasoning that can still be applied. It is even more interesting to notice that Kant himself started out from such a redefinition.

In a first movement, we will analyse this theory. Without doubt, this will take us on a detour, as Kant did not explicitly deal with the question of legal judgement. The Kantian approach, however, is of interest. Kant develops an original perspective which is not known enough and which concerns the type of analogy that lies at the heart of moral judgement. Our hypothesis holds that the contemporary acquirements of the philosophy of language allow us to extend this analysis to legal judgement. Without denying the differences between law and morality, legal judgement and moral judgement are moved forward by the same analogical operation, which Kant only describes on the level of the moral judgement. This analogy (we can call it symbolic) is specified by Kant vis-à-vis the analogy that characterises the theoretical judgement. In order to understand the nature of the analogy that defines, according to us, the legal judgement, we will make a detour by the Kantian theory of the role of analogy in moral (practical) judgement and, first, by the analogy in scientific judgement.

In a second movement, we will show how this Kantian approach applied to the legal judgement adequately clarifies the application of a rule and how this leads to what only Wittgenstein has been able to think in the XXth century, namely that paradox that constitutes such an operation of application.

2. The concept of analogy is central in Kant's work, even though its importance has only recently been emphasised thanks to the effort of F. Marty[24]. It is central because it's with leaning on this concept that Kant tries to redefine correctly the statute of human Reason. Leaving behind the classical solution of metaphysical dogmatism as well as the irrationalist solution, Kant will reformulate the theory of scientific judgement and of practical judgement. To do this, he will use the concept of analogy which becomes thus central in Kantian philosophy. Kant herein joins several

24 F. Marty, *La naissance de la métaphysique chez Kant – une étude sur la notion kantienne d'analogie*, Paris, Beauchesne, 1980.

earlier philosophers, of whom Aristotle is one of the outstanding. Aubenque demonstrated that the Stagirite turned to the concept of analogy to find an intermediate way between the sophistic scepticism and the platonic "dogmatism". The analogy thus presents itself as a "solution of the central aporie of the ontological discourse"[25]. The originality of Kant holds to this redefinition of analogy. In our analysis of this redefinition, we will understand why it is central in the Kantian theory of the practical judgement.

a. The transposition is double. It takes place in reference to the Humian concept of analogy, which is representative of the conceptions that were dominating at the time being. Hume distinguishes two kinds of analogy: the perfect analogy and the imperfect analogy. Both refer to the relation of causality and differentiate according to the probative value of the derived conclusions. All our reasonings concerning matter of fact are founded on a species of Analogy, which leads us to expect from any cause the same events, which we have observed to result from similar causes. Where the causes are entirely similar, the analogy is perfect, and the inference, drawn from it, is regarded as certain and conclusive. But where the objects have not so exact a similarity, the analogy is less perfect, and the inference is less conclusive; though still it has some force, in proportion to the degree of similarity and resemblance[26].
With the help of this distinction, Hume analyses the use of such reasonings in the phenomenal knowledge and in the knowledge of God. As far as the latter is concerned, it is known that Hume defends his sceptical thesis because the resemblance between the divine and the human is imperfect. The analogical proof of God is too weak. While in many cases phenomenal knowledge is characterised by "perfect analogies", the knowledge of God, as the theists allege it, only rests upon an analogy that is much too imperfect.

25 P. Ricoeur, *La métaphore vive*, Paris, Seuil, 1975, p. 335.

26 J. D. Hume, *An Enquiry concerning Human Understanding*, in "Enquiries concerning Human Understanding and concerning the Principles of Morals", 3rd ed., L. A. Selby-Bigge (ed.), Oxford, Clarendon Press, 1975, p. 104

On these two plans as distinguished by Hume, Kant redefines the analogy. A first transposition is operated by Kant. It deals with the concept of perfect analogy that Hume uses to account for the scientific judgement (phenomenal knowledge).

As F. Marty states, "the analogy (of Hume) in the knowledge of the phenomenal world becomes (with Kant) the analogy of experience"[27]. In fact, Kant estimates that the concept of Hume is not rigorous enough and is equivocal to the understanding of the essential mechanism that structures scientific knowledge, namely the articulation of the intelligible and the phenomenal proper to the scientific judgement. The reason for this, Kant notes, is that Hume is framed by the concept of analogy conceived as the imperfect or perfect resemblance between two realities, while actually analogy has to be conceived of as the identity of relations between dissimilar realities. Kant thus redefines the analogy according to the model of mathematical analogy (a/b = c/d). This course was already set by Aristotle[28]. But even though he draws from the mathematical analogy the definition of analogy as identity of relations, he introduces certain modalities: the general form of Kantian analogy "consists of a transformation of the mathematical analogy of the fourth proportional in a philosophical analogy"[29]. Different from what happens in the mathematical analogy, a proposition in the philosophical analogy is of the type a/b = c/x: the fourth term is unknown and can not be derived from the knowledge of the three other terms. This transposition towards the mathematical analogy and its modalities finds its explanation in the necessary "synthesis" that the theoretical judgement provides between intelligible (necessary) and phenomenal (experience and contingency). Hume only succeeded in giving right to the second dimension (the indispensable submission of scientific knowledge to the control of experience), thereby hurting the first dimension (the construction of experience through the

27 *Op. cit*, p. 133.

28 On this see P. Ricoeur, *op. cit.*, p. 340 and also J. Vuillemein, *De la logique à la théologie – cinq études sur Aristote*, Paris, Flammarion, 1967, pp. 13ff.

29 F. Marty, *op. cit.*, p. 76.

mathematical relations that constitute the categories of understanding). Kant's definition of analogies of experience as constitutive of every scientific experience and regulatory towards the intuition translate the specificity of the Kantian analysis of the scientific judgement. "The undertaking of Kant consists in giving the relation of resemblance (Humian analogy) the rigour of mathematical expression without hurting the merely regulatory character of the analogies of experience. The primacy is confirmed of the experience which, as the experience of the phenomenal given, remains the instance to which theory must subject itself"[30]. If the three analogies of experience (principle of permanence, causality and reciprocal action) are only regulatory towards intuition (which is the meaning of the idea that the Kantian analogy is not mathematical but only philosophical) this acknowledges the radical finiteness of human Reason. The schematisation of categories of understanding does only provide a searching rule from the point of view of phenomenal knowledge. There are no guarantees that nature will let itself be "legalised" by the categories of understanding. There are no guarantees as to the systematic unity of nature. Existence does not construct them. Science is not a mathematical deduction. In this sense, the fourth term of the proposition is not deduced from the three first ones. There is no place for scientific dogmatism. The discourse of science is always open to the aleatory experience. The three analogies of experience that Kant puts forward as at the base of every theoretical knowledge express thus the critical solution of the scheme by which Kant avoids the dogmatism of Leibniz (who intellectualises the phenomenal) or the reductionism of Hume (who reduces the intelligible to the phenomenal).

This first transposition, bearing upon the Humian conception of analogy functioning in phenomenal knowledge, is joined by a second transposition that leads more directly to the Kantian approach of the practical judgement. This concerns Hume's approach of the theological knowledge with the help of the concept of analogy. One must bear in mind its scope. Hume denounced the traditional theistic proofs of the

30 *Ibid*, p. 133.

existence of God founded on the analogy of art and of nature[31]. The inference, according to him, did not have enough probative value, as the resemblance between the divine and the human is imperfect (maximal distanciation between the two fields of "reality"). Kant accepts this denounciation but reformulates its foundation, which he finds not rigorously enough analysed by Hume. To obtain this, he modifies again the concept of analogy. Furthermore, at the same moment where he reaffirms with Hume the failure of all possible theoretical knowledge of the existence of God, Kant reconstructs the basis of another possible discourse on God than that of science and theoretical knowledge. Against the idea that analogy consists in a more or less approximative resemblance, Kant reaffirms the necessary rigour of the concept of analogy: it is an identity of relation between dissimilar entities. This differentiation on two levels (similarity of present realities and similarity of relations) leads to a fruitful insight. The theory of regulatory Ideas (and of the practical Reason, as we will see) is entirely related to this distinction and this redefinition of the Humian analogy. Indeed, what does a correct appraisal of the dissimilarity of realities indicate? It indicates that the Idea of God as one knows, the synthesis of the Ideas of Me (of the soul or of the subject) and the world (or the system of nature)| is only an Idea of Reason. The idea of unconditionality that goes with it indicates that its reality is only logical. Hence it can not be temporalised and schematised like the categories of understanding. Therefore, we can not give a phenomenal content to Ideas of Reason. Only a theoretical knowledge of it can be produced. Even though it is simply an imaginary space that goes along with the movement of Reason, the Idea of Reason (God, Subject and System) does not lose every function: the regulatory function is still exercised. The impossibility of a categorical schematism of Reason does not make impossible any meaningful discourse on it. Exactly this allows us to conceive precisely the analogical relation: parallel with the dissimilarity of realities (the unconditional and the conditional) there is an identity of relation.

31 The analogy between the design of nature and that of works produced by human intelligence (art) is claimed to allow the inference of the existence of a cause of the same nature, that is, a Being endowed with intelligence (a divine Being as the cause of nature on the one hand, and a human Being as the cause of human productions on the other).

Kant states this explicitly when he tries to define how one can use in a legitimate way a determined concept of what the things as such can be. Two solutions are to be avoided, he says: the one that depasses the limits of Reason, considering that it is possible to obtain a knowledge, a theoretical apprehension of what things are as such; but also the one (empiricism) that pretends "to want to hold the principles of the possibility of experience for the universal conditions of things as such" and thus to see "our experience as the unique possible way of knowledge of the things" or, in other words, "our intuition in space and time as the only possible intuition"[32]. This leads to the question, clearly formulated by Kant: "how does our Reason act in this relationship between what we know phenomenal knowledgel and what we do not know and will never know the Ideas of Reasonl"[33]. In order to think this relationship and thus the specific and non theoretical "knowledge" that Reason can produce of these Ideas, Kant uses the expression analogy: "a knowledge of this kind is by analogy. This word does not mean, as often thought, an imperfect resemblance between two things, but a complete resemblance of two relations between things that are dissimilar."[34]

Without doubt we encounter here the same conception of analogy that Kant uses to define the structure proper to theoretical knowledge: the analogy is conceived on the model of mathematical analogy trans-

[32] *Prolégomènes à toute métaphysique future qui pourra se présenter comme science*, § 57, French transl. J. Rivelaygue, in Oeuvres philosophiques, vol. II, Paris, Gallimard, 1985, p. 134. This also lets us understand why Kant can say that empiricism or "scepticism, absolutely originally, takes its source in metaphysics and its undisciplined dialectics": by linking the thing-in-itself and experience, he talks about what the things-in-themselves are (*ibid.*).

[33] *Ibid.*, § 57. p. 138.

[34] *Ibid.*, § 58, p. 142; and Kant explains in a note: by this sort of analogy I can "give a concept of the relationships between things absolutely unknown to me, for instance: the advance in the happiness of children = a is to the love of the parents = b in the same proportion as the prosperity of the human race = c to something unknown in God = x which we call love; not that the latter has the least resemblance to any sort of human inclination, but we can take its relationship with the world to be similar to that which things of the world have among themselves. But this concept of relationship here is a simple category, namely the concept of cause, which has nothing to do with the feelings".

formed in philosophical analogy. However, its use as far as the specific "knowledge" of the Ideas of Reason is concerned gives a scope at analogy that is very different from the analogies of experience. The Ideas of Reason can theoretically not be conceived, as they can not be put into a scheme. Where the analogies of experience, at the principle of all scientific knowledge of the phenomenal world, are regulatory towards the intuition but constitutive, for experience, the analogy that is at the principle of the "knowledge" of the Ideas of Reason is purely regulatory. No experience allows to "present" (darstellen) a phenomenal content that permits theoretical knowledge of the Ideas of Reason. This does not mean that all meaning is denied to these Ideas of Reason. A certain objective value can be maintained in their use. A certain "intuition"[35] corresponds to it. To qualify their effects, Kant uses in the "Prolegomena" a term that he will employ again to specify the practical judgement, namely the term "symbolical"[36]: "...we will not attribute to the Supreme Being any of the proprieties by which we think the objects of experience, and we avoid thus the dogmatic antropomorphism[37]; but we attach it at the relation it bears with the world, and we permit ourselves a symbolic anthropomorphism that actually only concerns language and not the object itself".

The term of symbol allows Kant to define the positive effect of the use that can be made of the three Ideas of Reason, and at the same time to differentiate this effect from every theoretical pretension. The Ideas of Reason are purely regulatory: they are but a "necessary rational concept without any corresponding object as far as the senses are concerned"[38]. However, they have a certain efficacity. They orientate human action, be it the theoretical action of understanding (science) (regulatory use of

35 Kant himself uses the term intuition, cf. *Critique de la Faculté de juger*, French transl. by A. Philonenko, Paris, Vrin, 1984, § 59, p. 173.

36 *Prolégomènes*, § 57 *in fine*, *op. cit.*, p. 142.

37 Justly denounced, as Kant admits, by sceptical empiricism.

38 *Critique de la Raison pure*, French transl. by A. Tremesaygues and B. Pacaud, Paris, PUF, 11th ed., 1986, p. 270.

the Idea of systematic unity of the world), or be it our practical action (regulatory use of the Ideas of subject or of freedom concerning morality and law). The reference to Ideas of Reason and particularly to the Idea of God does not produce a knowledge, a determination of these ideas as of ourselves. In this sense, the discourse remains anthropomorphic. But it is symbolic because, as it is related to language and not to a determined object (God, the World, or the Subject), it opens an indefinite reconstruction: every discourse that pretends to say what world and subject are (in other terms, to say what God is, synthesis of the Ideas of the system and Me), rests upon a metaphysical illusion and is polluted with dogmatism. Such is the symbolic effect of the analogy that structures the use that one can make of the Ideas of reason.

A propos the idea of God (but the two other ideas are included there in) F. Marty has pointed out very well: "In the end, if it is true that we think less God than the world, it is all about the world, as offered to man. Even if not explicit with Kant, the Idea of God is not lost: it enters in the relation itself of man and world. Man seems, under his initiative and in freedom, as the image of God, where the real makes see in imprevisibility, like a transcription of the sovereign independence of God. The anthropomorphism is symbolic, at the same time because it opens a world to invent and closes the way to phantasies of the arbitrary."[39]

b. What is the use of this long detour by the Kantian conception of analogy? The complete theory of the practical judgement is with Kant articulated around the mechanism of the analogy. A form of analogy structures and specifies the moral judgement. We will now proceed to see how this central place must be recognised in the heart of legal judgement, another species of practical judgement. In a first movement, we will limit ourselves however to the level of the moral judgement, the only one explicitly analysed by Kant.

One of the main problems that poses, according to Kant, the analysis of the practical judgment is the one of application of the moral law. In

39 *Op. cit.*, p. 196.

its basic formulation, this problem is easy to grasp. It deals with the concrete application to an action of what is enounced in a general rule, in case the moral law. F. Marty clearly described this as to "discern in several possibilities of action for which one finds himself, the one that responds to the moral exigencies"[40]. This problem is a problem of judgement and poses what Kant calls a problem of schematism, which means a problem of presentation of the concept in the phenomenal. The difficulty mounts when one notices that the solution envisaged by Kant to resolve this problem in the framework of the scientific judgement can not be applied to practical judgement. Indeed, the solution of the categorical scheme, namely the one of operationalisation of categories of understanding allowing to construct objects of experience and knowing them, can not be maintained when facing the construction of the "objects" of practical Reason. It is not difficult to comprehend why.

In the case of the scientific judgement, we have to understand the connection, the conjunction of the understanding and the sensibility. The Kantian solution is the one of schematism, this method that allows to procure an image to a concept. Hence we dispose of a means to represent a universal concept in a particular image, and thus to present a phenomenal object under the concept. This connection is made possible by the fact that the two 'terms' to be joined belong entirely to the order of time[41].

A very different question is the problem of the practical judgement. On the one side, the moral good is something "supra-phenomenal" and therefore "by consequence, there is no phenomenal intuition in which

40 *Op. cit.*, p. 248.

41 One should in fact recall the necessary link between the concept and pure intuition, which itself is nothing other than time. This is what allows Kant to say that the schemes of the categories (the whole set of which constitutes the concept) "are, then, nothing other than determinations of time made *a priori* in accordance with rules" (*Critique of Pure Reason*, *op. cit.*, p. 155). It would, moreover, be well to stress that time is that within which every intuition of the senses is presented.

one can find any correspondence"[42]. On the other side, this moral good must be applied to actions that do take place in this phenomenal world. The moral good is defined as the object of free will, namely an autonomous and auto-regulatory will. This is the meaning of the law of autonomy and of the maxim of formal universality that is related to it. In other words, the concept of the moral good is connected with this Idea of Reason that is the Idea of subject (identity to oneself) or the Idea of freedom, which is its teleological translation.It is thus easy to understand the impossibility to use the solution of the categorical schematism. Facing the problem of application of a moral rule (the law of freedom) and the maxim of universality to a particular case, one is in a certain respect (even if it's on the practical level) confronted to the problems that Kant met in the knowledge of God and, more generally, of the three Ideas of Reason. For this reason Kant employs in his enquiry of the practical judgement the solution that already operated before in *Appendix to Transcendental Dialectics*, Kant names this solution to the problem of application of moral judgement "typic", in order to differentiate it of the schematism, the solution to the problem of application that poses the theoretical judgement.

The typic of the practical judgement functions on the basis of the mechanism of analogy that Kant applied as the principle of the discourse that Reason can validly hold on God and on the Ideas of Reason in general. The analogy that structures the typic is in no way whatsoever the one that functions in the analogies of experience. Undoubtedly, we deal in both cases with relations and identity of relations between dissimilar realities. The difference, however, is that Kant considers the analogy that sustains the scientific judgement as producing a theoretical knowledge, even if it remains permanently open to a reality of which nothing can guarantee its *a priori* intelligibility. The analogy constitutive of the discourse one can hold on the Ideas of Reason is of a purely symbolic nature. Therefore Kant qualifies the moral judgement as symbolic hypotypose, as opposed to the theoretical judgement that is qualified as a schematic hypotypose.

42 *Critique de la Raison pratique*, transl. by L. Ferry and H. Wismann, Paris, Gallimard, *Oeuvres complètes*, vol. II, 1985, p. 691.

We will not continue on a technical examination of these appellations. However, it is useful to bear in mind this explicit reference Kant makes to the term of symbol to characterise the nature of the application of a practical judgement. We encounter this reference two times: first marginally in *Critique of Practical Reason*[43], and more extended in *Critique of the Faculty of Judgement*[44]. As revealed by F. Marty, these occurrences bear relation to the fragment of Prolegomena where, also in an isolated way, Kant utilises the term symbol to characterise the narrow limits to which the exclusively regulatory function of the Ideas of Reason confine the discourse that man can develop on those Ideas with the intention of presenting them in the phenomenal reality.

As the practical judgement is so impregnated by this second category of analogy, it is justified to reject any dogmatic approach and to reject any formalistic approach of the practical judgement.

First, any dogmatism is denounced. The correct appraisal of the difference between type and scheme, between symbolic schematism (practical Reason) and categorical schematism (theoretical Reason) leads to the recognition that moral behaviour (the moral object) can not be known in the way a phenomenal fact is known (object of science). Utilitarian empiricism as well as moral intuitionism (Kant calls this "mysticism") must be rejected, as they both fail to recognise the difference between the typical and the schematical. Kant, on his turn, defines the type of the moral law starting from the law of causality which rules the phenomenal world. The law of causality serves as a model in order to represent better which are the determinations of free will, it is to say the will directed by the moral law (which also means a subject

43 *Critique de la Raison pratique*, *op. cit.*, p. 694.

44 "All intuitions that one brings under *a priori* concepts are therefore either *schemata* or else *symbols*, and of these intuitions, the former contain direct presentations of the concept, while the latter contain indirect ones. The schemata effect <the presentation> demonstratively; the symbols do it through the mediation of an analogy (for which one also uses empirical intuitions), through which the faculty of judgment effects a double operation consisting in applying, firstly the concept to the object of an intuition of the senses, and secondly the simple rule of reflection on this intuition to a quite different object of which the former is only the symbol", *Critique de la faculté de juger*, *op. cit.*, § 59, p. 174.

transparent to itself and identical to itself). Kant defines the type of the moral law as follows: "Ask yourself if, considering the action you plan to undertake as subject to a law of nature from which you are part, you can still regard it as possible for your will."[45] (This means, if the meaning of this law of nature is transposed in terms of the law of causality: could you consider this action as caused by your free will?). However, (this is only a type, a symbolic and metaphorical presentation, to indicate the precarity and the imperfect, indirect and not assured character of such a presentation. It is exactly this symbolic, metaphorical and precarious dimension that is not recognised by utilitarian (empirical) or intuitionist interpretations of the moral law. Utilitarian empiricism, which uses as a criterion of the moral law the happiness caused by the planned behaviour, would like to find a rule of decision in the experience itself. This disregards that the model of the law of causality is only a type and not a scheme. Kant describes this as "to place amongst the concepts what simply belongs to the typic of concepts"[46].This thus definitively disregards the gap between the phenomenal world and the intelligible world to which the free will belongs. This accounts for the dogmatism of the utilitarian solution that presupposes theoretical knowledge of moral action. The same mistake – though inverse – contaminates moral intuitionism or "mysticism". Here, the moral universe is not brought back to that of phenomenal nature, but it is supposed to be possible for human reason to find access to theoretical knowledge of the pure intelligible, to determine theoretically what a free will demands. This is again an affirmation of a dogmatism that disregards the finiteness of human Reason.

In the matter of practical Reason, the dogmatism consists in "making a scheme of what could only serve as a symbol". This does not mean that the moral discourse is drowned in scepticism. The analogical nature at the heart of the decisions of practical Reason allows to provide meaning to the moral judgement. This is an intermediate position between scepticism and idealistic or empirical dogmatism. The rule of

45 *Critique de la Raison pratique*, *op. cit.*, p. 692.

46 *Ibid*. p. 693.

Freedom always has to be conquered; the discontinuity between the phenomenal and the moral obliges to a constant reprise of the determination of the exigencies of the moral law. The discourse is a search. These determinations are a task for human Reason and not a given of knowledge. As F. Marty aptly underlines, for Kant moral reflexion has as its own place the decision. "This place is not some kind of Idea of the Good, nor the Idea of a God as supreme legislator, and not some kind of consideration on the essence of man of which one searches the perfection or the advantage. It is freedom, but as freedom of action and hence ... man in his historical reality." In this place, the historical rules or the attempt to identify good action "do not dispense us from difficult and risky scrutinies, as the real as it is given must be taken into account, in its complexity. The difficulty of the moral starting point lies in the multiplicity and constant renewal of the decisions that we live in and that figure as explosions"[47]. History as place of Freedom becomes thus the place of an open task, which always has to be redefined.

In the same movement, we understand the rejection of a formalistic lecture of the moral law. However, this denounciation is not explicitly present in Kant's text, and, even more, the interpretation of Kant is traditionally formalistic. It is customary to rampage against the legalism of Kantian morals, completely based on the unconditionality of a moral law, which by nature doesn't care too much for the phenomenal conditionnement of human action. Peguy clearly formulated this formalistic interpretation of Kantian morals: "Kantism has clean hands, but has no hands"[48]. Even though it is innovating, the interpretation that F. Marty proposes of the Kantian approach of the practical judgement seems more adequate, if not according to the letter then according to the logics of the Kantian enterprise. Indeed, the appraisal of the purely symbolical character of the presentations that human Reason can produce of the exigencies of the moral law indicate that they are function of historical circumstances of life-situations where the

47 *Op. cit.* pp. 274-275.

48 Quoted by F. Marty, *op.cit.*, p. 306.

moral decision has to open up. The analogical undertaking that Kant inscribes in the heart of the moral judgement refers, as demonstrated, to the analogy that traverses the human discourse, moved by the regulatory ideas of Reason. It characterises this discourse with a precarity that condemns it to a constant reprise of the meaning that these Ideas bear. One of the features of the finiteness of the subject is the irreducible openness of the moral discourse to the imprevisibility of the real[49]. What is more, Kant's text invites to such a denounciation of formalism, as F. Marty reveal. How can otherwise the presence be interpreted of the "exception" in the Kantian table of categories of freedom? This is Kant's indication that the moral law can not be automatically applied. The moral destination of the human subject, reasonable and ending being, is always historically situated. The conciliation of the necessary recognition of the law and the "diverse of desires" that characterises the phenomenal nature of human action is logically expressed by the importance of the category of exception. Kant joins here a long tradition that Aristotle already expressed with his idea of *epieikeia*. The general and abstract law is in its rigidity by nature incapable to seize the diverse reality, always changing and unpredictable. The moral judgement would not recognise its nature, if it enclosed in a legalistic rigidity. Such a legalistic perspective would on its turn be a

49 "It may in fact be said that Kantian morality does not state specific determinations of moral action, and is therefore 'formalist', if this specific determination is understood as being that which makes up an idea of man from which one could in every circumstance deduce what has to be done in order to realize it. On the basis of this sort of 'anthropology', it is not possible for Kant to construct a morality. We may speak of 'Kantian formalism', meaning by that that the whole of the moral law comes down to this single requirement: be a man, do what any man would see it possible to do at the place and time that are yours. But – and here we restore what formalist interpretation disguised – this should be in attention to reality, which is primarily that of the human world. Kantian 'formalism' is, then, no longer the legalistic rigidity so explicitly condemned by Kant. It is openness to the unpredictability of existence, in a world of free subjects. To Peguy's formula: 'Kantianism has no hands', we must add: 'because it has a multitude of them' – the multitude of functions that the human hand can perform, by contrast with the rigidity of the tool. It will, moreover, be hard for him to declare that he 'has clean hands': the man whose being is in time cannot give himself this satisfaction, which would be that of possessed sainthood" (*op. cit.* p. 309).

sign of metaphysical dogmatism (reduction of the phenomenal to the intelligible).

Departing from what preceded, three observations can be made. These will lead us to the question that more directly concerns us, namely the question of the legal judgement.

a. The Kantian analysis of the practical (moral) judgement boils down to the thesis that, for logical reasons (of transcendental logic) the construction of a moral object (namely the recognition of a certain behaviour as moral) remains purely symbolic. The concept of such an object remains characterised by an irreducible indetermination. The judgement presents a phenomenal intuition under a concept, but that operation remains indirect and precarious. Facing the inconditionality that the moral rule implies, the finiteness of our human reason and thus the conditioned and phenomenal character of our human existences explain that we will never be guaranteed "in truth" if our judgement is just. No general formulation of the rule can produce the economy of its eventual inapplicability in a specified situation (theory of *epieikeia*)[50].

b. This basic precarity of the moral judgement implies that it can not be analysed as a determining judgement, namely as the application of a known universal to a particular case. The moral judgement is a particular form of

[50] Let us recall the essential scope of Kant's entry in the category of exceptions to the table of categories of Freedom. It does not only mean, it would seem, that determination of the field of application of a rule does not depend on a pretended meaning given to the rule which could be defined independently of an awareness of the specific features of each case in point. The meaning of the rules is on the contrary constructed from contact with the cases that have to be solved. This also implies, in our view, that application of a rule posited *in abstracto* each time requires a value judgment, with the norm of reference being constituted by the universality that is characteristic of normative discourse: normative justice, as Habermas calls it. This ultimate norm, on the basis of which the meaning of each particular rule is defined, is a universal, neither given nor posited, but always only sought for. We shall see that this same mechanism characterizes not only moral discourse, but also the legal discourse which, at the level of the judge, is accordingly not prevented from being pronounced under the twofold constraint of the rule of argumentation and of the signs that constitute the rules of law" (see below).

the reflective judgement: the universal is not known but searched. This is the meaning of the symbolic nature of the "application" of a general concept of the moral rule to the particular. Without doubt, Kant distinguishes the moral judgement from the aesthetic judgement, another form of the reflective judgement[51]. However, it is important to reveal that both, as they are reflective, are distinguished from the scientific judgement. Again, the lecture of Kant may not be reduced. The reflective dimension of the moral judgement does not lead to the complete absence of legality or of scepticism and does not lead to moral cognitivism. The position is intermediate. The universal, even if not given and not known, is not absent: the judgement is taken in a constant search for the universal, which can only be attained along the incomplete model of the symbol. The universal functions in a purely regulatory way, which demands for its unconditional nature (Idea of the Subject or identity to oneself, presupposed by the concept of autonomy that signifies the moral law). This also explains why Kant carefully precises that the rapport between the moral judgement (symbolic hypotypose) and the scientific judgement (schematic hypotypose) is itself an analogy[52]. Again, we establish the transposition that Kant has converted to science the *Critique of Pure Reason*, analysing the difference between the analogy figuring in the "knowledge" that human Reason can produce of the Ideas of Reason and the analogy functioning in scientific knowledge. The moral judgement taken in the purely regulatory mechanism of the Idea of Subject is traversed by an analogy in the second degree: the "synthesis" of the general and the particular is only analogous to the analogy that lies at the base of the schematism of scientific knowledge.

It is also on this point that the difference between moral judgement and legal judgement is situated, according to Kant. Even though he did not examine this question profoundly, the latter judgement was certainly ranked in the category of determining judgements: the mechanism of symbolic hypotypose and of the typic and the category of the exception (*epieikeia*) would not be transferable to the legal judgement. In law, the judge must be

51 This emerges clearly from the passages of the *Critique de la faculté de juger, op. cit.*, where Kant describes the symbolic hypotypose (section 59), on this see also, F. Marty, *op. cit.*, pp. 355-356.

52 *Critique de la Faculté de juger, op. cit.*, section 59.

content to apply a rule, posed by the public authority. The concepts that this rule uses are purely empirical. The indeterminate character of the concept of moral good (Idea of the Subject conceived as Idea of the Reason) and the related impossibility of categorical schematisation would hence not exist in the framework of the legal judgement.

c. We consider this differentiation between moral judgement and legal judgement as inadequate. The Kantian analysis of practical Reason, of the type of analogy that traverses it and of its consequences (rejection of a knowledge "in truth" and rejection of any legalistic formalism) constitutes a theoretical gain towards the empirical (utilitarian or sceptical) or intuitionist analyses. This theoretical opening remains, however, conceptualised in the framework of a philosophy of conscience, as K. O. Apel and J. Habermas perceived. The developments of the philosophy of language during the 20th century allow for a more adequate redefinition of the solution Kant outlined. This solution is an intermediate way, as the finiteness of human Reason obliges to criticise every metaphysical pretension of a discourse that wears itself out to "say" the universal, and as the necessity of the universal as a simple horizon of meaning is not denied. This is the issue of the most recent philosophical thinking, which, at the same moment where it notices the conceptual insufficiencies of Kant, however perceives the symmetric insufficiencies of phenomenological or positivist perspectives, both incapable to do justice to the statute of the universal that the pragmatics of the discourse reveal. This is not the place[53] to develop this reformulation, starting from the philosophy of language, of the critical position that Kant frameworked. We only indicate its importance for the question of the practical (moral) judgement and of its distinction with the theoretical (scientific) judgement and the legal judgement.

The analogy that Kant discovers at the principle of the practical judgement must be read again, from the perspective of language. Kant constructs this analogy referring to the problem that poses the schematisation of the Ideas of Reason. This schematisation is called symbolic in order to differentiate it from the categorical schematisation proper to scientific knowledge. Every time that Kant tries to grasp this analogy that is at the

53 On this see our work, cited, A. Berten and J. Lenoble, *op. cit.*

heart of the human discourse on the Ideas of Reason, the question of language rises at the same time[54]. However, Kant does not explore this issue. Only in the 20th century language becomes really the object of systematic reflection and the support of new philosophical paradigms. The analysis of language or, more exactly, of the discourse (namely language driven by the subject of enounciation) reveals that the Kantian "symbolic" analogy is an analogy that is indissociable of every discourse-act. The objective of unconditionality is at the base of every enounciation and participates in the auto-referentiality that is constitutive of the discourse. To speak implies the objective of a universal where language, in a metalinguistic reappraisal of itself, tries to express itself and thus obtain this guarantee of truth, this self-foundation where sense and reference join together. At the same moment, however, this enquiry is paradoxical[55]: the objective of reference (which P. Ricoeur therefore even calls metaphorical reference)[56] is always lacking. This paradoxical search is itself the motor of the enounciation and the production of meaning. This is the logical operator that Kant named symbolic analogy even if, not at all starting from language to construct it, he did not perceive its exact extension and limited it to the discourses of metaphysics (analogy of theological discourse) and morals. What are the effects of this relecture of symbolic analogy in terms of philosophy of language and of a redefinition of its extension?

First, it has an effect on the Kantian theory of the practical judgement itself. For sure, we noticed, Kant constructs the practical judgement as reflective. However, this construction remains a little ambiguous. The Kantian text exposes itself to formalistic interpretations. F. Marty is right

54 On this see F. Marty, *op. cit.*, pp. 160-161; pp. 360 ff.; the same author thus states that Kant had made "a symbolic hypotypose play a part in the constitution of language" (*op. cit.*, p. 532).

55 On this paradoxical logic of statement, see *Droit, politique et langage*, *op. cit.*,. It is because he does not adequately construct this paradoxical dimension of universal pragmatics that Habermas misses the dogmatic aspect of modern law and returns to idealize the argumentative character of it (see above, and below).

56 In the same perspective, one might say that analogy is only the mark of the law of discourse that condemns truth to be only "metaphorical truth", again taking up an expression of P. Ricoeur; on this cf. P. Ricoeur, *La métaphore vive*, *op. cit.*, p. 310 and especially pp. 374-399.

to denounce them as incompatible with Kant's theoretical premisses. But Kant himself did not always perceive its consequences. For example, he let believe in the possibility to define *a priori* certain rules as universally valid (prohibition to lie), independently of a phenomenal framework asking for their application. Habermas' reformulation[57] of the maxim of universality, starting from universal pragmatics, constitutes, from this point of view, a better theoretical approach to inscribe the symbolic character of practical judgement and thus its purely reflective nature. Such a perspective on ethics opens up for purely procedural ethics. The last normative criterion of universality (which is searched for) is the rule of argumentation. Ethical cognitivism is purely procedural: this is the way to leave scepticism, utilitarianism and intuitionism in morality.

There is also an effect on the theoretical judgement. We will only mention the problem here. Is it without doubt that Kant's approach in the first Critique is ontological (theory of objectivity) and not epistemological? The two points of view are partly connected: a physical object only exists if it is constructed by experience, i.e. if it is known on the basis of a scientific judgement. Now, the cardinal distinction between determining and reflective judgement that Kant utilises to differentiate between theoretical judgement (schematic hypotypose)[58] and practical judgement (symbolic hypotypose) risks to fail to recognise the purely linguistic and consensual character of scientific truth. At the contrary, the reformulation of finiteness of Reason in terms of a theory of language (finiteness as a result of an irreducible gap

[57] "...it is not enough for an individual to ask himself, thinking about it twice, whether it would be possible for him to adhere to a norm. It is not even enough for all individuals to do that thinking, each in his own corner, and then to record their votes. What is needed is "real" argumentation in which the persons concerned participate... On the basis of this perspective, it is necessary to change the formulation of the categorical imperative to go along the lines suggested: instead of imposing on all others a maxim that I could wish to be a universal law, I must submit my maxim to all others so as to to examine in discussion its claim to universality. A slippage is thus brought about: the centre of gravity lies no longer in what each may wish to assert without being contradicted, to be a universal law, but in what all can unanimously recognize as a universal law". J. Habermas, *Morale et Communication*, French transl. by Chr. Bouchindhomme, Paris, Cerf, 1986, pp. 88-89.

[58] Even though Kant did point out the reflective aspect of scientific reasoning – as testified by his theory of the analogies of experience conceived of as philosophical analogies – (see above).

between meaning and reference) helps to perceive the intersubjective and communicational logics that are at the basis of every judgement, including the scientific judgement.

Last but not least we examine the effect on the legal judgement. Also here the frontier between moral judgement and legal judgement must be reformulated. Legal judgement (application of law in a particular case) is now also caught in this reflective structure that is the universal that is not given and known but searched for. The distinction between conditioned and unconditioned is now perceived as written into the game of every discourse: it functions in the operation of the production itself of meaning that moves forward the paradoxical logic of the enounciation[59]. As a result from this, the analogy that Kant pointed out that well as the basis itself of the practical judgement, also runs through the legal judgement. In every application of a legal rule by the judge to a particular case, the universal is not given but searched for. In Kantian language, we would say that the concepts to be applied to the phenomenal conceal a supra-phenomenal dimension. The process of application of law is in this sense metaphorical. Law does not stop to express and produce itself in contact with every particular case that justifies its application. This does evidently not mean that law and morals are confounded. Undoubtedly, the judge must make his decision by the application of rules (theory of sources of law). These rules, formulated by the social body, are of a very different nature than those enounced by the moral discourse on the basis of the idea of autonomy. But, and Kant could not foresee this, the operation of the constitution of the meaning of legal "rules" conceals itself a paradoxical mechanism that is only the manifestation of the paradox of enounciation functioning in every human discourse and is related to the auto-referentiality that lies at its base. It is this paradox of application of a rule that Wittgenstein, as the first, has tried to construct. The pragmatic theory of language allows us now to grasp it better. To close our enquiry, we will now outline this Wittgensteinian approach and its effects for legal interpretation.

The hypothesis of the paradox of the operation that consists in the ap-

59 On this see our work, cited.

plication of a rule is not new. As J. Bouveresse[60] well demonstrated, this hypothesis finds its roots with Wittgenstein and its most assured expression with Kripke. We will only proceed on the general idea. J. Bouveresse formulates the Wittgensteinian question to know what it is to follow a rule: "The problem he wants to resolve has the form of a dilemma of the following type: or the rule determines the action in such a way that there is some kind of supra-empirical fact from which it results that it is impossible to follow a rule otherwise than in this precise way, or the rule does not determine the action and in principle everybody could follow the rule as he understands it. In other words, or there is, beyond the chain of all the reasons that the user might successively invoke, one last and true reason that justifies him in the facts to follow the rule as he does, or what he does in the application of the rule results only from an arbitrary choice without motivation. It is equally evident that, for Wittgenstein, the platonic illusion and the sceptical illusion both stem from the same origin-: the tendency to artificially install (while we are philosophising) a problematic distance between the rule and its applications which, in reality (this means, from the point of view of practice), does not exist at all"[61]. The paradox is thus evident. This results entirely from the rejection of the platonic conception of the rule. The application of the rule depends upon the interpretation that I give. But how can we control this interpretation if it is itself that upon which the criterion of evaluation is based? Without doubt Wittgenstein considers the sceptical solution equally unacceptable. Bouveresse is right, however, to note that Kripke's paradoxical formulation is difficult to eliminate and that the problem remains open with Wittgenstein. Without doubt the reference to the socially established use to decide what is correct is inscribed in the horizon of this paradoxical perspective. But this is itself a false explanation that does not resolve the paradox at all, as Bouveresse, only seeing this solution, demonstrates.

In fact the paradox of the rule, luminously intuited by Wittgenstein, seems to us a simple case of application of the paradoxical that moves hu-

60 J. Bouveresse, *Le paradoxe de Wittgenstein ou Comment suivre une règle*, in "SUD", special issue dedicated to L. Wittgenstein, 1986, pp. 11-55, this study was taken up again and developed in J. Bouveresse, *La force de la règle*, Paris, Minuit, 1987.

61 *Ibid.* p. 48.

man speech and the operation of meaning. Wittgenstein is right to refuse both the platonic and the sceptical interpretation. Is the logic of meaning not forced by the truth, as it is inscribed in the horizon of an ideal? Even though the sceptical perspective does not conceptualise it correctly, it nevertheless indicates that this constraint of the truth is empty: the ideal is inconsistent[62]. The logic of meaning is condemned to constantly depend on every dogmatic fixation, while every turnover is made under the constraint of rational argumentation. Also the legal rule is subordinated to the logic of the discourse: its meaning is the effect of an interpretation that is always susceptible of reconstruction by arguments on the purely procedural horizon of rational consensus. This is how the narrow tie between the application of the rule and the argumentative openness or reflective structure of the legal judgement is understood. The application of the rule is in itself paradoxical. Considering the game of paradox, the discourse of the judge is taken, or should be taken, in a permanent operation of hermeneutic reconstruction that guides the logic of the argumentative discourse.

A theory that assumes this paradox of the application of the rule hence acknowledges the radical interpretative character of the legal judgement and, correlatively, abandons every semantic approach to law. Legal norms have no meaning in themselves. Law is the meaning of legal enounciations that the community produces and keeps on producing. In this sense, law never stops being expressed on the level of the judge. The theory that best takes this logic of meaning into account is the narrativist model as Ricoeur tried to think through for historiography. We have elsewhere tried to outline the fecundity for law of Ricoeur's approach in "Temps et Récit"[63]. In this sense, we think R. Dworkin well understood the radical narrative structure of the legal judgement. However, ambiguities subsist with Dworkin. They risk to re-introduce a "platonic" conception of the rule, to use Wittgenstein's expression. This is demonstrated by the reference to the concept of "integrity". It is not made clear that it must only be thought as a purely regulatory idea and as purely inconsistent. Therefore it is not wrong

62 On this see *Droit, politique et langage, op, cit.*

63 On this see J. Lenoble, *Philosophie contemporaine du droit et modèle herméneutique*, in "Etudes d'anthropologie philosophique, IV", Bibliothèque de l'Institut Supérieur de Philosophie, Louvain, ed. Peeters (forthcoming).

to see under the Dworkinian concept of "integrity" the risk of restoration of the postulate of rationality of the legislator. This is a principle of the dogmatic effects of the legal hermeneutics inherited from the French Revolution. Without doubt, the rationality of law functions as an ideal; but it is precisely not a postulate but an ideal, in itself empty. This allows us to return to the contemporary neo-Kantism in law.

The argumentative perspective that Habermas develops rejoins our own conceptions. We are convinced that legal hermeneutics that acknowledge this interpretative openness on the basis of a discourse regulated by communicational ethics correspond to the exigencies of modern democracy. This evidently implies an increased role of the judge that does not correspond to the model inherited from the French Revolution, which was haunted by the vision of a government of judges. We already remarked, however, that signs of evolution appear in our societies, which are not without any relation to the actual crisis of the Welfare-State. Is this crisis not due to diverse traces of dogmatism that our misinterpretations of the democratic modernity have generated in our political and legal structures? From the point of view of law, the lack of recognition of the paradoxical character of the application of the rule has lead to hypostasiate its meaning and to dogmatise legal interpretation. The neo-Kantians, with Habermas as one of the prominent, perpetuate on this point the insufficiency of their theoretical lecture of the legal judgement. This explains their idealising lecture of the dogmatism always present in our legal hermeneutics. Inversely, the positivist or systemic (e.g. N. Luhmann) positions, even if they grasp more adequately what generates the systemic pre-comprehension of our actual legal discourses, lack the criticism that can be made on it and the inadequacy of such a functioning of law with respect to a full appraisal of democratic exigencies. The reason herefore is also the disownment of the paradoxical logic of the enounciation and its consequences for the operation of application of a rule. They lack the interpretative radicality which is well high-lighted by the narrativist model that P. Ricoeur tried to circumscribe. We have already stated that Dworkin has partly well understood this. Maybe this privilege is due to his experience with American law, which has always stressed the central role that had to be given to the judge, and more fundamentally to law, to avoid the political dogmatism of a State that would be the sole owner of the interpretations of democratic legitimity.

In the end, it is this same critical insufficiency of positivist and systemic position that explains their difficulty to account adequately for the moral dimension of the legal judgement. In fact, as they do not perceive the statute of the ideal that is implied in the paradoxical logic of the enounciation, positivist and systemic positions lack the dimension of transcendence that should command legal hermeneutics in our democratic society. The moral element of the legal judgement must be conceived on this basis. It must exclusively be understood in terms of procedural rationality. On this level, the position of Habermas on the practical judgement is an adequate view. Of the numerous traces of an inadequate view that can be found with the positivists, we will only mention one here. The limits that Hart attributes to the moral element of law remain connected to a substantial conception that lacks the proper modern reconstruction of morality that contemporary philosophy permits. The identification of law and morals, without which law is not complete, must be understood as inductive to the reflective dimension that is proper to the rationality of action regulated by norms.

We will not return, under the guise of a conclusion, to all the different insights that we have tried to draw from the role of analogy in legal reasoning, but will consider two of them.

The first insight refers to the double insufficiency of the recurring approaches of legal theory on this question.

Undoubtedly jurists have always pointed out the irreducible rhetoric use of the argument *a pari* in law. But, as we demonstrated, with the best of them this is accompanied by ambiguity, if not to say by aporia. Legal theory too often economically avoids the proper philosophical statute of Reason and the question of articulation of meaning. We engaged in this detour, which is long and harsh, and revealed that the analogy in law gains a more essential role through it. While rhetorics consider it as an argument amongst others, opposed to the argument *a contrario*, we have seen that a correct appraisal of the radical finiteness of human Reason obliges to recognise therein the essential form of all practical judgements-: moral, political or legal. It is the logic of language, which we denominate elsewhere as the paradoxical logic of enounciation, that makes that the legal judgement is by nature reflective and not determining. Just like the moral and political judgement, the legal judgement, even though it has its own constraints (theory of sources of law), does not function on the basis of a given universal, incarnated by rules put by the authority, but with the objective of a universal that is searched and that regulates the unending production of meaning of these same rules.

This last reflection also explains the second insufficiency of legal theories of the analogy in law, and more generally of theories of legal reasoning. In fact, they aim to describe the logical functioning proper to the legal judgement. Our lecture of the function of analogy in legal judgement does not rest upon the same objective. We do not believe that every legal judgement functions on the basis of a "symbolic analogy", to convert to the Kantian approach. Such a functioning, according to us, results only from an account of the radical finiteness of human reason. Without such a recognition, the moral, political or legal judgement is bound to metaphysical illusions and generates dogmatism. In other words, our own undertaking is in some way "normative", as it indicates what would be of a legal judgement (and of a concept of practical Reason) that would rest upon an appraisal of the presuppositions that work in the discourse, vector of meaning and of human Reason. This leads us to our second insight.

Our analysis of the role of the form of analogy in law also allows us to return to the actual debates of legal philosophy. It allows us to validate the position of authors as Habermas, Alexy, or Dworkin, who tried to refute the phenomenological points of view of deconstruction[64] and the dominant points of view of positivism. They are right to reveal the structural kinship between moral and legal judgement, even if they restore cognitivist ethics on a constructivist and purely procedural basis. These positions adequately perceive the necessity to take into account, beyond the criticism of metaphysics, the horizon of universality that moves the operation of meaning at work in the discourse. The role of analogy in law is only the logical translation of this fundamental articulation of human discoursivity.

However, also here, beyond the fundamental correctness of their philosophical orientation, a dogmatic flavour appears with these authors. Indeed, as they lack the link that the Wittgensteinian problematics of the paradox of

[64] In a sort of framework that tends in France to be used by such authors as Ewald or Nerhot, or in English-speaking countries, though often in oversimplified fashion, by *Critical Legal Studies*.

application of a rule ties together with the Kantian theory of the analogy of the practical judgement, these authors risk, in one form or another, to restore the dogmatic presupposed of a rule of which the meaning would be a given, presupposed and imposed. The meaning of the legal rule is, on the contrary, the effect of a construction, even if not arbitrary, of the community of jurists. Two constraints are featuring. First, the objective of a universal that is searched, even though it is empty; the normative constraint of argumentation follows from it. Further, the obligation to construct this meaning in reference to the existing signs and discursive practices. Contrary to the dogmatic presupposition that continues to traverse our European legal models, the legal system is not rational. The "integrity" of the system, to turn to Dworkin's expression, does not exist. It is a simple Idea of Reason on the basis of which the meaning of rules is always susceptible of being reconstructed and recreated, even though this reconstruction rests upon a justification that will never have any other guarantee than only the consensual argumentation of the social community[65].

65 Even the one inherited from Hart, like the institutional theory of Law of N. MacCormick and O. Weinberger, which we have called hermeneutic.

ANALOGY IN LEGAL SCIENCE: SOME COMPARATIVE OBSERVATIONS

BERNARD S. JACKSON

In this paper, I shall offer no answers to the question: "What is the nature of analogy in legal science?" Rather, I shall offer some observations, drawn from work in which I am engaged in Biblical Law and the early history of Jewish Law, designed on the one hand to illustrate the cultural-contingency of our problem, and on the other to indicate some non-traditional perspectives which we may usefully add in our search for understanding of the rational and reasoning processes of legal systems in the West.

The term "analogy" has no universal or fixed meaning. We find it used in different senses both as applied (by Western writers) to different legal systems, and indeed even in the analysis of our own legal system. We therefore have a preliminary methodological problem, in identifying the object of our inquiry (Section l).

But the problem is more than merely methodological. We must be clear as to whether we wish to make any *universal* claims about analogy, or whether our claims are restricted to the cultural-contingency of modern Western systems (one or more of them). Self-evidently, we ought not to be making universal claims merely on the basis of common features identified within Western systems of law. The problem here is more than merely empirical: we would not solve it by increasing to the maximum possible extent the number of legal systems we were able to investigate. Rather, we have a conceptual problem. Any claims of universality must be supported by philosophical or other reasons as to why the phenomenon in question is apparently universal. We may draw upon other disciplines, such as cognitive psychology, to help us distinguish between those forms of reasoning which are likely to be universal, and those which are not. And if we seek such a universality, I suggest that we are more likely to locate it in the sphere of narrative competence, rather than that of political justification. The closer we get to the universal in law, the further we travel from the "scientific" forms in which it is clothed by particular specialist groups within particular cultures (Section 2).

Setting aside, provisionally, the search for any such universals, and adopting as a methodological criterion (Section l) non-formal modes of reasoning actually used in different legal systems, irrespective of the names attached to those modes either by the culture concerned or by the Western observer, we may greatly enrich our investigations. In the process, we may also find reason to doubt the universality of one basic, underlying presupposition of Western analyses of legal science, namely the distinction between "form" and "content" This underlying presupposition is very frequently expressed in our practices of formalisation. The formal or logical accounts of reasoning presuppose that rationality is not located in the linguistic expression of legal rules, or even of legal arguments: it consists in a series of underlying moves, which receive particular manifestations in the discourse of legal reasoning. Again, we continually contrast the levels of logic on the one hand and rhetoric on the other. But some of the phenomena which I shall examine from the Jewish tradition indicate the existence of a culture in which the logic of the level of expression was taken very seriously indeed. In short, the literary presentation of rules was treated as an argument. I shall look particularly at examples of chiasmus and collocation (Section 3).

I conclude (Section 4) with some preliminary remarks about the distinction between "analytical" and "analogical" reasoning, in the light of the examples here discussed. By relating these forms to what may most plausibly be claimed to be universal, we may gain further insight into the forms of cultural contingency – not merely between societies, but also within them.

1. THE TERM "ANALOGY"

The problem of analogy is summed up by the lexical definition provided by the Oxford English Dictionary. It catalogues (I hesitate to say distinguishes) nine different usages, some of them attributed to specialist disciplines such as mathematics, language, and natural history. In this last, for example, "analogy" is taken to mean:

> Resemblance of form or function between organs which are *essentially* different (in different species), as the analogy between the tail of the fish and that of the whale, the wings of a bat and that of a bird, the tendril of the pea and that of the vine.

In language, analogy is taken to be the:

> similarity of formative or constructive processes; imitation of the inflexions, derivatives, or constructions of existing words, informing inflexions, derivatives, or constructions of other words, without the intervention of the formative steps through which these at first arose.

In maths, it is "proportion: agreement of ratios", leading to a conception of "due proportion; correspondence or adaptation of one thing to another". More generally, the OED defines the term as:

> equivalency or likeness of relations; 'resemblance of things with regard to some circumstances or effects', 'resemblance of relations' (Whately); a name for the fact, that, the relation borne to any object by some attribute or circumstance, corresponds to the relation existing between another object and some attribute or circumstance pertaining to it.

More vaguely, it continues, the term means: "agreement between things, similarity." As a figure of speech, the statement of an analogy is a simile or similitude. As for logic, two senses are distinguished: "resemblance of relations or attributes forming a ground of reasoning"; and "the process of reasoning from parallel cases; presumptive reasoning based upon the assumption that if things have some similar attributes, their other attributes will be similar."

The common feature to all these senses is that each one of them, as it stands, is purely formal. Throughout, the terms "resemblance", "correspondence", "agreement", "equivalency", "likeness", "similarity", "parallel", are used, without any indication as to the criteria for determining the degree or nature of such resemblance, equivalency, similarity, etc. But there is also a second, and equally important, formal criterion implicit in these conceptions. Analogy cannot exist between two phenomena if the two phenomena are the same: analogy exists only as between different phenomena.

These two characteristics of the range of lexical uses of the English word "analogy" (of course, I make no claim in respect of the French "analogie", the Italian "analogia" etc.) find reflections in descriptions of the reasoning processes of the Common Law.

To take the first, albeit negative, point: the application of a *binding* precedent to a new case is *not* conceived as the use of analogy. From the formalist viewpoint, what we have here is replication: the two cases are the same. Application of a binding precedent, once the legally salient features of the facts in issue have been identified, is taken to be a deductive process[1], diferent from the application of a statutory rule. The major premise to be applied is the same both in the precedent being applied and the case to which it is applied; the minor premise claims precisely that the facts of the two cases are "the same", in that they are instances of the general class constructed in the major premise, in the sense that the facts of the two cases, once all their legally irrelevant features (such as most of the particularities of person, place and time) have been stripped away, are indeed the same; and equally that the logical process of application of minor premise to major premise, resulting in the same conclusion, is equally the same. Thus, the precedent being applied and the case to which it is applied are not different things; the new case reiterates the same thing.

It is a different feature of the processes of Common Law reasoning which is sometimes described as "analogy". In "hard cases", the major premise may itself be indeterminate, and may have to be constructed from existing materials within the legal system, which do not themselves constitute *binding* precedents for this case. A celebrated example is the case of *Rylands v. Fletcher* (1868 L. R. 3 H. L. 330), which introduced into English law a principle of strict (no fault) liability where damage is caused by the escape of a dangerous entity brought on to land. The case involved the escape of water from a privately-constructed reservoir through the under-

[1] E.g. N. MacCormick, *Legal Reasoning and Legal Theory*, Oxford, The Clarendon Press, 1978.

ground workings of an abandoned coal mine, the existence of which had not been known. Vinogradoff writes, of the reasoning process used by the court:

> The court had to discover the major premise under which the case should be brought: it had to reason by analogy from the liability for other kinds of dangerous things, e.g. wild animals; and finally it set up the principle ...that 'the person who for his own purposes brings on his lands and collects and keeps there anything likely to do mischief if it escapes, must keep it at his peril, and if he does not do so, is *prima facie* answerable for all the damage which is the natural consequence of its escape'[2].

Here, the materials from which the new rule was to be constructed were clearly regarded as "different" and not "the same". Wild animals which escaped were different from water which escaped from a reservoir; the pre-existing principles of liability for nuisance were also "different". We are not told why. Within the culture concerned, there is no need to do so; the classifications are taken as self-evident. But these different phenomena are taken to be sufficiently similar to justify application of the same consequence to the case of the reservoir (and to a category of cases for which, according to the *ratio decidendi* of the case, the reservoir stands). Hence, the description by Vinogradoff of this principle as the use of analogy.

There are, however, theorists who have described the whole process of decision by precedent as being based upon, or perhaps justified by, analogy, in the sense that precedent relies upon the feeling that "like cases ought to be treated alike". But care must here be exercised. What the account I have provided above indicates is not that "like cases ought to be treated alike" (since this aphorism is used not of the construction of new principles, as in the case of *Rylands v. Fletcher*, but to justify the "deductive" process of legal reasoning, where the major premise is already established). In that latter context, the aphorism should really read: "identical cases ought to be treated identically," since it is the *same* legal conclusion which is applied to the two cases, and this can be done only once the later case has been *subsumed*

2 P. Vinogradoff, *Common Sense in Law*, London, Oxford University Press, 1946, 2nd ed. by H. G. Hanbury, p. 136f. (The Home University).

under the major premise, i.e. judged to be an instance of the *same* category as that specified within the major premise.

But to say this is to look at the facts of the later case only from the viewpoint of their legal construction. If "like cases ought to be treated alike" has any application to the normal process of the application of binding precedent to new cases, it can mean only this: factual situations which, in all their particularity, are different, ought nevertheless to be treated as if they were the same, provided that we judge that these cases are sufficiently alike. Of course, on this analysis, a vital discretionary element enters into the application of precedent[3]. We next have to ask: "Who exercises this discretion, and on the basis of what criteria?"

I would maintain that analogy does enter into the legal process at this point. It is not, however, the analogy of legal science, but rather a much more popular, perhaps subconscious, analogy, which in my earlier work I have discussed under the headings of "Subconscious Rationality"[4] and "Narrative Coherence"[5]. Of this, more again anon.

The differences between these uses of the term "analogy" in the context of English law (analogy in the construction of new principles, analogy (or the claim to its absence) in the application of binding precedent) take on some perspective when we look at other cultures. I have long been fascinated, but have never systematically investigated, the following claim made by the leading Western Islamic law scholar of the last generation, Joseph Schacht:

> There are two methods by which legal subject-matter can be brought into a system, the analytical and the analogical. The analytical method,

[3] MacCormick would not deny this.

[4] "Rationalité consciente et inconsciente dans la théorie du droit et la science juridique", *Revue interdisciplinaire des études juridiques* no. 19 (1987), pp.1-18; "Conscious and Unconscious Rationality in Law and Legal Theory", in *Reason in Law, Proceedings of the Conference Held in Bologna, 12-15 December 1984*, ed. Carla Faralli and Enrico Pattaro, Milan, Giuffrè, 1988, III, pp. 281-299.

[5] "Narrative Models in Legal Proof", International Journal for the Semiotics of Law I/3 (1988), pp. 225-246; *Law, Fact and Narrative Coherence*, Merseyside: Deborah Charles Publications, 1988.

> the classical example of which is provided by Roman law, leads to the creation of logically organised legal norms in an ascending order. The analogical method leads to the organisation of legal subject-matter by parataxis and association. Islamic law represents this latter type of systematising in great purity, and this corresponds with the type of thinking expressed by the Arabic language. Closely connected with this way of thinking is the casuistical method, which is indeed one of the most striking features of traditional Islamic law. All these features are manifestations of a typical way of thought which pervades the whole of Islamic law and which has determined the organization of the legal subject-matter in all its aspects[6].

Let us leave aside, for the moment, the notion of casuistical method[7], which does not seem to present a self-evidently strong distinction between Islamic law on the one hand and either Roman law or English Common Law on the other. What is certainly important in Schacht's claim is the distinction between a system of "logically organized legal norms in an ascending order" (which seems to indicate the apparatus of a conceptual hierarchy) and on the other hand "the organization of legal subject-matter by parataxis[8] and association". It might appear that Schacht here fails adequately to distinguish between two different phenomena: modes of reasoning on the one hand, methods of presentation on the other. Whether Schacht had in mind the deconstruction of that distinction, or its inapplicability to the culture he was studying, may be left aside. I shall argue from Jewish materials, to which the Islamic may well be closer than they are to our modern legal systematics, that such a distinction ought to be deconstructed, and that we may well view the method of presentation of the law as itself constituting a form of reasoning. In contrast to Schacht's hierarchical model (the analyti-

6 "Law and the State – (a) Islamic Religious Law", in J. Schacht and C. E. Bosworth, *The Legacy of Islam*, 2nd edition, Oxford, Oxford University Press, 1974, p. 397.

7 But see my "Legalism", *Journal of Jewish Studies* no. 30 (1979), pp. 1-22, esp. 14-16.

8 "Parataxis" is the "placing of propositions or clauses etc. one after another, without indicating by connecting words the relation (co-ordination or subordination) between them" (OED).

cal model, which he attributes to Western legal science), which I have termed "conceptual", I propose to use the term "literary" rationality, to refer to those phenomena which use the forms of presentation as modes of argument.

I take as a first example one of the thirteen "hermeneutical rules" (*middot*) used in classical rabbinic texts: *hekesh* (sometimes compared with the Islamic *qiyas*). Louis Jacobs has provided the following brief description:

> [S]imilar to the *gezerah shavah* but not identical with it are the rules of *hekkesh* (comparison) and *semukhim* ("juxtaposition"). *Hekkesh* refers to the presence of two laws in the same verse, from which it may be inferred that whatever is true of one is true of the other. For example, "thou shalt eat no leavened bread with it; seven days shalt thou eat unleavened bread therewith" (*Deut.* 16:3). Although women are exempt from carrying out positive precepts associated with given time, they are nevertheless obliged to eat unleavened bread on Passover, since the verse, by combining the two laws, compared the duty to eat unleavened bread with the prohibition against eating leaven, which, being a negative precept, is binding on women[9].

Here, the analogy is based not upon substantive likeness between the two cases, but rather upon their collocation in the authoritative biblical text. Some examples I shall offer later suggest that this conception was not an invention of the post-biblical interpreters, but that it exists in comparable forms within the biblical text itself.

My principal point at this stage, is, however, terminological. Although Jacobs uses the term "comparison" to describe *hekkesh*, this has frequently been regarded as the Jewish form of reasoning by analogy. Such a conception is, indeed, distant from the assumptions of modern Western legal scholarship (if not, to the same degree, from those of literary scholarship).

[9] "Hermeneutics", *Encyclopedia Judaica*, Jerusalem, Keter Publishing House, 1972, VIII, p. 368: "The *argument by comparison* is the deduction of a rule, not stated explicitly, from an accepted teaching to which it bears a strong resemblance." He gives as examples arguments introduced by *hainu* (Pes. 9b-10a), *yalfinan* (Yev. 57), *shema'minah* (Pes. 5b). See *The Talmudic Argument*, Cambridge, Cambridge University Press, 1984, p. 14.

As a result, some comparative lawyers (such as Maine in the nineteenth century) saw analogical reasoning as somehow less strict, more distant, more loose and more primitive than Western "analytical" reasoning. It is important to be aware of this cultural prejudice, if we are to rid ourselves of its malign effects.

2. UNIVERSALITY OF ANALOGY?

If the object of our inquiry is to identify the elements of some universal legal rationality (a modern version of natural law?), we must do our best to avoid attributing this status to culturally-contingent forms of rationality found in Western law. I take it that the proposals of Patrick Nerhot when he presented some tendencies of legal dogmatics in his pre-conference paper, illustrates this latter category. Legal dogmatics categorise analogy as "logical reasoning based upon the resemblance of terms". If by "terms" it means the presence of the same lexical item in two laws, which provides a basis for analogising between them, then this presupposes a form of legal rationality which is text-based, and for this reason alone is unlikely to command the status of a universal. This conception of *analogia juris*, representing the rational *and unitary* force of a body of legislation, again presupposes something (the postulate of unity) which may appeal to legal philosophers as a model, but which has weaker claims for the comparative lawyer, for whom increasingly the notion of "legal pluralism" (even within a single nation state) has attracted increasing assent. The function which Nerhot attributes, speaking once again about legal dogmatics, to such rational and unitary force also resides, in my view, on the *philosophical* rather than the *empirical* level. It sees it as providing the origin and justification of general principles of law. My difficulty here resides not in the identification of the "general principles" as the object of justification, but rather with the assumption that the function of analogy is indeed justification. This assumption, of course, is part and parcel of a wider vision of legal reasoning, endorsed by many legal philosophers, for whom the justification of decisions is either synonymous with the grounds for decision-making itself, or represents the sole interest of legal philosophy (relegating the grounds of decision-making to the sociologists of law). But if we are seeking universals, I suggest that we are far more likely to find them at the level of decision-making rather than that of justification: the former is more likely to be influenced by psychological and sociological universals; the latter is an explicit, conscious cultural product. Should I invoke an analogy with Marxist conceptions of base and superstructure?

The pre-conference paper about legal dogmatics does attribute to analogy the function of providing a ground for decision-making in unforeseen cases and this is possible only if we attribute rationality to the body of laws, and conceive of them in the form of (a unified?) system. In line with most contemporary legal philosophy, this makes the assumption that decision-making is an exercise in the explicit use of rationality by experts. To some, this vision of legal decision-making is faulty only on the grounds that it is overly idealistic; to others, even the idealism is ill-founded. From a semiotic point of view, the discourse of legal scientists is simply a set of speech-forms which legal scientists use to attempt to persuade each other of particular propositions which have pertinence within the universe of their discourse; it is not to be equated with "the law", which is a plurality of interlocking discourses, which may exert mutual influence. Moreover, legal scientists themselves, though they may indulge in the discourse of legal science, do not inhabit a world of legal science alone. They are part and parcel of the general culture, and even (strange as this may often seem) of humanity in general. They are therefore not immune to the use of non-specialist forms of reasoning and discourse.

Idealism of this kind of dogmatics continues when it proposes that analogy may function as a means of filling gaps in a legal system, in accordance with the general spirit of that system, and avoiding "arbitrariness". But what do we mean by "arbitrariness" in this context? Clearly, we cannot mean that reasoning by analogy eliminates the need for choice. I noted earlier the presence of discretion as a common feature in different conceptions of "analogy", as the term is used in English. At best, then, analogy may be conceived as a mode of the exercise of (in Dworkin's terms) "weak" discretion. But how weak can it be when it depends upon formal criteria like "resemblance", "similarity", etc.? Are we really here operating in the sphere of an explicit (even universal) rationality, or rather in that of social, intuitive, experiential feelings of "fit"? Models of narrative coherence, based upon social psychology and semiotics (rather than explicit practical reasoning), seem to me to come closer to an explanation of this social, experiential dimension of "fit"[10].

Bennett and Feldman have argued that stories have implicit structures that enable people to make systematic comparisons between them[11]. This would seem to imply that people carry around with them a stock of socially-constructed narratives, acquired through the whole range of their social experience (including their education). A significant factor affecting the plausibility of a newly-communicated story is the degree to which it fits a narrative which already exists within this stock of social knowledge. This should not be understood as claiming that we carry around with us an immense stock of substantive stories as concrete and as detailed as the stories told in court, whose credibility the jury has to assess. Rather, Bennett and Feldman maintain that it is the "implicit structures" of stories which enable people to make comparisons. We then have to ask about the character of these narrative structures. How general are they? And how far do they depend upon some *narrative competence* – comparable perhaps to the Chomskyan model of a linguistic competence which allows the child to learn a grammar, and thence to recognise as grammatically well-formed (or not) an infinity of "sentences", despite the relatively limited data actually presented to the child for the construction of such models. In other words, our practice of narrative recognition may depend upon some form of universal narrative competence, notwithstanding the fact that the structures of narrative recognition (like the rules of a particular grammar) will be socially and culturally contingent. Elsewhere, I have argued against the proposals that we can identify a "deep structure of law" along Chomskyan

[10] *Law, Fact and Narrative Coherence*, *supra*, no. 5, esp. ch.3.

[11] Bennett, W. L. and Feldman, M. S., *Reconstructing Reality in the Courtroom*, New Brunswick, Rutgers U. P., 1981, x.

lines, in terms of structural characteristics of systems of legal rules[12]. However, Chomskyan-type deep structures may well be relevant to law, insofar as law makes use of the same narrative structures as other parts of culture.

Greimasian semiotics provides an account of such a narrative competence in its theory of "basic structures of signification" (*structures élémentaires de la signification*), which are universal from one culture to another (although this does not necessarily involve adoption of an innate competence)[13]. Through a re-analysis of Vladimir Propp's Russian folk-tales, and the thirty-one narrative structures derived by Propp from them, Greimas inferred a more abstract, general (and, as he claimed, universal) "actantial" model, which (in combination with a paradigmatic level, inspired by de Saussure and Hjelmslev) he takes as representing the "deep level" of all discourse. This actantial model, sometimes now described as semio-narrative, consists in a "narrative syntagm", with three elements: the setting of goals ("contract"), the achievement (or non-achievement) of those goals ("performance"), and the acknowledgement of the performance (or non-performance) of those goals ("recognition"). Involved in this narrative syntagm are a set of *actants*, subject-object, sender-receiver, helper-opponent. A sender invests a receiver as "subject" of the story, by communicating a goal to him. In achieving this goal ("object"), or performing his task, the subject may be assisted by a "helper", or obstructed by an "opponent". At the end of the syntagm there is another communicational element, the sending and receiving of recognition of what has occurred. The *actants* and *fonctions* which make up the semio-narrative level may be expressed at the level of manifest discourse by a variety of *acteurs* (real people in social life; "characters" in literature), and each one of these may perform different actantial roles at different times. But the fact that we are able to make sense of social action (whether real or literary) at all is due to the fact that these ba-

12 "Can One Speak of the 'Deep Structure' of Law?", in *Theory and Systems of Legal Philosophy*, ed. S. Panou et al. (Stuttgart: Franz Steiner Verlag, 1988), pp. 250-261 (ARSP Supplementum III).

13 For a fuller statement, see my *Semiotics and Legal Theory* (London: Routledge and Kegan Paul, 1985), Part 2, esp. ch. 3; see also A.J. Greimas, *On Meaning: Selected Writings in Semiotic Theory* (Minneapolis: University of Minnesota Press, 1987).

sic structures underlie the discourse. This theory of the universal level of discourse does not claim to provide a theory of universal *reason*, except insofar as "intelligibility" – the capacity of something to "make sense" – requires fundamental structures of understanding, which include categories which inform the making of judgments of similarity between phenomena.

In the course of legal decision-making, judgments are made on both facts and law. They are made, it is suggested, in terms of "fit" with narrative models of typical behaviour patterns, and typical legal responses to those behaviour patterns. "Analogy" may well be a suitable term to use to describe such judgements of similarity or fit. But before any such (socially and culturally contingent) judgments can be made, both the narrative typifications and the data on which decisions are to be made have to be intelligible. Narrative structure may therefore represent a necessary, and universal, condition for the application of decision-making by analogy.

3. SOME EXAMPLES OF LITERARY ANALOGY FROM BIBLICAL LAW

I turn now to consider some examples of non-formal (in the sense of non-deductive) reasoning encountered in Biblical legal texts. Of course, our very perception of the Biblical texts, in modern Western scholarship, is necessarily mediated through our own cultural concepts and methods. This, I suggest, is reflected in an important methodological debate amongst students of Biblical law in recent years.

In 1960, Professor Moshe Greenberg published an article entitled, "Some Postulates of Biblical Criminal Law"[14]. He argued that comparison between Biblical and Ancient Near Eastern laws should proceed not on the basis of possible influence of one concrete law upon another, but should compare the underlying principles of the different systems. On this basis, he maintained, a marked difference between Biblical and Ancient Near Eastern law emerges. In particular, he inferred the existence of a principle within Biblical law of the "incommensurability of life and property": life was not forfeited for property offences, and property was not regarded as a proper compensation for loss of life. In both respects, Ancient Near Eastern law

14 *Yehezkel Kaufmann Jubilee Volume*, Jerusalem, The Magnes Press, pp. 5-28.

differed from this postulate. Some years later, I pointed out difficulties in Greenberg's methodology: his inferences from the particular to the general were uncontrolled, and non-necessary[15]. At that stage, I was prepared to concede that the search for such "postulates" (as Greenberg conceived them) was legitimate; the problem (perhaps insoluble) lay in the method by which he proposed to find them. More recently, however, I have come to doubt the underlying conceptual structure. Greenberg, I suggest, is seeking to attribute to the biblical text a rationalist model of values, which derives from our own cultural experience. Without evidence of the presence of such a structure, we have no sufficient reason to assume its presence[16].

To say this is not to deny the presence of underlying values in biblical law (or, more exactly, in the texts of biblical law: since that is all to which we have access)[17]. But the values of biblical legal texts may relate to one another in different forms of system than those of modern Western legal science. Our model may not be a conceptual, hierarchical one; it may be a literary and analogical one. By literary and analogical, I mean that its mode of expression may be found in the *form* of the biblical legal texts, rather than in their content; and that the systematicity of these values may be more a matter of narrative fit than of reasoning through different levels of abstraction.

I shall present two examples, both of which may (I hope will) read rather strangely to Western legal scientists. The first is the principle of arrangement which governs the presentation of the first section of laws in the "Book of the Covenant" of *Exodus* 21-23, which appears in the biblical narrative as the law-book revealed to Moses by God on Mount Sinai immedi-

15 B. S. Jackson, *Essays in Jewish and Comparative Legal History*, Leiden: E. J. Brill, 1975, ch. 2, which largely reprints, with some revision, "Reflections on Biblical Criminal Law", *Journal of Jewish Studies* 24 (1973), pp. 8-38.

16 This argument is advanced in different forms in "The Ceremonial and the Judicial: Biblical Law as Sign and Symbol", in *Journal for the Study of the Old Testament*, no. 30 (1984), pp. 25-50, at 35ff.;"Some Semiotic Questions for Biblical Law", in *The Oxford Conference Volume*, ed. A.M. Fuss, Atlanta, Scholars Press, 1987, pp. 1-25, at 16ff. (*Jewish Law Association Studies* III); and in my forthcoming *Wisdom Laws*.

17 Moreover, the values of biblical legal discourse are not necessarily the same as the values of biblical legal practice insofar as we can reconstruct the latter.

ately after the Decalogue. The arrangement of these laws has long provoked puzzlement amongst legal historians: it seems to conform to no known set of legal concepts. As a result, some have concluded that the arrangement is either "chaotic", or that it is based merely upon some primitive principle of association. In fact, what we have is a sophisticated *literary* presentation, which uses a literary artifice found elsewhere in biblical writings, namely the chiasmus. This is a pattern in which a series of elements is repeated in reverse order, with the first and last elements also often forming the centrepiece of the group. Thus, in Exodus 21:2-27:

A1	Exod. 21:2-11	Liberation of male and female slaves
B1	Exod. 21:12-17	Capital provisions
C1	Exod. 21:18-19	Injuries from a brawl
D	Exod. 21:20-21	Fatal assault on one's own slave
C2	Exod. 21:22-23	Brawl affecting pregnant woman
B2	Exod. 21:24-25	Talionic provisions
A2	Exod. 21:26-27	Liberation of male and female slaves

Of course, I have myself presented this schema in the form which I hope will most readily persuade my readers that the pattern does indeed exist. The phrases which I have used to categorise the various elements of the law are my phrases; the biblical text itself includes no headings revealing the categorisation of the original biblical writers. But chiasmus is a well-known feature of biblical literature, and other examples are beginning to emerge also in the "legal" texts. In the absence of any other credible principle of arrangement, the scheme here proposed has some plausibility.

But what, precisely, are the resemblances or analogies upon which this scheme is based? Here is the full text of the passage, as translated by the New English Bible.

2 When you buy a Hebrew slave, he shall be your slave for six years, but in the seventh year he shall go free and pay nothing.

3 If he comes to you alone, he shall go away alone; but if he is married, his wife shall go away with him.

4 If his master gives him a wife, and she bears him sons or daughters, the woman and her children shall belong to her master, and the man shall go away alone.

5 But if the slave should say, 'I love my master, my wife, and my children; I will not go free',

6 then his master shall bring him to God: he shall bring him to the door or the door-post, and his master shall pierce his ear with awl, and the man shall be his slave for life.

7 When a man sells his daughter into slavery, she shall not go free as a male slave may.

8 If her master has not had intercourse with her and she does not please him, he shall let her be ransomed. He has treated her unfairly and therefore has no right to sell her to strangers.

9 If he assigns her to his son, he shall allow her the rights of a daughter.

10 If he takes another woman, he shall not deprive the first of meat, clothes, and conjugal rights.

11 If he does not provide her with these three things, she shall go free without any payment.

12 Whoever strikes another man and kills him shall be put to death.

13 But if he did not act with intent, but they met by act of God, the slayer may flee to a place which I will appoint for you.

14 But if a man has the presumption to kill another by treachery, you shall take him even from my altar to be put to death.

15 Whoever strikes his father or mother shall be put to death.

16 Whoever kidnaps a man shall be put to death, whether he has sold him, or the man is found in his possession.

17 Whoever reviles his father or mother shall be put to death.

18 When men quarrel and one hits another with a stone or with a spade, and the man is not killed but takes to his bed;

19 if he recovers so as to walk about with a stick, then the one who struck him has no liability, except that he shall pay for loss of time and shall see that he is cured.
20 When a man strikes his slave or his slave-girl with a stick and the slave dies on the spot, he must be punished.
21 But he shall not be punished if the slave survives for one day or two, because he is worth money to his master.
22 When, in the course of a brawl, a man knocks against a pregnant woman so that she has a miscarriage but suffers no further hurt, then the offender must pay whatever fine the woman's husband demands after assessment.
23 Wherever hurt is done, you shall give life for life,
24 eye for eye, tooth for tooth, hand for hand, foot for foot,
25 burn for burn, bruise for bruise, wound for wound.
26 When a man strikes his slave or slave-girl in the eye and destroys it, he shall let the slave go free in compensation for the eye.
27 When he knocks out the tooth of a slave or a slave-girl, he shall let the slave go free in compensation for the tooth.

The main organising theme of the chiasmus is slavery, and particularly liberation from slavery. That fits well with the wider narrative context of the revelation of these laws, which occurs very soon after the liberation of the Israelites from their Egyptian slavery. And indeed, the memory of that liberation is sometimes used in the Bible quite explicitly as a motive for Israel's obedience to the law. However, "liberation from slavery" can be said to be the principal theme or topic of only Al of these provisions. In D, the "liberation" is figurative – release by involuntary death; while in A2, such liberation is provided as a sanction for assault resulting in the loss of an eye or tooth. In terms of theme, verses 26-27 seem to follow much more directly upon their immediate context, since the preceding paragraph (my Cl) involves assault by one free man upon another. Nevertheless, the element of liberation from slavery is present, and this is sufficient to provide connection for the purposes of the chiasmus.

Bl and B2 are connected more by literary form than by content. In both, the provisions are (atypically, as has been widely noted) presented in forms which differ from the casuistic (in the sense of biblical form criticism) formulation of the rest of the collection. Both sets are formulated in variations of what is called the "apodictic" form. Moreover, the principle of equivalence receives its literal, talionic form in both of these sets of provision: death for homicide at the beginning of Bl; and eye for an eye etc. in B2.

Cl and C2 are linked in terms of their internal narrative setting, rather than their legal theme. Both involve assaults causing serious bodily injury. But the first involves a deliberate blow, while the second concerns an incidental, and unintended, injury to a bystander. The link between the two resides in their internal narrative contexts: the setting of both is a brawl, a quarrel which suddenly erupts and results in blows being traded. Contrast this narrative image with that of the ambush, where the wrongdoers lay in wait (verse 13, in Bl).

My second example concerns a subtle literary feature of this collection, which is embedded within the collocation of provisions regarding male and female slaves respectively, in Al[18]. The first paragraph deals with the male Hebrew debt-slave (Ex. 21.2-6); the second with the special status of the female *amah* – transferred permanently from the house of the debtor to that of the creditor, in order to become a wife (or concubine) to a member of the family (Ex. 21.7-11). The period of enslavement of the male Hebrew debt-slave is temporary – a maximum of six years (unless the slave himself opts to make the relationship permanent), while that of the *amah* is of its nature permanent, unless she is rejected from the family. There is, however, a *casus omissus* – the female debt-slave who is not to become an *amah*, but is to perform non-sexual (domestic and agricultural) duties. We have good evidence to suggest that this, in practice, was the most common case of debt-slavery of all. So why should it have been excluded?

The answer is that the editor, in this way, is able to emphasise what is seen as a fundamental difference between the legal positions of men and women. The first paragraph includes a rule that the creditor may give a woman to the male debt-slave, but that at the termination of the period of service he must leave her (and any children she has borne to him) in the house of the creditor. In effect, therefore, the master may use the temporary

18 See further my "*Biblical Laws of Slavery: a Comparative Approach*", in *Slavery and other Forms of Unfree Labour*, ed. L. Archer, London and New York, Routledge, 1988, pp. 86-101 (History Workshop Series).

male debt-slave for breeding purposes without altering his status. There is no suggestion anywhere that he may do the same to the temporary female debt-slave. The second paragraph of the Covenant Code tells us under what circumstances a female debt-slave may be used for breeding purposes: it is only if she enters into the special status of *amah*, which at the same time gives her a permanent status within the family. In other words, by juxtaposing these two paragraphs, and by omitting any mention of the case which was the most common in practice, the message is conveyed that the status of a man is not affected by sexual services, whereas sexual services may not be demanded of a woman without altering her status. Here, analogy is used in order to emphasise difference despite apparent similarity; and it is done through literary mechanisms – collocation, combined with suppression of that which would interfere with the message of the juxtaposition.

4. THE ANALYTIC AND ANALOGICAL

In conclusion, some tentative suggestions as to the significance of the material here studied.

The distinction between analytical and analogical approaches to legal reasoning (Schacht's distinction above) might appear at first sight to be the following. In the analytical approach, a hierarchy of concepts is built up, each such concept being made up of a set of elements which are individually necessary and jointly sufficient to constitute an instance of that concept. As a consequence, every single variable is significant. No two phenomena can be instances of the same concept if they vary even in one significant element. Analogical reasoning, on the other hand, might appear to be looser, in the sense that the presence of any one common element between phenomena might appear sufficient to justify the assumption of a resemblance (analogy) between them. If so, the creation of such analogies becomes relatively arbitrary.

This, I believe, is a fair representation of the attitude of a number of Western commentators upon non-Western legal science.[19] The examples I

[19] Legal science is a term of art which I use only for convenience; I believe it is as misplaced for Western as for non-Western systems.

have discussed perhaps provide some hints as to the areas in which that conventional view proves inadequate. Three such aspects have been noted:

1. Analogy can be used in the construction of overall literary meaning, through the arrangement of material.

2. Analogy does not have to rest upon explicit terminology, and does not have to be explicit in the advancement of its own argument; it can proceed by the collocation of different sets of binary oppositions.

3. The resemblances and differences with which the text plays may be based upon social-experiential narrative frames, rather than abstract legal concepts.

By taking account of these three aspects in combination, we begin to take account of social content of legal rules on the one hand, and the specialised rhetoric of their presentation on the other.

These suggestions clearly require considerable elaboration. But the effort will be worthwhile, since these issues are far from the parochial concerns of a student of ancient Near Eastern law. The study of analogy in the West should not be straightjacketed into the confines of a formalist conception of Western legal science. To do so is to risk impoverishment – precisely the impoverishment which results from the appropriation of the law by the legal scientist and the abstraction of law from both its social and rhetorical foundations.

LEGAL ANALOGY BETWEEN INTERPRETIVE ARGUMENTS AND PRODUCTIVE ARGUMENTS

VITTORIO VILLA

1. LEGAL ANALOGY AND SELF-REFERENCE

In this paper I will try to discuss, taking as a specific example the *argument by analogy*, the problematic relationship between *legal interpretation* and – juristic and judicial – *legal integration*, that is between the two activities which are traditionally qualified as, respectively, "law finding" and "law creation".

Before going into the details of this kind of critical analysis, I have prejudicially to clarify the main features and the quite complex internal articulations of discourses potentially referring to analogical arguments. In so doing, I will not need at all to give, in advance (supposing that it could ever be possible), a precise and complete definition of the concept 'argument by analogy'. Even for the class which these arguments surely belong to (the class of legal *arguments*), this kind of definition is out of order. Here, on the contrary, it will be enough to give a sort of – not rigorous and not accomplished, from an analytical point of view – "pre-definition" of legal arguments in general. With regard to this, I suggest to qualify as *legal arguments* the outcomes (in terms of *structured sets – or chains – of propositions*) of a complex socio-linguistic practice whose main task is to offer *justifications* of legal interpretations and decisions.[1]

[1] This configuration of legal arguments' task is a sort of "common place" in analytical jurisprudence. See, for instance, N. MacCormick, *Legal Reasoning and Legal Theory*,

What kind of argumentative discourse is legal analogy? In which way can it be suitably defined? The answer to these questions depends largely, of course, on the kind of definitional approach that we choose to adopt. This last one, in its turn, depends on more general epistemological premises. In other terms, the "background" epistemological framework at least blocks some definitional approaches and leaves open other ones. For instance, if we accept, as I think we should, a *constructivist*[2] epistemological perspective, then we will be obliged to leave out any kind of *essentialistic* definitional models, and particularly that one called *definition per genus et differentiam*. From a "constructivist" perspective, as a matter of fact, we cannot ever speak of – or refer to – "something" (a thing, an event, a process, etc.), belonging to a given – natural, social, linguistic, etc. – domain, as if it was *per se* (that is, because of its "objective internal structure" or "autonomous configuration") provided with *essential properties* and included in a *natural kind*, because that "something" (at least as an autonomous entity with its equipment of "essential" and "contingent" properties) is not the point of departure, but, on the contrary, *the result*, among others of course, of one of the – potentially – many possible selective and "theory laden" reconstructions of that domain. This kind of "global interpretive reconstruction" is explicitly performed by the *working* conceptual scheme (that is, by the framework used for that domain's theoretical representation) or, anyway, it is implicitly presupposed by all the kinds of operations and activities accomplished inside that scheme[3]. It is just in the light of this reconstruction that

Clarendon Press, Oxford, 1978, pp. 14-15 and R. Guastini, *Lezioni sul linguaggio giuridico*, Giappichelli, Torino, 1985, pp. 94-96.

[2] I suggest to qualify as *constructivist* all those post-positivist epistemological trends which try to take a sort of "middle way" between *realist* positions on one side, and *anti-realist positions* on the other. See, as very good examples of this kind of perspective, H. Putnam, *Reason, Truth and History*, Cambridge University Press, Cambridge Mass., 1981, and N. Goodman, *Ways of Worldmaking*, Harvard University Press, Cambridge Mass., 1978. See also, for a more detailed examination of constructivism, a recent book of mine, titled *Costruttivismo e teorie del diritto*, due to be published (in its final draft) by Giappichelli.

[3] Almost all the recent meta-theoretical conceptions, of *holistical character*, which conceive scientific theories as a sort of *structural wholes* (in the more specific terms of, respectively, "research programmes" (Lakatos), "paradigms" (Kuhn), "world versions" (Goodman), etc.), pay a great debt to the seminal work of Quine; see particularly W. V. O.

it is possible, not only to isolate that "something" from a still undifferentiated and quite amorphous empirical background, but also to equip it with "relevant" properties and to put it into one or another "pertinent" kind.

If, therefore, our task was that of defining legal analogy, or legal arguments in general, on the basis of constructivist epistemological premises, then we could not rely on some essential and aprioristically defined features of these arguments; we, rather, should better put at work a conceptual scheme (in this case, a theory of legal reasoning), whose aim should be that of offering a global interpretive reconstruction of a given domain (in this case, of certain specific and context-bounded argumentative practices). From this point of view, therefore, we should avoid to use, in legal reasoning's domain as well as, generally speaking, in law's domain, the classical definition "per genus et differentiam". In fact, this kind of definition rests heavily on *realist premises,* because it presupposes, to a certain extent, that legal arguments, and even "law" as a whole, constitute some sort of natural "genus", endowed with "essential" properties of transitive character. We should, on the contrary, if we wanted to remain faithful to that epistemological perspective, prefer to adopt a different definitional approach, and precisely that one based on the *research, guided by paradigmatic cases, of relevant similarities between specific instances belonging to a given domain*[4].

According to this approach, therefore, the problem that all theories of legal reasoning must confront is that of singling out some "genuine" *paradigmatic instances of legal arguments' concrete uses,* and, afterwards, that of finding out, of course in the light of the conceptual framework adopted, some "relevant" similarities between the first ones and other "borderline"

Quine, *From a Logical Point of View*, Harvard University Press, Cambridge Mass., 1953, and *Word and Object,* MIT Press, Cambridge Mass., 1960.

4 The "paradigm shift from essentialist theories of definition to a "family resemblance" approach, which is taking place in contemporary analytical philosophy, is strongly affected, of course, by the work of "later Wittgenstein" on the ways in which we learn to apply "words" to "things"; see, for instance, L. Wittgenstein, *Philosophical Investigations,* transl. by G. E. M. Anscombe, Blackwell, Oxford, 1983 (first edition 1953), par. 65-66, and *Culture and Value*, ed. by G. H. von Wright and H. Nyman, trans. by P. Winch, Blackwell, Oxford, 1980, p. 14. A good scrutiny of Wittgenstein's theses on this subject can be found in D. Bloor, *Wittgenstein. A Social Theory of Knowledge*, MacMillan, London, 1983, pp. 22-49. Coming back, now, to legal theory, we can notice a strong Wittgensteinian influence in Hart's criticism of "per genus et differentiam" definitions of law (H. L. A. HART, *The Concept of Law,* Clarendon, Oxford, 1961, pp. 13-17).

cases. It is just the "background" conceptual framework that determines the "working pattern" for the evaluation of the similarities' relevance. We can suitably speak, in referring to the set of paradigmatic instances, of the *concept* of legal argument, and, in referring to the – competing – conceptual frameworks, of *conceptions* of legal argument[5]. In my view, the last ones contain, among other things, some *normative ideas* on the features that make legal arguments "good" or "genuine"; these ideas, in their turn, give a guidance and a unifying purpose to selective and biased processes which amount to the reconstruction of "argumentative practices" performed in a given context[6]. I would like to stress, by the way, that this mixture of descriptive and normative elements is unavoidable in theoretical contexts presenting competing conceptual schemes which are "undermined by the facts"[7], even more so in those contexts in which "social practices" (law, scientific method, argumentative discourses, etc.) constitute the specific object of description.

[5] The distinction between *concept* and *conception* is is very useful, in philosophy of natural sciences as well as in philosophy of human sciences, in order to offer an adequate solution to the so called problem of "incommensurability" of theories (that is, "how to explain the fact that different theories – conceived as global interpretive reconstructions of a given domain – can sensibly refer to the same "thing" ?). For the same purpose the distinction is introduced, for instance, by H. Putnam (*Reason, Truth and History*, *op. cit.*, p. 116), albeit in a slightly different way (he, as a matter of fact, assigns to the term 'concept' a different meaning). My proposal, on the contrary, comes much closer to that of W. B. Gallie (*Essentially Contested Concepts*, in "Proceedings of the Aristotelian Society", vol. XVI, 1955-1956, pp. 167-198), and, with specific regard to jurisprudential field, to that of R. Dworkin (*A Matter of Principle*, Harvard University Press, Cambridge Mass., 1985, pp. 153-154, and *Law's Empire*, Fontana Press, London, pp. 65-66, 70-73, 92-94).

[6] For a good example of a meta-jurisprudence according to which a theory of legal reasoning should not offer a "exhaustive description" of all the arguments actually performed in a given context, but should, on the contrary, bring to light the "fundamental features of legal argumentation", see N. MacCormick, *Legal Reasoning and Legal Theory*, *op. cit.*, p. 13.

[7] For a good rendering, in general terms, of the "underdetermination thesis", cf. M. Hesse, *Revolutions and Reconstructions in Philosophy of Science*, Harvester, Brighton, 1980, p. VIII; a quite interesting application of this thesis to legal theory is proposed by R. Dworkin, *Law's Empire*, *op. cit.*, p. 52.

It is important to note that this definitional approach becomes, to a certain extent, *self-referential*, whenever it is applied in legal analogy's definition. I think we can easily notice this as soon as we realize that research of similarities between "paradigmatic cases" – those explicitly provided for by enacted rules – and "borderline cases" – new and unruled "hard cases" – is just what constitutes the *undisputed concept of legal analogy* (that is, the non-contested paradigmatic instances of the argument's use by judges and jurists). But this amounts to say that, in taking into account legal analogy, this definitional approach refers, to some extent, to itself, that is, just to the same features shared by itself. From this point of view, therefore, we can rightfully say that legal analogy is an important example – as an institutionalized and public kind of argument – of this extensively growing and successful (at least in recent analytical philosophy) definitional approach. Owing to these features, legal analogy is more and more becoming a model for methodological and/or argumentative discourses whose nature and main characters are much more questionable. I'm thinking, in particular, of the case of "scientific method", whose nature and peculiar features are strongly disputed in contemporary meta-science. With regard to this methodological controversy, it happens quite often that those post-positivist philosophers of science who maintain that scientific method works through research of similarities "in nature", and requires "practical" arguments and decisions, look very carefully to legal analogy, and to legal arguments in general, as a useful explanatory model in order to clarify adequately these contested features of the scientific method itself[8]. It is not true, therefore, that, as some hold, there aren't significant relations between legal analogy and analogy "as it is used in scientific method[9]; I maintain, on the contrary, that there is a "network" of relevant similarities between the two procedures, whose acknowledgement, however, depends largely on the adoption of a

[8] I try to show that this is not an abstract hypothesis, but, on the contrary, a thesis strongly backed by empirical evidence (that is, by the fact that many post-positivist philosophers of science look at legal reasoning as a model for scientific reasoning), in a recent book of mine (V. Villa, *Teorie della scienza giuridica e teorie delle scienze naturali. Modelli e analogie*, Giuffrè, Milano, 1984, ch. V)

[9] This is, for instance, the opinion of L. Gianformaggio, *Studi sulla giustificazione giuridica*, Giappichelli, Torino, 1986, p. 139.

"constructivist" conceptual framework in the representation of both scientific practices and legal practices of argumentative character.

2. LEVELS OF DISCOURSES REFERRING TO LEGAL ANALOGY

Coming back, now, to the observations regarding the "stratifications" of discourses potentially referring to legal analogy, and to legal arguments in general, I am of the opinion that these discourses' point of departure should be constituted by *specific and context-bounded argumentative practices* performed by jurists and judges belonging to a given spatio-temporal region. By this I mean that the multi-levelled discourses referring, in the last analysis, to legal arguments, should have, as their direct and immediate object of analysis (which takes always, of course, the form of an interpretive reconstruction), the concrete uses of these arguments – included, obviously, all that which is involved in these operations – by "legal agents" in question. This kind of methodological prescription does not imply, anyway, that *theories of legal reasoning* (that, after all, constitute the outcome of these discourses of reconstructive character) cannot have – as in fact have – a larger scope, in the sense of their referring to those argumentative practices performed in legal domains which can be considered as *sufficiently similar* (as such can be considered, today, western legal systems, leaving apart the obvious differences between "codified law" and "case law").

My analysis, however, is not located at the level of legal reasoning's theory, but, rather, at that of meta-theory's. From this point of view, my specific task will be that of critically discussing the "standard" way in which some current theories of legal reasoning face the problem of legal arguments' – and, particularly, legal analogy's – *function* inside the legal system. Here, therefore, the main question is: can legal analogy be legitimately characterized as part of *legal interpretation* (in a "strict sense" of interpretation), or, rather, has it to be qualified as part of *law creation* (in a "strong sense" of creation)? My observations, as a matter of fact, concern analogy's function rather than structure. By *analogy's structure* I mean the "internal discursive mechanism" exhibited by this kind of argument. For a "structural approach", the main problems to investigate are those regarding the *form of the argument* ("has it a logical, or a quasi-logical, or even a rhetorical structure?"), the *nature and the features of its working procedures* ("which kind of similarity relationship are we speaking of?"), etc. By *analogy's function* I mean the role played by the argument inside legal system, especially in terms of the legal outcomes eventually produced by its juristic or judicial adoption ("which kind of – legal or extra-legal – standards are justified through analogical reasoning?"; "which kind of results does it bring about inside the system?").

From a "functional" point of view, what mostly interests me is legal analogy as an important instance of a certain class of arguments currently called *productive arguments*[10]. This class of arguments is usually contrasted, at least by analytical jurisprudence, with another class of arguments, the so called *interpretive arguments*[11].

In the next sections I will try, *firstly*, to bring to light and critically to survey a "standard" version of this conceptual opposition, and precisely that one explicitly or implicitly connected with analytical theory of law (in its "positivist" and "realist" versions); *secondly*, to suggest an alternative way of drawing this distinction, which, of course, relies on a different perspective (a "broad" legal positivism).

3. LEGAL ARGUMENTS AND LEGAL POSITIVISM

There are at disposal many – and not always competing – ways of defining *legal positivism*. In my opinion, it is important to distinguish, at least, between legal positivism *in a broad sense* (in terms of a general conceptual scheme which gives rise to a sort of "research program") on one side, and various theoretical versions of that framework (as specific interpretations of that program's hard core) on the other one.

In a *broad sense*, legal positivism expresses a general philosophical and theoretical standpoint according to which (all) law is conceived as a *integrally human artefact*, that is a socio-cultural product of human communities, whose "normative" existence and content are not bounded at all by *trans-cul-*

10 See particularly R. Guastini, "Produzione di norme a mezzo di norme", in *Etica e diritto*, ed. by L. Gianformaggio and E. Lecaldano, Laterza, Bari, 1986, pp. 187-188, and *Lezioni sul linguaggio giuridico*, *op. cit.*, p. 95.

11 *Ibid.*, pp. 95ff.

tural, external (in respect of that given legal community) *constraints*. This is, as we can easily notice, more a philosophical presupposition (which marks a strong opposition with legal naturalism in all its versions), than a fully accomplished theoretical hypothesis. As such, therefore, it can lead, by way of hard cores interpretations, to different – even competing – legal theories.

Among them, legal realism and "strict" legal positivism are undoubtedly two of the most important ones. Apart from many obvious differences, they have much in common (perhaps more than it is usually held). One of the commonly shared theses is of great interest for my paper's aims; we may call it, in Dworkinian terms, the "plain-fact view".[12] According to my interpretation, this thesis holds that the existence of "law" (whatever "object" may fall under law's definition) is, in the last analysis, a "question of fact", in the sense that it can be every time – empirically or, at least, quasi-empirically – decided with reference to single authoritative decisions, performed "all at once" by legislators (for positivists) or by judges (for realists). In the light of this view, it is perfectly legitimate to say, in both logical and temporal terms, that *one thing* is empirically to ascertain the "objective" existence of certain legal sentences (the task is accomplished making reference to the empirically observable acts which are responsible for their production), *another thing* is to manipulate the same sentences through the necessary but subsequent intervention of interpretive and argumentative operations, which are, without any doubt, "value-laden" and – at least partially – subjective.

I am persuaded that the opposition between interpretive and productive arguments constitutes – sometimes implicitly – an integral part of this conception. I hold, in other terms, that it derives from the thesis mentioned above, according to which we should always distinguish carefully, in judicial activity (and even in juristic one), between "to discover an already existing positive law" and "to create a completely new law". It seems that could not be found a way in the middle: on one side, we have a passive, quasi-empirical ascertainment of something "existing" *independently* of this recognitive activity and *prior* to the necessary interpretive and evaluative operations which shall take place only later upon that "something"; on the other side,

12 R. Dworkin, *Law's Empire*, *op. cit.*, pp 7ff.

we have a process of law creation that, although it could not be qualified as "completely free", it is not, anyway, constrained by legal standards.

At this point, we can easily see the connection between this general distinction and the more specific one between legal arguments. The first one, as a matter of fact, opens the way to the establishment of the opposition between interpretive arguments and productive arguments. In other terms, it is on the basis of the distinction between "law discovery" and "law creation" that it is possible to qualify: as *interpretive* all those argumentative discourses giving, in the context of *easy cases,* justifications, to legal interpretations or decisions, which presuppose, at the beginning of the reasoning's chain, legal sentences which can be qualified – with the help of the acts which are responsible of their production – as objectively and autonomously existing prior to any interpretive intervention; as *productive* all those discourses which, in justifying decisions on *hard cases*, develop a complex "argumentative network" having, on one side (as starting premises), *extra-legal standards,* and, on the other one (as reasoning's final conclusion), a totally new legal rule.

I will not try, now, to distinguish among different kinds of legal arguments, putting immediately at work the dichotomy between interpretive arguments and productive arguments. I will only assume, for argument's sake, that, from the point of view of who accepts this opposition, legal analogy constitutes, without any doubt, an undisputed instance of "productive argument".

For this kind of perspective, as I said before, productive arguments end up by creating new law. It is important to stress that this is a "strong" sense of law creation, which should be carefully distinguished from – at least – two other weaker senses: a) law creation in a *very weak sense,* that is as a – formal – characterization properly given to the judicial activity which, in applying a general norm to a specific case, turns to a new individual norm's production[13]; b) law creation in a *weak sense*, that is as a legal interpretation's theoretical qualification, according to which "to interpret" means always "to create a new rule", in the sense of the ascription, by way of interpretation, of a meaning (the "norm-proposition") to a legal sentence[14]. Here the concept of 'law creation' is analytically contained in the concept of 'legal interpretation'.

Law creation in a *strong sense*, on the contrary, can be considered as the outcome (the new rule) of a productive process in which the interpreter behaves just like the legislator, because he doesn't draw at all the new rule from the inside of legal domain (that is, from other legal rules or standards), but completely from the outside of it.

If we, from now on, go along with *constructivist* epistemological premises, then we have to admit that the opposition between interpretive and productive arguments doesn't lie "outside in reality", waiting to be discovered; it is, rather, at its best, the result of a theoretical and normative (and, therefore, always partial and biased) reconstruction of some "current" argumentative practices, performed in our contemporary legal systems. As such, it stands or falls on certain *ontological and epistemological presuppositions*, which now I will try to put into light.

a) When I speak here of "ontological presuppositions" (always in a "anti-realist" and relativist configuration of ontology), I want to refer to those *linguistic objects* ("normative sentences") which, as we have seen before, constitute the outcome of certain legal domains' selective and biased reconstructions performed by some influential analytical theories of law (both in strictly positivist and in realist versions). The theories in question hold that these objects represent in fact *all* that we can say and observe of law when we attend to the problem of its "empirical existence" (in a stage that is, of course, logically and temporally prior to that one in which take place the necessary "manipulative interventions"). In so doing, these theories perform – explicitly or implicitly – an operation which is precisely "theoretical" in

13 This is, for instance, Kelsen's opinion; see H. Kelsen, *Reine Rechtslehre*, F. Deuticke, Wien, 1960, pp. 239ff., 350ff.

14 See, as a very important and influential example of this position, G. Tarello, *Diritto. Enunciati. Usi*, Il Mulino, Bologna, 1974, pp. 167ff., 389ff.

character: that is, they carry out a sort of identification between *concept of law* (the set of paradigmatic instances accepted as such by all competing legal theories) and – a specific – *conception of law*. According to this conception, legal domain is filled *only* with paradigmatic instances, that is with normative sentences produced "all at once" by single authoritative decisions.

b) The "epistemological features" of this framework concern the theory of knowledge not only presupposed in general terms by these analytical legal theories, but also currently put at work and heartily suggested for all legal operations which are deemed as "cognitive" in character. For this conception, the only viable cognitive approach to law is that which, maybe after many theoretical or practical intermediations, has anyway an *empirically ascertainable and fully objective* point of reference in social reality (the single human acts which are responsible for the normative sentences' production). These characters mark off very sharply this cognitive approach from another alternative approach (we may call it the *creative* or *productive* approach), which, without referring at all to pre-existing legal materials, brings about completely new ones.

4. LEGAL ARGUMENTS AND POST-POSITIVISM

These two – ontological and epistemological – presuppositions have been radically put into discussion, firstly, in more general terms, by post-positivist trends in philosophy of science; secondly, with specific regard to legal domain, by certain contemporary jurisprudential and meta-jurisprudential perspectives, belonging, among others, to (post-)analytical legal theories and to continental legal hermeneutics. I think that, owing to the critical debate provoked by these new perspectives' intervention, it becomes to appear, sometimes quite unsistematically and confusedly, a different way of theorizing on legal arguments, and, more specifically, of distinguishing, from a functional point of view, between kinds of arguments.

Among this large amount of critical observations, I will select, obviously, those which come closer to my meta-theoretical "view of the matter". With regard to this, my choice will be specifically addressed to criticism coming from *constructivist theories of knowledge* on one side, and

Dworkin's theory of legal reasoning on the other one. The fact is that, in my opinion, there is a strong and not at all fortuitous convergence between some general features of the two theories, in the specific sense that Dworkin's theory can be fruitfully reinterpreted and analytically refined on the basis of constructivist – or, at least, post-positivist – epistemological premises[15].

Starting from this hardly sketched critical approach, which can be aptly called *post-positivist* in a double sense (that is, together from an epistemological and legal-theoretical point of view), I will now make some observations against the ontological and epistemological features mentioned in the last section.

a) I am persuaded that most part of doubts raised against those ontological presuppositions regards the basic thesis according to which "positive law" (in the sense of normative sentences produced by legal authorities) is located in a pre-theoretical, non-interpreted, and neutral dimension. Main problems come from the fact that this dimension, filled with legal materials produced "all at once" by single human acts, is conceived as totally independent from that other one in which take place all the – however necessary – interpretive and argumentative manipulations of the same materials. In other terms, for this conceptual framework it is as if law's features could really "exist" prior to the intervention of whichever conceptual scheme we decide to adopt in representing and classifying those "materials". This is the crucial point of the matter, toward which, and certainly not by chance, ontological and epistemological criticism begin to conflate: as a matter of fact, post-positivist theories of knowledge and post-positivist legal theories[16] converge in recog-

15 I try to argue in favour of this interpretation of Dworkin's theory in a recent book of mine called *Costruttivismo e teorie del diritto*. The book is due to be published by Giappichelli, Torino.

16 On this subject, see Dworkin's very significant and influential criticism of "plain-fact view" (R. Dworkin, *A Matter of Principle*, Harvard University Press, Cambridge Mass. 1985, pp. 154ff., 169ff. and *Law's Empire*, *op. cit*., pp. 13ff., 48ff., 70ff., 91ff.), which clearly presupposes, in my view, "constructivist" epistemological premises. We can easily notice that this is the case if we take carefully into account what Dworkin says (in many places) against "external skepticism"; Dworkin says, for instance, in general terms, that "none of the beliefs we have, about the world and what is in it, is forced upon us by a theory-independent recalcitrant reality; ...we have the beliefs we do only in consequence

nizing that law (like any other object, however) can never be a pre-theoretic and non-interpreted given, because the only correct way of speaking of its "positive existence" passes necessarily through the adoption of one or another conceptual scheme, specifically referring to certain interpretive and argumentative practices performed by members of a "legal community". According to this point of view, law does not gain its "positive status" in "all at once way", but, rather, through the continuous work of a cluster of representative, interpretive, argumentative practices, which take place at different – but interacting – levels (the "common sensical" level, the judicial one, the juristic one, the strictly theoretical one).

b) With regard to criticism of that conceptual framework's *epistemological features,* we need only to develop, to the ultimate consequences, the arguments exhibited at ontological level. The real core of the matter is that behind the theoretical discourses on positive law mentioned before lies a very influential and historically lasting *image of descriptive language.* According to this image, descriptive language, and, particularly, scientific one (as the "real" descriptive language), represents, for all other kinds of languages, the model of "genuine" discourse, because it is the only language which succeeds in objectively and unbiasedly "keeping in touch" with a reality conceived as if it could have an autonomous configuration independently of the scheme adopted. In my opinion, this "normative idea" constitutes the unchanging epistemological foundation of analytical philosophy, with very few – but important – exceptions, from the twenties up to the fifties. I am persuaded, for instance, that great part of the analytical trends (liberalized empiricism, prescriptivism, "ordinary language" philosophy – at least in some important version, etc.) which, from the forties onwards, reacted strongly against "strict" neo-positivism, nevertheless went on sharing firmly these epistemological presuppositions[17].

of having accepted some particular theoretical structure" (R. Dworkin, *A Matter of Principle, op. cit.* p. 169).

[17] Good examples of this kind of attitude are the "prescriptivist" and "divisionist" approaches which, from the fifties up to the sixties, are prevailing in analytical theories of ethics and of law (see, for instance, for ethical theories, R. M. Hare, *The Language of Morals*, Oxford University Press, Oxford, 1952, and for legal theories, U. Scarpelli, *L'etica senza verità*, Il Mulino, Bologna, 1982).

Leaving apart the pioneering – and strongly undervalued till recent times – work of "later Wittgenstein", it was only in the sixties, exactly when the first "post-positivist wave" in philosophy of science went to surface, and, afterwards, in the seventies, with the constructivist epistemologies' arrival (as a critical answer to the attacks coming from "realist" perspectives), that this image of descriptive language began to be submitted to a very damaging critical scrutiny[18].

As I have already tried to show before, the core of this critical work is constituted by the thesis according to which every "descriptive linguistic activity" (in whatever domain be it performed) requires always a prior "constructive intervention" into the portion of reality in question, that is it unavoidably presupposes the implicit or explicit adoption of a conceptual scheme whose basic function is to give a global "interpretive reconstruction" of the empirical domain which the particular object – or objects – to be described belongs to[19]. This kind of "interpretive reconstruction" basically ends up by "cutting out" that – prior amorphous – portion of reality into *specific entities* equipped with "relevant properties", and then grouped together into "pertinent kinds"[20].

18 For a good analysis of this controversy between realism and post-positivism, cf. R. Rorty, *Consequences of Pragmatism*, Harvester Press, Brighton, 1982, pp. XVIIff.

19 This crucial point is stressed very clearly, for instance, by Hesse when she says that every set of predicates, in a descriptive language, implies always a classification of the "furniture of the world" (M. Hesse, *Revolutions and Reconstructions in the Philosophy of Science*, *op. cit.*, p. VIII). A good elucidation of the "constructivist approach" to the relationship between conceptual schemes and reality is given by Hollis and Lukes: these scholars, in critically referring to what they call *conceptual relativism* (which resembles very much what I mean by "constructivism"), say that, from this perspective's point of view, "experience undermines what is rational to believe about the world ... (and therefore) schemes of concepts provide grids on which to base belief"; and they keep on noting that "the thought is that each scheme ... organizes or fits nature or the world" (M. Hollis-S. Lukes, "Introduction", *in Rationality and Relativism*, ed. by M. Hollis and S. Lukes, Blackwell, Oxford, 1982, p. 7).

20 These kinds of sophisticated processes are very well analysed by Goodman: he says, for instance, that "identification (of objects and events) rests upon organization into entities and kinds" (N. Goodman, *Ways of Worldmaking*, *op. cit.*, p. 8), and, afterwards, that the kinds in question are not "natural" at all, but "are rather habitual or traditional or devised for a new purpose"(*ibid.*, p. 10).

Here the crucial point is that, according to constructivism, there is "no reality" which we can refer to independently of the "interpretive filter" provided by conceptual schemes; from the same point of view, therefore, we can legitimately say that there is "no positive law" independently of some conceptual scheme's intervention, that is independently of one or another competing legal theory giving a certain kind of "theoretically laden" reconstruction of some specific and context-bounded legal practices of productive, interpretive and argumentative character (together with the normative outcomes of these activities).

5. INTERPRETIVE ARGUMENTS AND PRODUCTIVE ARGUMENTS

What kind of implications can be derived from this "double-edged" post-positivism for theory of legal reasoning, and, particularly, for the "standard" conceptual distinction between interpretive arguments and productive arguments? One of the most important implications is, I think, that which leads to the radical revision of this dichotomy. The reason is that the opposition in question is firmly rooted in those ontological and epistemological presuppositions which we have criticized in the last section. What this opposition implies is, as a matter of fact, that there are cases in which legal arguments rely, as normative premises of the reasoning's chain, on *pre-existing positive law*, conceived as a *pre-theoretic and non-interpreted given* (here the arguments used are classified as "interpretive arguments"); and, furthermore, there are cases ("hard cases") in which legal arguments do not rely at all on positive law (in the same sense as before), but, rather, on certain "extra-legal standards" (here the arguments used are classified as "productive arguments").

But, if we adhere to a post-positivist (in the "double" sense explained before) conceptual scheme, then we have to recognize that very often in legal practice it is extremely difficult to draw this strong "demarcation line" between these different kinds of arguments. By this I mean that in many cases (perhaps in most cases) legal interpretive and argumentative practices *at the same time find and create positive law*, in the sense that they refer to "preexistent" (in respect of subsequent theoretical and manipulative interventions) legal materials which, however, need always some kind of interpretive and reconstructive work (performed in the light of a conceptual scheme) in order to be included in a given legal domain as "genuine instances" of positive law[21].

The refusal of this conceptual opposition between legal arguments does not certainly imply at all that we should not need to employ, in theory of legal reasoning, any kind of distinction; it implies, rather, that we should try to build different – maybe more refined – kinds of distinctions. Anyway, in pursuing this task, we should take care of avoiding to draw a *qualitative distinction* between legal arguments in question; we should, rather, introduce the more flexible criterion which leads to a *distinction by degrees* located in the "continuum" constituted by legal discourses of argumentative character. This kind of *quantitative distinction*, which I am provisionally speaking of, prefigures a sort of threefold functional difference among legal arguments located in that "continuum":

a) on one side of the spectrum stand argumentative discourses (of logical or quasi-logical character) adopting, as normative premises, legal materials which are not only undoubtedly part of what we have called "paradigmatic instances of positive law", but also whose normative content does not give rise to serious interpretive problems. But, again, this does not mean at all that, in these cases, there are not at work, standing in the background, "theory-laden constructive interpretations" coming from one or another of – often competing – legal conceptual schemes, but only that the outcomes of these processes of a given legal domain's theoretical representation (that is, the resulting "objects") are commonly shared by anyone of the competing frameworks, at least in the sense that they are not put into question ;

b) in the middle of the spectrum stand argumentative discourses which rely, too, on " paradigmatic instances of law" (that is, whose identity, as positive law, is not contested), whose normative content, nevertheless, poses serious interpretive questions, because it is susceptible of different – sometimes alternative – interpretations, each of them being equally able to pass the test

21 I would like to stress again that this way of conceiving the relationship between "law finding" and "law creation" pays a great debt to Dworkin's legal theory (see particularly R. Dworkin, *A Matter of Principle*, *op. cit.*, pp. 158ff., and *Law's Empire*, *op. cit.*, pp. 6ff., 227ff.).

of "normative coherence"[22]. I suggest to call these "middle course" situations *hard cases in a weak sense;*

c) on the other side of the spectrum stand just those argumentative discourses which have been called, wrongly in my opinion, *productive*, without further qualifications. These arguments are required in cases where paradigmatic instances of positive law are completely lacking. It is for these situations that we can properly use the label *hard cases in a strong sense.* Here the difficult matter, which anyway, in this paper, I will not examine further on, is that of finding the "pertinent" law for the cases in question, going beyond the "paradigmatic" legal dimension, up to the deeper dimensions which legal principles and values belong to[23]. Just in order to accomplish this complex and multi-faceted task, the so called "productive arguments (*argument by analogy, argumentum a contrario, argument from principle*) come quite often to the fore.

But I cannot pause here on a detailed survey of these different kinds of legal arguments; I would like only to emphasize the fact that, according to my definitional proposal, legal arguments are placed in a single scale, without solution of continuity. Anyway, it is enough, for my paper's aims, to have shown that the opposition between interpretive arguments and productive arguments should be given up.

Of course, this conceptual analysis of legal arguments is not at all able to mirror (as a sort of "epistemological impossibility") the arguments' concrete uses in legal practice; but this holds for any kind of analysis (at least when the object to be analysed is a social practice). More generally, the fact

22 On this subject, see my essay *Normative Coherence and the Epistemological Presuppositions of Justification*, in "Law, Interpretation and Reality", P. Nerhot, General ed., Reidel Publishing Company, 1989.

23 To take into account the complex ways in which judges and jurists handle with these matters is one of the most important tasks of contemporary theories of legal reasoning. And, of course, the answers to these questions will vary very much in relation with bigger differences in the conceptual schemes adopted. Cf., for instance, the different answers given by A. Aarnio, *The Rational as Reasonable. A Treatise on Legal Justification*, Reidel, Dordrecht, 1987, ch. IV; N. MacCormick, *Legal Reasoning and Legal Theory, Clarendon, Oxford, 1978, chs. VII and VIII;* R. Dworkin, *Law's Empire*, *op. cit.*, p. 239ff.

is that theories of legal reasoning are not able to "describe" all what happens in argumentative practices, nor are they interested (even if it could be possible) in assigning the same weight to all these concrete uses; in any case they are obliged, implicitly or explicitly, to take sides on them, trying to recognize, for instance, *wrong uses*, or, better, uses that cannot be considered as instances of good or *genuine* legal arguments. Putting it very briefly, a fully accomplished theory of legal reasoning should always contain some *normative ideas* on what is to be considered a "good legal argument"[24].

In conclusion, I think it is worth to display the main outcomes of my paper. *Firstly*, I have tried to show the recoursive and self-referential character of analogical method, in the sense that the method chosen in describing legal analogy is also analogical in character. *Secondly*, I have striven to put into question the distinction, currently held in analytical legal theories, between interpretive arguments and productive arguments. With regard to this topic, I have subjected to critical scrutiny the ontological and epistemological presuppositions which that distinction is based on, trying contextually to suggest a different way of distinguishing among legal arguments, inspired by a "double-edged" post-positivism. According to this perspective, the difference among legal arguments is only a "question of degree": as a matter of fact, many legal arguments are, to some extent, both interpretive and productive, in the sense that, with their help, *judges and jurists together and contextually find pre-existing law and create new law*. Even argument by analogy, therefore, in its "genuine" form, does not merely create, in opposition to a current opinion, new law (at least, in a "strong" sense of creation), but, rather, brings about normative results that constitute, together and contextually, the product of "law finding" and "law creation".

24 This seems to be, albeit with some hesitation, MacCormick's opinion (see N. MacCormick, *Legal Reasoning and Legal Theory*, *op. cit.*, pp. 13, 75-77).

LEGAL KNOWLEDGE AND MEANING (THE EXAMPLE OF LEGAL ANALOGY)

PATRICK NERHOT

For Bobbio, it is beyond doubt that analogical inference must have a logical foundation, and only a logical one; reasoning by analogy would accordingly be logical reasoning where "formal logic will be more important than the teleological approach"[1]. Bobbio's study is, then, presented in two separate parts: one dealing with the logical aspect of analogy (formal logic), the other with analogical inference in legal science[2].

Analogy in logic consists in linking two terms by a resemblance, with the predicate attributed to the first of them being then attributed to the second. This relationship of resemblance between the two terms leads to a conclusion. In what may this resemblance lie? Here there cannot be a trivial response. There is an analogy between two objects in virtue of *properties* they have *in common*, but these properties already belong to the theoretical order[3]: the examples of the analogy between the earth and the moon, be-

[1] N. Bobbio, *L'analogia nella logica del diritto*, Turin, 1938.

[2] The methodological problems of this approach are obviously numerous, and we shall repeatedly have occasion to come back to some of them. Let us emphasize merely that on this approach, history is a discourse of truth; the distinction between empirical sciences and social sciences is accepted on a positive basis like the one the Vienna circle was able to define; recognition of the active subject comes about on the basis of a rationalist philosophy of law.

[3] This pre-theoretical aspect of the acceptance of "properties common to two objects" is not explicit in Bobbio. For instance: "resemblance is a concept of relations: resemblance

tween light and sound, in a classificatory system (cf. Aristotle) or in political rhetoric ("the father is to the son what the State is to the citizen") are examples which show this. Constructing an analogy in the form of logically rigorous reasoning requires the setting of the limits and extension of the "relationship of resemblance" (which *a priori* risks leaving untouched the question of resemblance as such), an operation that has to be done in two stages. Firstly, by positing that reasoning by analogy, "broken down into its simple elements", can be reduced to "ordinary syllogistic reasoning"[4]. For this reason, the argument will not be regarded by the author as a special type of reasoning but "only a particular formulation that may cover any kind of reasoning whatever"[5]. Secondly, by stating that "between the (major and minor) premises there is always something implied" and that "the validity of argument is also bound up with the validity of this general proposition"[6]. Bobbio would say that the proof of this can be found in the reality of our discourse through the use of rhetoric, "where persuasion comes more from an example than from the rigour of a universal law"[7]. However, this very idea of example, understood in the sense of "*model*" settles nothing, since here too it would be hard to give an exhaustive definition of the concept of model, given that we have many meanings for this term, all very different. Stressing one particular sense of the term "model" implies adopting an epistemological connection that extends not merely to

means relation between two or more objects *said to be similar* (our emphasis); two objects are said to be similar when they have something in common", N. Bobbio, *op. cit.*, p. 88.

4 N. Bobbio, *op. cit.*, p. 93.

5 "Deductive or inductive". This is perhaps not all that obvious, and would merit some clarification, it being understood that in the natural sciences, for instance, analogy is accepted as an inductive inference.

6 "The war of x against y is an evil; the war of y against z is an evil; the war of x against z is an evil. Implication: war against neighbours is an evil", N. Bobbio, *op. cit.*, p. 94.

7 The author continues "all this is proved by previous cases in case law, where a particular situation provided for by the legislature is not adopted very exactly, but as a model situation to be extended to all similar cases", *op. cit.*, p. 95. On this notion of "creative imitation" in the act of pronouncing justice see P. Nerhot, "The Notion of Narrative Coherence in Legal Interpretation" in *Law, Interpretation and Reality*, ed. by P. Nerhot, Reidel, 1989; French version in *Revue de Synthèse*, no. 2, 1990.

the meaning or the use of models in the sciences (natural or social) but to the very structure of scientific theories, to their explanatory capacity, to their relationships, in other words, with the phenomena they are intended to explain[8].

We can, moreover, observe this throughout the author's own statements, where the need to discover an "implied" universal proposition (without which no conclusion would be necessary) leads him to speak of the *validity* of reasoning by analogy, using theoretical elements taken from formal logic. Since the concept of resemblance, says the author, is in itself indeterminate and indeterminable in abstract and absolute fashion, the concept must be regarded as relative and as setting its limits in terms of the "given reference point". In other words, for an argument from analogy to be valid, "that is, necessarily conclusive", the relationship of resemblance has to be endowed with "a definite meaning".

"Q is P. S is similar to Q. S is P. The something in common, M, by which Q and S are similar, is at the same time the sufficient reason for P and Q"[9]. *This sufficient reason* is, then, the definite meaning; it is the "necessary and sufficient condition for the similarity to be a probative postulate"; it is the "*general law of validity* of argument by analogy"[10]. What Bobbio reproached analogical inference with was, according to him, its capacity to lead to arbitrariness, since "the naked resemblance, while it may have a force of historical persuasion, does not by itself offer a rigour of argument until it has been taken in a sense in conformity with the law of validity"[11]. Analogical inference must, then, be an *argument of certainty*,

[8] Mary B. Hesse, *Models and Analogies in Science*, University of Notre-Dame Press, Notre-Dame, Indiana, 1970; Italian version: *Modelli e analogie nella scienza*, introduction by C. Bicchieri, Giangiacomo Feltrinelli Editore, Milan, 1980. Mary Hesse thus presents the logical model, the mathematical model, the theoretical model, the imaginary model and the analogical model, the last being defined as the three-dimensional physical representation of an object or a system. "In this category we find the planets, electrical circuits considered from the viewpoint of acoustic models, some mechanical models and graphs. All these models have in common that they are representations based on isomorphism between the laws governing the two processes considered" (p. 8).

[9] N. Bobbio, *op. cit.*, p. 96.

[10] *Ibid.*

[11] N. Bobbio, *op. cit.*, p. 97.

once taken in the form conforming with the law of validity, and empirically therein.

It is, then, formal logic which, according to Bobbio, enables a certain result to be arrived at: Q is P *because* M; "because" means: either a relationship of consequentiality (all M – type – are P – predicate) or a relationship of cause and effect (M causes P). The underlying argument in the first case is a piece of deductive reasoning, and in the second an empirical observation (that we observe that the cause of P is M). Let us nevertheless note that there is no *certain result* that follows from these two propositions.In the first case, the idea of resemblance is posited as obvious on the basis, we feel, of an analogical inference internal to the classificatory system[12]. M.Hesse[13] stated that in this type of analogical inference the horizontal relationship may be constituted by one or several resemblances in structures or functions, and each column may contain elements with no *obvious correspondence or resemblance*. The vertical relations in turn may be conceived simply as part of a whole, or be interpreted as causal relationships depending on some theory, or as an interrelation between a part determined by an evolutionary origin or an adaptation to the environment. Analogical inference may thus serve either to make predictions or to infer, for instance from the structure of a bird's skeleton, which we know, the missing parts of a fish skeleton. But the most important thing to clarify is once again the *nature of the analogical relationship (in our example, then, this would be a classificatory system expressing a certain state, a certain form of knowledge) before coming to consider the validity of the analogical inference as such*. Which Bobbio would seem not to have done.

In the second case, finally, the resemblance would be the result of an observational process, amounting to explaining nothing from everything or, which comes to the same thing, a tautology.

[12] E.g.:

Bird	*Fish*
wings	fins
lungs	gills
feathers	scales.

[13] M. Hesse, *op. cit.*, p. 82ff.

Similarly, to continue this question of the certainty we are supposed to secure from purely formal logical argumentation, a mathematical proposition would not to any greater extent be the formal process of reasoning thanks to which an analogical inference in legal science might be regarded as certain. This might be an analogical inference of the type: a is to b as c is to d.

By contrast with the mathematical proposition, we shall never be able to show the *transitivity* between three pairs of terms as follows:

$$\text{if} \quad \frac{a}{b} :: \frac{c}{d} \quad \text{and} \quad \frac{c}{d} :: \frac{e}{f} \quad \text{then} \quad \frac{a}{b} :: \frac{e}{f}$$

This is simply because the analogical inference is suggested by a criterion of resemblance, which amounts to positing once again the problems relating to relations of resemblance and causality, problems which, I repeat, have to do with the *nature* of the analogical relationship – constituted by mathematical reasoning itself, or in other fields constitutive – and not the validity of the analogical inference. We have seen (p. 4, note 10) that the validity of an argument of this type was bound up with the validity of a general *implied* proposition. In Bobbio's conception, it is the notion of "sufficient reason" that must be gone into further; this is the concept that seems to have to determine the nature of the analogical inference. We shall see that here too he does not seem to arrive at the result he hopes for. "In order for predicate P to able to be transposed in formally valid and substantively certain fashion from situation Q to situation S, it is necessary for Q and S to be similar, not generically, but by having in common M, understood as the sufficient reason for Q and P"[14]. The relationship of resemblance is, accordingly, well expressed by the "sufficient reason", through an argument of either deductive or inductive type. Deduction will take place where the particular situation provided for by the law that has to be extended to a similar case is understood not as an absolute binding value but as an example of a general proposition, i.e. as a "*species representing a genus*"[15].

[14] N. Bobbio, *op. cit.*, p. 101.

[15] N. Bobbio, *op. cit.*, p. 102, our emphasis. It becomes increasingly clear that the conception the author has of analogical inference within a classification system is rather

Induction, for its part, takes place where the validity of the first proposition is based on the empirical finding of a necessary causal network (rather than on the cause of a principle), that is, that "it refers to the cause of the representation the relevance of which to the case provided for is also noted"[16].

The "sufficient reason" is, then, this interpretive principle on the basis of which the continuous "plot" of a legal order that sometimes appears fragmentary will be "created" (i.e. *discovered*). Thus, the author says that the function of of analogical argument in law consists in filling the lacunae of the positive order. "The two forms of analogy considered hitherto can be regarded as the typical ways in which the *two typical lacunae* (our emphasis) of any legal order come to be filled: the subjective lacuna (resulting from inadequate legislative regulation) and the objective lacuna (resulting from the new formation of the relationship and of an institution"[17]). However, this "rigorously logical", this seeing analogical inference as argumentation of formally binding certainty, leads, as the author advances in his ideas, to pushing ever further back the referent of resemblance, to avoiding, in some way, this question of resemblance, thus leaving oddly disarmed someone seeking to discover what makes a resemblance be accepted. It is rather as if one had come all this way to get back to the starting point.

In fact, analogical inference to fill a subjective lacuna means in the author's eyes that when the law does not exactly – or partially – express the whole of the doctrinal or case-law elaboration of law, "thereby bringing about an imbalance between the legislative and the judicial order", then analogical extension is brought about on the basis of general principles set by case law or worked out by doctrine[18]. Analogical reasoning then takes on the aspect of a deduction, drawing its initial impulse from a specific case governed by the law, seen as an example, but basing its validity on the

inexact. What emerges from all these definitions intended to define analogical inference is more of a progressive definition of what law is, rather than a definition of what this type of reasoning sets up.

16 *Ibid.*; our observation in the foregoing note is still more plainly illustrated here. Through these definitions, what is in fact happening is preparing the ground for the theory known as that of "lacunae" in law.

17 N. Bobbio, *op. cit.*, p. 104.

18 *Ibid.*

general principles that form a common legal heritage[19]. When instead one has to deal with a new case ("produced by social situations that did not exist when the laws were laid down"), analogical extension proceeds inductively. Identical qualities between the new cases and the case regulated by law are noted, and this partial identity is exactly what constitutes the resemblance of the two terms destined to justify the extension. The fact that the resemblance does not refer to a common type is therefore not deduced but merely *noted, that is, induced from comparative observation*[20].

In the first case the "logical rigour" comes about in the form of a syllogism in which the "general principle" will be the major premise: let us note, then, that the question of "certainty" will relate to the inference of this general principle. In the second case the logical rigour comes from the opposition between theory and observation. But in both cases we derive the validity of the inference (which may be presented as an argument of formal logical type) from the nature of the analogical inference – which is the real problem. Moreover, the opposition between theory and observation would seem today to raise more problems than it solves[21]. If we wish to stay close to a model used in *some* of the natural sciences, the problem will become that of the relation between what constitutes part of theory and what part of observation[22].

This long road pursued by Norberto Bobbio has accordingly brought us to the following point: in order for legal analogy to be perfect and the conclusion to be certain, it is necessary for the resemblance established between the case provided for by the legal provision and the one not provided for to

19 *Ibid.*

20 N. Bobbio, *ibid.*, our emphasis.

21 See e. g. C. Bicchieri, *op. cit.*, p. 14, for this type of opposition and analogical inference.

22 C. Bicchieri gives an example: the temperature of a gas (measured with a thermometer) is proportional to the average kinetic energy of the molecules making it up. This rule of correspondence brings into relation something ***unobservable***, the kinetic energy of the molecules, with something observable, the temperature of the gas. The "modellist" thesis of Mary Hesse consists in giving the notion of model an essential role in the construction of the theory; it is to guide the choice of formal structure (see C. Bicchieri, *op. cit.*, p. 24f.).

consist in the fact that both cases have as common term of reference the "sufficient reason" of the provision itself. What might the sufficient reason of a legal provision be? What is traditionally called the "*ratio legis*", where the *ratio* is identified with the final cause, that is, the object of the law.

For Bobbio, the *ratio legis* means the sufficient reason for the law, but this is to have a double sense (which we shall find again later in Betti). The sufficient reason for the law will be *either* the reason for its existence *or* the reason for its truth. Reason for existence means "reason for existence of a fact", and is identified with the principle of causality. The reason for the truth of a proposition will be identified with the relationship of consequentiality underlying it. Thus, a legal norm will according to the angle one looks at it from be conceived of either as "a historical fact" the cause of which has to be sought, or as a judgement the basis of which has to be sought [23].

Analogical deduction can accordingly be made in two ways. The search for the cause of a norm regarded as a historical fact will be done on the basis of the idea that the legal norm is a human fact regarded as a manifestation of intent (or expression of a thought). Accordingly, along with the efficient cause, there will be a final cause to be identified with the reason for the norm[24]. The search for the foundation of the norm will consist in understanding the norm as the consequence of a principle. The norm is no longer seen under the aspect of fact, but under the aspect of a judgement the justification for the truth of which has to be found[25]. *The norm as historical fact has an object; as judgement it has a foundation.* Faced with a situation not provided for, analogical inference may be effected by showing that the two situations have an *identical object* or that they have the same foundation[26].

But once again all these arguments Bobbio pursues only shift the problem of resemblance, push it further back, without ever approaching it directly. In the generality of cases, in fact, the reason for the law is not ex-

23 N. Bobbio, *op. cit.*, p. 107.

24 *Ibid.*

25 *Ibid.*

26 N. Bobbio, *op. cit.*, p. 108.

plicit; it has to be "drawn" from a legal provision, and we are almost always faced with either the "obscurity" or the multiplicity of the object[27]. As for the foundation for the truth of a norm, Bobbio thinks it may derive from a general principle regarded as a dogma by doctrine[28].The certainty of the object and the validity of the foundation lie outside the argument from analogy; we may even say that they constitute the *presupposition* we do not know the reason for.

Perhaps we can after all find an answer to this question in Bobbio when he opposes the voluntarist conception of law in order to affirm a "rationalist" conception[29]. The positive system contains a very specific rationality, which will be the foundation for the analogical inference. If the law is rational, and its rationality consists in correspondence with a historical requirement, this will apply in the area of its historical function, but there is no need to attribute to it, through a fiction, a different intent from the one it displays; the point is to draw from it, to extract from it, its "intimate rationality"[30]. The foundation of the analogical inference will thus be the "*intimate* rationality" of a legal provision, and a hermeneutic will be its introspective technique. Once the foundation of analogy is set in the presumption of legal order and by reason of this presumption, one may then say that the interpreter, when he offers an analogical argument, does not emerge from the legal order but on the contrary remains within it, since ultimately he does no more than "make the immanent rationality of the system explicit"[31].

27 In any case, the idea of a search for the object of a law implies an interpretative act. It is only this that can bring into play the principle of resemblance, but Bobbio tells us nothing about this.

28 This would, then, be the general principle that determines resemblance in the analogical argument, but Bobbio does not tell us why, still less how, the idea of certainty emerges from this.

29 "Law is thought in movement, not an intent that has stopped", *op. cit.*, p. 115.

30 N. Bobbio, *op. cit.*, p. 121.

31 N. Bobbio, *op. cit.*, p. 10.

So defined, analogy is effected within stable limits, clearly defined; it departs from any activity of a creative nature. However, the proof remains uncertain, fixed to pillars about which one may doubt whether they support anything at all. What is ultimately an "immanent rationality" of law conceived of as a system? How is this rationality recognized, how is it stated? Moreover, the fact that it is expressed through a historicism obliges us to ask about the way this history is constructed. All these questions are left in the dark by Bobbio, which does not however mean that they are not present, since in a certain sense he speaks about them, but only implicitly. All these categories are in fact not starting points for methodological reflection, but endpoints of an entirely political concern, a construction (reconstruction) on the basis of a present. The past (history of law is in this sense inescapable) is what illuminates the present meaning; it is like the foundation of a present position[32]. Let us here content ourselves with giving the first clues to the plot[33].

"The whole change in traditional systems of interpretation had to be made by way of analogy every time it was necessary to move beyond the scope of legislation, to change the – stuffy – air of the codes, to fill up the gaps left by the legislative formulae. It was forgotten that this procedure was very old, and that the novelty consisted merely in assigning a fundamentally empirical meaning and value to it. With romanticism, analogy made a great leap forward, moving progressively away from interpretation of law, with which it had always remained bound previously in law, to end up becoming a synonym of legal creation.

"Analogy has become the typical expedient for remedying the shortcomings of legislation, and the justification for all the revolutionary innovations. Analogy opened up the gates to arbitrariness, or at any rate masked the advent of the judge as law-maker"[34]. Bobbio's essay, which started out intending to locate itself in a logical formalist tradition, ended up being shot through with historicism.

32 We shall not develop here this question, which is one of the major points of our current study on Legal Interpretation (publication planned before autumn 1990).

33 N. Bobbio, *op. cit.*, p. 35.

34 N. Bobbio, *op. cit.*, p. 78.

II

Let us leave this epistemological question aside in this paper and act as if every event, however manifest, was not retrodictive; as if it presented itself positively in all its truth; and let us also assume, with Bobbio, that the jurists of the old law ("diritto comune") posited extensive interpretation as primary, and regarded analogy "or better similitude"[35] as the most appropriate means of legislative extension. At one time, then, ("diritto comune"), this "similitude" was central to all interpretive doctrine. Bobbio then goes on to present us with his history of analogy, through a *precomprehension of law in which the two major principles we have already mentioned are at work, namely that law is a system in which the body of laws is rational.*

Extensio a simili, a method of reasoning antecedent to the period when Bobbio begins his study, is dealt with on a logical basis[36], opposed explicitly to the traditional mode of reasoning, namely argument from equity, since henceforth the point will be to organize into a system the arguments used by jurists. Here we are in the 16th century; Bobbio analyses the phenomenon, explaining that in order to bring the notion of resemblance under the requirements of legal logic, the specific qualitative element of the legal case in point, the *ratio legis*, has to be identified, and the similitude must thus be understood as an *identitas rationis*[37]. It is mainly through similitude that the *passage from the case provided for to the case not provided for* is accomplished. Referring to an author of the time, J.Hopper, Bobbio posits that in the scholastic interpretation the method of analogy aimed at eliminating the contradictions in a body of law, at making a legal system into a logically linked system. Although slightly in contradiction with what he had said earlier, Bobbio concludes that analogy is not an extensive interpretation but first and foremost a *comparative*[38] one, an understanding

35 N. Bobbio, *op. cit.*, p. 10.

36 N. Bobbio, *op. cit.*, p. 29.

37 N. Bobbio, *op. cit.*, p. 35.

38 N. Bobbio, *op. cit.*, p. 48.

which, moreover, seems to us to be in conformity with the archaeological analysis done by Foucault on that period. For Bobbio, the point was to "grasp the unity of the multiple, *the rational element in the apparent, or actual, logical disorder*; to make a set of laws held together by the illogical logic of history into an authentic legal order, bound by the schemes of formal logic"[39]. The law, the author points out, is no longer isolated, but confronted with other laws, which explains why comparison is systematic and symptomatic of something: it is no longer an isolated, unrepeatable desire, but the specific moment of a reason in process of development. Let us note that here once again it is more that historical plot itself brought out by Bobbio that makes this causality among events possible than the logical force as such of the elements brought together that forces this conclusion. But it is true that at a certain point in the history of law[40] *the idea of unity of a "body" of laws* arises, just as the spirit of system (Domat, Vico, Leibniz) comes to be the driving force of any research programme. Natural law brought new vigour and supplied solid justification for this spirit of system. With Bobbio, however, a continuity is postulated that may perhaps raise a problem. From the uncertain and timid sense of the rationality of the laws (the hermeneutic clue that guided the jurist in reconciling antinomies, on which generations of jurists cut their teeth) to the unitary and complex sense of the laws, over the long period running through the 16th, 17th and 18th centuries, Bobbio wishes in fact to see a simple, gradual passage. This passage, understood as substitution of a comparative interpretation by an *analogia iuris*, a substitution that remains for him the expression of one and the same phenomenon, thus allows him to locate the historical origin of analogy in an interpretation of comparative type.

The archaeological enquiry carried out by Foucault into "words and things" was, as we all know, on the contrary to show two discontinuities in the episteme of Western culture: one located in the classical period (more specifically, the mid-seventeenth century) and the other at the start of our modernism (the nineteenth century). These two discontinuities do not reflect some sort of improvement in reason, but instead show that "*the mode of*

39 N. Bobbio, *op. cit.*, p. 52. Our emphasis.

40 Under the impetus of monarchy's action against feudalism, and in order to develop trade and commerce still further.

being of things and the order which by dividing them up offers them to knowledge has been profoundly altered"[41]. The continuity posited by Bobbio must accordingly appear as suspect, or at any rate not possessed of an identical logic.

It is in fact resemblance, understood as similitude, a term Bobbio was right to use, that in large part guides exegesis and interpretation of texts in the sixteenth century; but the question Foucault raised was that of *the way this similitude was conceived of,* how it was able to organize the figures of knowledge. We know his answer; we know that the four figures of knowledge (convenentia-aemulatio-analogia-sympathia) that he identified teach us how the world the world has to be reflected in order for things to resemble each other: *the sign is bound up with the resemblance.* The sign of affinity, what makes it visible, is analogy (for instance, a nutshell and the human brain), and what constitutes the basis for the value of the sign is resemblance[42]. A sign signifies to the extent that there is a resemblance with what it indicates (i.e. similitude), which made Foucault say that semiology and hermeneutics were super-posed in the form of similitude: seeking meaning meant bringing out what resembled it. At this point in history knowledge must be imagined as an interpretive process consisting in going from the visible mark to what is said through it[43], but signs designate the hidden only through a resemblance. "The specific feature of knowledge is neither seeing nor showing, but interpreting". The whole of thought is shifted into the element of resemblance; analogy can only be comparative interpretation (cf. Hopper), and belongs to this episteme. Where Bobbio saw continuity, Foucault discovers discontinuity, the "limit" to use M.de Certeau's term: at the start of the seventeenth century thought was no longer shifted into the world of resemblance; a break had come about with what might be called *divinatio*, which revealed a *prior* language distributed in the world by God. With the seventeenth century, it is *within knowledge* that the sign begins to signify, and it was from it that it took its certainty or its probability. *Analysis comes to replace*, rather than to extend, the analogical hierarchy;

41 M. Foucault, "Les mots et les choses", *op. cit.*, preface, XIII.

42 M. Foucault, *op. cit.*, pp 40-41.

43 *Ibid.*

for the classical episteme, what is fundamental is the relationship with "mathesis".

"Henceforth the relations among beings were to be conceived of in the form of order and measure, with the fundamental imbalance that problems of measure can always be reduced to those of order"[44]. This relationship with mathesis as a general science of order was to bring out a number of empirical areas that had not hitherto existed. *This relationship with order* is just as essential for the classical age as the relationship with interpretation was for the Renaissance. There is a dissociation between sign and resemblance; thought is henceforth to function in strictly binary mode. This is a fundamental feature of the mode of knowledge that brings knowledge of things under the possibility of representing them in a system of norms. Natural history, the new science of the period, assumes the idea of continuity in nature[45], and has no history except to the extent that it is capable of continuity. *The search for order as the basis and foundation of a general science of nature is posited.* This epistemological feature of knowledge soon begins to appear very plainly in other, more traditional areas: thus, *the idea that all laws are united in a logical system emerges, and analogia iuris* becomes established during this period. This *analogia iuris* fundamentally expresses the idea that the value of legislation is unitary and rational (Bobbio saw in it, wrongly in my view, the origin and justification of what are today called general principles, maintaining this conception of history as a long continuum in a continuous process of rational improvement). If "natural law" becomes predominant, this is no longer in order to interpret similarities; nature becomes a homogeneous space of identities and differences. *Analogia will henceforth indicate to jurists* no longer the organic connection of laws (proper to an episteme that has disappeared, namely comparative interpretation) but *the truly rational system of law*, which is thus beyond positive statutes and independent of them: the "system" of natural law. From the organic connection of statutes it was claimed to extract a system; henceforth it would be a rationality of law, of its systematic nature, that would seek to extract an organic unity. In classical knowledge, the sys-

44 M. Foucault, *op. cit.*, p. 71, referring to Leibniz.

45 M. Foucault, *op. cit.*, p. 158.

tem expresses the idea that the knowledge of empirical individuals can be acquired through the continuous, ordered universal table of all possible differences. The idea of continuity in nature is central. Analogy comes thus to operate in accordance with a radically new feature of the episteme; it comes to express a *continuity in nature through the idea of break* (the naturalist method is founded on this idea of continuity in just the same way); it comes to take on the practical value of a reference point to remedy the deficits of legislation.

In this new arrangement of knowledge, then, we may be able to find the two principles of cognition that guide the statement of the law. Firstly, there is the statement that *all laws are united in a logical system*, which is continuous (and complete). This principle supplements the one from the previous epoch, of the impossibility for one law to contradict another. Between these two principles one has to see something more than a gradual transition, even if it is quite clear that they can *a posteriori*, on a purely technical approach, appear as complementary. For the view that all laws are united into a logical system means endowing oneself with the possibility of imagining new interpretive principles (for instance, that there are no lacunae in the system) *that would have meant absolutely nothing previously*.

Secondly, there is this new situation facing the interpreter of having to create informative principles which will be presented as the "legal spirit". The analogical principle quite clearly has to do with the first principle insofar as it *reproduces* the continuous system of law. It is its formal aspect, or its logical aspect as we now say. But over and above this formal aspect, we shall find it again in the very structure of our knowledge; this is what Foucault's work shows, and it is plainly the whole mysterious aspect of analogy. *Ratio legis*, for instance, is extracted from the principle of the systematic nature of law; it intends to reflect a unity, but this unity will always be expressed on the basis of a particular structure of knowledge, the periodicity of which has to be located. In the early nineteenth century, we know that biology came to supplant the history of natural sciences, providing us with the category of the alive, a special structure of knowledge that was pregnant with consequences for the definition of the notion of resemblance. This is where we come to the creative aspect of analogical reasoning, which however still remains rather mysterious. It is our archive, our virtual identity.

ANALOGICAL REASONING AND LEGAL INSTITUTIONS

ZENON BANKOWSKI

I start by looking at what is involved in moving from a snail in a ginger beer bottle, through sulphites in underpants and antimony sulphide in manganese, to a lift in a shaft. Lawyers from the Anglo-Saxon jurisdictions will recognise these facts as coming from cases in the law of delict or tort and they will recognise that I am starting with the famous case of *Donoghue v Stevenson*. Here it was held that Mrs. Donoghue, who was made ill by starting to drink, in a cafe, a bottle of ginger beer in which she claimed there had been a decomposing snail, had a remedy in negligence against the manufacturer with whom she had no contractual relation. Lord Atkin said:

> A manufacturer of products, which he sells in such a form as to show that he intends to reach the ultimate consumer in the form in which they left him with no reasonable possibility of intermediate examination, and with the knowledge that the absence of reasonable care in the preparation of putting up the products will result in an injury to the consumer's life or property, owes a duty of care to the consumer to take reasonable care. ([1932] A. C. at 599)

The next situation concerns an Australian doctor who bought some underpants in which the manufacturer had negligently left iron sulphites during the washing process. Grant bought them and contracted dermatitis from which he was severely ill. He sued the manufacturer:

> If the foregoing are the essential features of Donoghue's case they are also to be found, in their Lordship's judgement, in the present case. The presence of the deleterious chemical in the pants, due to negligence in manufacture, was a hidden and latent defect, just as much as the remains of the snail in the opaque bottle: it could not be detected by any examination that could reasonably be made... It was argued, but perhaps not very strongly, that Donoghue's case was a case of food or drink to be consumed internally whereas the pants were to be worn externally. No distinction, however, can be logically drawn for this purpose between a noxious thing taken internally and a noxious thing applied externally. (Lord Wright in *Grant v Australian Knitting Mills* [1936] A.C. 35)

The third case, *Kubach v Holland* [1937] 3 All E. R. 907 is rather more complicated. Here a school teacher bought from the second defendant some manganese dioxide which was in fact that and a quantity of antinomy sulphide. This had in turn been bought from a third party but the invoice stated that the goods "must be examined and tested by user before use". This was not told to the teacher and neither he nor the second defendant did so. There was an explosion in the class. In an action by a schoolgirl injured in the blast the second defendant was held liable but the original manufacturer was judged not liable. Lord Hewart CJ, having discussed Donoghue, said:

> The case which is there contemplated is, I think, in essential respects the opposite of the present case. The manganese dioxide which the third party ought to have supplied here to the second defendants might have been sold for a variety of purposes... It was common ground that a very simple test, if it had been carried out, as the third party's invoice prescribed, and as the first defendant was not warned, would immediately have exhibited the fact that antimony sulphide had erroneously been made up and delivered as manganese dioxide.

In *Haseldine v Daw and Son Ltd.* (1941) 3 All E. R. 156. Haseldine was injured by a lift in a block of flats. This had just been been serviced by a company, A. & P. Steven Ltd., who had a contract to service the lift and report any problems to the owners of the block of flats. This they did negligently and did not give a report to the owners. Goddard L. J. said:

> If there was any doubt about the governing principle of *M'Alister (or Donoghue) v Stevenson*, Lord Wright has dissipated it. The manufacturer was held liable not because he was interested in his product being used as it left the factory but because he had no reason to contemplate an examination by the retailer or ultimate user before use... On what sound principle then, can the case of a repairer be distinguished from that of the maker of an article? Of course, the doctrine does not apply to the repairer of any article any more than to its manufacture. If I order my tailor to make me a suit, or a watchmaker to repair my watch, no one would suppose that anyone but myself was going to use the suit or watch. If the tailor left a large needle in the lining, and it injured a person to whom at some time I lent the coat, I should think that the latter could not recover against the tailor. The relationship would be altogether too remote... The case of a lift repairer, however, is very different. A lift in a block of flats is there to be used by the owner and his servants, the tenants and their servants, and all persons resorting thereto on lawful business. Blocks of flats and offices are frequently owned by limited companies, who would be contracting parties with the lift engineers. In a such a case, the employer would be the one "person" who could by no possibility use the lift. If the repairers do their work carelessly or fail to report a damage of which, as experts, they ought to be aware, I cannot see why the principle of *M'Alister (or Donoghue)* should not apply to them.

Looking at these cases and the reasoning that is employed in them we can see that the analogical reasoning used in the law seems to be a version of the reasoning by analogy that we use in our everyday lives. What we require is first of all a base line or point from which we can start and by reference to which we can compare and contrast any particular problem case or situation. In this instance we can see that the base point here is a "manufacturer of products, which he sells in such a form as to show that he intends them to reach the ultimate consumer in the form in which they left him with no reasonable possibility of intermediate examination". We can see constant reference to it in the other cases and it is their implicit similarity or dissimilarity to that case that is important. Thus the "deleterious chemical in pants, due to negligence in manufacture, was a hidden and latent defect just as much as the remains of the snail in the opaque bottle"; in Donoghue it was a "case of food and drink to be consumed internally whereas the pants were to be worn externally". In *Haseldine* it was a repairer rather than a manufacturer. In *Kubach* there was a possibility of examination which was not afforded in the other cases. But it is not just a retelling of the similarities and dissimilarities of the factual circumstances that are important but also a judgement of which factual similarities are important and which factual dissimilarities are to be ignored. Thus "on what sound principle can the case of a repairer be distinguished from that of a manufacturer?" and no distinction can be drawn between "a noxious thing taken internally and a noxious thing applied externally". The fact that a schoolgirl was injured by a latent defect in a good supplied by a manufacturer was not the same because there was, between the manufacturer and schoolgirl, as it were, the possibility of the very examination which the manufacturer advised.

So we look for a base point, one where the correctness of a decision can be established, and then look to the similarities and differences with other cases. At this stage a decision is made depending upon the importance and relevance that we ascribe to the differences and similarities. How is this to be selected? If we look at common law systems at least, one can see that the doctrine of precedent or *stare decisis* provides the institutional setting for analogical reasoning. In the idea that courts should follow past relevant decisions of appropriate courts in the hierarchy, we not only get the keystone of analogical reasoning – like should be treated alike – but also a natural base point, that previous decisions of an appropriate court in the hierarchy are to be taken as authoritative, i.e. as correct. This might be called the system's central idea of justice, if not a central idea of justice in general. But all this still rests on whether we can give some content to this way of looking at things. As Hart (1961) says,

> "Treat like cases alike and different cases differently" is a central element in the idea of justice, it is by itself incomplete and until supplemented, cannot afford any determinate guide to conduct... [U]ntil it is established what resemblances and differences are relevant, "Treat like cases alike" must remain an empty form. To fill it we must know when, for the purposes in hand, cases are regarded as alike and what differences are relevant. (p. 155)

We can give a more formal account of the type of reasoning involved here thus. The base case has facts Á, Å, È, as does the problem case. We can therefore make the decision because there is a rule that says, "whenever facts Á, Å, È, decide X". But there is a problem here for it depends upon the assumption that all cases that are alike have facts in common and that these correspond to legal rules. If we take the examples with which I began my paper, then we can see that on one view of it the cases do not really have that many facts in common at all. Thus the snail in the ginger beer bottle which features in our base line case does not appear in any of the other cases; lifts and underpants also seem unique to their particular cases. Chemicals appear in at least two of the cases but they do not correspond to any legal rule. This would seem to imply the unique particularity of each case. But we did, in our discussion, see other facts that were in common. Thus there were latent defects, articles bought by third parties and this can correspond, with some emendations to a legal rule of the type formulated in *Donoghue v Stevenson* :

> A manufacturer of products, which he sells in such a form as to show that he intends them to reach the ultimate consumer in the form in which they left him with no reasonable possibility of intermediate examination, and with the knowledge that the absence of reasonable care in the preparation of putting up the products will result in an injury to the consumer's life or property, owes a duty of care to the consumer to take reasonable care. ([1932] A. C. at 599)

But this leaves us with some problems. First of all it seems to imply the unique particularity of every case which would make analogy impossible. We can make these facts more abstract and thus more general, an "ultimate consumer" instead of an "a lady of a certain age", a "manufacturer" instead of a ginger beer maker. But in doing this we are having regard "for the purposes in hand" what cases are to be seen as similar and what different. This implies that these fact categories do not correspond to legal rules but that they are constituted by them. It is the universal rule that is important and not the actual facts of the case. Thus we talk of the "facts" of *Donoghue v Stevenson* but we almost always use the principle that I have quoted above and indeed used as at least part of the "facts" of the case. But if this is the case then we do not really need the facts of the case at all and we can dispense with analogies and work with the rule in deductive form. Thus the examples of analogical reasoning that I have shown above are merely deductions from the original rule set out in *Donoghue*.

This does not capture the flavour of reasoning in the common law. There certainly is deduction, but the case by case method does seem somewhat different from that and particular facts of particular cases are important. As Detmold (1984) says,

> The first function of a judicial precedent is to stand as an example. The example is the decision of the case and the particulars on which it is based. There is a temptation to think that one reads a law report merely to learn of the (universal) properties and relations that obtained in the facts of the case with a view to constructing an appropriate norm; that one's interest in and knowledge of the particulars is irrelevant. But this is a mistake. One can know particulars as well by reading as by seeing, touching and hearing... And since it is particulars that give the intrinsically practical response which constitutes reasons, it is to the particulars of the precedent that I must attend if I am to learn the practical business of judging hard cases... The weight of reasons is unstatable. If I am to learn how to weigh reasons in law cases it can only be from the example of precedent cases. Thus does institutional history educate. (*The Unity of Law and Morality*, p. 179)

Detmold puts an extreme form of this view of particularity, holding that it is the facts of a practical case and nothing else that gives me a reason for deciding it one way or another. But, he goes on to say, the weighing of particular facts implies comparison and, though they are unique, the weighing can only be done by virtue of their attached universals. We weigh particulars with certain universals "particularly attached". Thus, even for Detmold, what is important in common law reasoning are both facts and universals and it is to the relationship between "institutional history educating us" and rules that we must look to get some answers to the problem. Here we can see the general problem of the universal and the particular, how far does our reasoning depend upon the unique individual case and how far does it depend upon general and universal rules or principles drawn therefrom and the relation between these. This is often expressed in terms of the conflict between substantive and legal justice but I want to put it in this more abstract way because, as I will point out at the end of my paper, it is the relationship of the universal and particular that is the key question not just in legal reasoning but in political and social arrangements in general.

Golding (1984) puts forward a more complex formalisation which might be able to encompass both the particular facts and the universal rules. He suggests that analogical reasoning might be reconstructed as follows:

1 X has characteristics Á, Å
2 Y has characteristics Á, Å
3 X has characteristic È,
4 Á, Å are È relevant characteristics
5 unless there are countervailing characteristics Y has È
6 there are no countervailing characteristics
7 Y has È

Let us see how Golding's formalisation would work with our examples:

1 A provider of ginger beer is one who produces a product which is intended (i) to reach the ultimate consumer (ii) in such a form as to leave him with no reasonable possibility of intermediate examination.
2 A provider of a lift is one who produces a product which is intended (i) to reach the ultimate consumer (ii) in such a form as to leave him with no reasonable possibility of intermediate examination.
3 A provider of ginger beer is one who (iii) owes a duty of reasonable care to that consumer notwithstanding the lack of contractual relationship.
4 Being the provider of a product which is one which (i) is intended to reach the ultimate consumer (ii) in such a form as to leave him with no reasonable possibility of intermediate examination is relevant to (iii) owing a duty of reasonable care to that consumer notwithstanding the lack of contractual relationship.

5 Unless there are other countervailing characteristics the provider of a lift is one who (iii) owes a duty of reasonable care to that consumer notwithstanding the lack of contractual relationship.

6 There are no countervailing characteristics.

7 The provider of a lift is one who (iii) owes a duty of reasonable care to that consumer notwithstanding the lack of contractual relationship.

8 A. & P. Steven Ltd. is the provider of a lift.

9 A. & P. Steven Ltd. owes a duty of care notwithstanding the lack of contractual relationship.

The above can be taken as describing how *Haseldine v Daw* was decided by analogy with *Donoghue v Stevenson*. Let us now look at some of the ways that we might want to challenge the result. It was argued in that case that:

6 there was a countervailing characteristic here in that A. & P. Steven Ltd. was a repairer.

How does one argue for this? We can see this by looking at how the argument was defeated in this case. It was rejected in effect by another argument from analogy which said that though the first two premises should read:

1 A provider of ginger beer is one who produces a product (0) of which he is the manufacturer and which is intended (i) to reach the ultimate consumer (ii) in such a form as to leave him with no reasonable possibility of intermediate examination.

2 A provider of a lift is one who produces a product (00) of which he is the repairer and which is intended (i) to reach the ultimate consumer (ii) in such a form as to leave him with no reasonable possibility of intermediate examination.

We can say that that characteristic 00 is not a countervailing characteristic because it is analogous to characteristic 0. Thus the distinction between a repairer and a manufacturer is not a relevant distinction for the purposes of owing a duty of care. And we can show this by another argument from analogy which enumerates characteristics of a manufacturer and repairer.

But other forms of reasoning come into play also. Thus premise 3 was a problem when *Donoghue* was first of all being decided; was a provider of ginger beer one who owes a duty of reasonable care to that consumer notwithstanding the lack of contractual relationship? Now this might be solved by other forms of legal reasoning, such as reasoning from principles, consequences and rules. What is important here is whether the analogy is relevant or not. We might argue that being the provider of a product which is one which (i) is intended to reach the ultimate consumer (ii) in such a form as to leave him with no reasonable possibility of intermediate examination is *NOT* relevant to (iii) owing a duty of reasonable care to that consumer notwithstanding the lack of contractual relationship.

Here is the key point in the argument, for it is here that we must decide whether to apply the analogy or not. The way we do this, it is argued, is by claiming that we apply the analogy if the consequences are good or if it instantiates a good principle etc. But this would have the effect, as we noted above, of dispensing with the analogy altogether and working from the consequences of the particular situation or the principles involved. This is not the case for the following reasons. Firstly, when arguing as to the relevance of an analogy what we are often saying is that the analogy is not perfect and that the resemblance, if we look deeper is not really there. Thus when we looked at the "provider" of ginger beer and the "provider" of a lift we saw that there was an argument that claimed that this was a superficial resemblance and that if we looked deeper we could see that this was not the case because one was a "repairer" and the other a "manufacturer". In that case the argument did not work. However we can see how the form of the argument here is still one of analogy by way of refining a seeming "brute fact" into more characteristics to see whether there really is a resemblance. What is at stake here is the "bruteness" of the particular fact or situation. If we do not find it "brute" enough then we can "split the atom" and get down to characteristics where we do or do not see analogy and similarity. This is not merely a sort of inductive exercise, enumerating more and more characteristics in order to get a "true resemblance", rather it is the quality of the resemblance that we are looking for. Obviously, at all these levels, differing forms of reasoning take place. So our unhappiness at a certain level of "bruteness" can stem from our views of the relevant rules of law or consequentialist or principled reasoning. But this does not displace analogical reasoning for it is quite often a way of showing a deeper resemblance. And so analogical reasoning is not displaced by the other forms of reasoning but rather they co-exist in an interlocking mixture. To the claim that the principle has priority over the analogy we may say that if you do not know how to answer the particular case you will not know the principle. Consequentialist reasoning, as put forward by MacCormick, claims, *inter alia* that sometimes in a hard case you find your answer by looking to the consequences or implications of the instant case and then answering a hypothetical case based upon it. It has been argued that if you can do that then why bother with the hypothetical case. The hypothetical case is important because we know the answer, for whatever reason, to that and from there we can work back by analogy. However, does this not appear like our earlier formalisation of the analogical argument namely; the base case has facts Á, Å, È, as does the problem case therefore make the decision because there is a rule that says, "whenever facts Á, Å, È, decide X'? And if this is the case it follows that we fall into the analogous trap of not needing the analogy since we can work deductively from the rule. Again this is not really the case for it is the analogy that gives us the answer and the rule or principle that enables us to make sense of the analogy. Perhaps the rule or principle will enable us to go on to construct other analogies but only in so far as we do not find an analogy that will alter that rule or principle. Rather like the series 2, 4, 6, 8, 10 where we know that the principle is +2 until we find that the next number is 14.

At the base of this form of legal reasoning then is the single instance, the legal analogy, even though it functions within an interlocking network of reasons, principles and rules. This view of it seems to me to fit the institutional framework and tradition of the common law with its insistence on arguing through the cases and *stare decisis*. But if somewhere at the bottom of all this is the single instance, the analogy, and this depends, as we saw, upon the quality of the resemblance, then how are we to judge that quality? Though we are in a network of interlocking reasons and principles which all help to create the notion of "sameness", at the bottom of all of this there is still some characteristic which we say is just the "same" as another. How do we know this? Hume thinks that the argument by analogy and therefore precedent works through the faculty of imagination. There is no matter of fact outside of the practice of legal reasoning and the body of the law that enables us to say that the one case is like the other. For Hume, what allows us to make these judgements is not what he would call reason but rather the faculty of the imagination. This is not to be seen as merely a "brute fact" about human psychology but rather some social fact about humans or a society in general (see Postema, 1987). What this means is that imagination is something that can only work within the context of a social practice. Thus the judgements of analogy are not idiosyncratic and objective for they take place within a strategic social context. Thus we may say, by analogy from Wittgenstein, that there is no private reference to the idea of "sameness", nothing that is our own to which no one else has logical access to. "Same" is a public concept which makes sense only within the context of a particular language and form of life. Thus we do not understand the "same" by adding any new facts but, by looking at it from within a context and tradition, we make valid and rational choices (see Kripke, 1982). It is within the context of this legal tradition then, with its interlocking network of principles, rules etc. that we find the conditions for making valid assertions of analogy and disanalogy. Analogy is at base a social concept.

What is the "tradition" or context wherein the analogy that I am talking about finds its social base? Martin Krygier has a useful analysis of what "tradition" might mean here. He claims that traditions have three main elements which are pastness, authoritative presence, and an element of social transmission. What do these mean?

(i) Pastness – a tradition sees the past as important for every tradition is made up of elements from the real or imagined past. You cannot start a tradition intentionally *de novo*. What is important here is the institutionalisation of past maintenance; the legal past is made important to the legal present by the practices, *inter alia*, of recording certain writings, giving authoritative status to some, ranking them in ways that can be understood by initiates but might seem mystical to the "rational" outsider etc. This gives the legal past power in the legal present. Arguments are expected to be justified in terms of past traditions and arguments. But that is not to say, however, that the past becomes a dead hand upon the present for it is a matter of interpretation of the past and, as the hermeneutic tradition shows us, that is not fixed. What is important is justifying a present decision by emphasising and showing its continuity with the past.

(ii) Authoritative presence – this follows on from the above point. The past is not simply part of the law's history, rather it is a recognised part of its present. Douglas Hay 1984 argues that "thinking like a lawyer" involves what historians might call "presentism", "the fallacy of working from present concerns to past origins is anathema to historians, but necessarily half the lawyer's method". As Maitland said:

> "What is required of the practising lawyer is not, save in the rarest cases, a knowledge of medieval law, but rather a knowledge of medieval law as interpreted by modern courts to suit modern facts." (Fisher, p. 491)

In other words, for the lawyer, as opposed to the historian, Whig history is something to be welcomed. The "legal history" of a particular doctrine or principle as it is excavated by the practising lawyer is something different as looked at by a historian. The former is a participant in the tradition, the latter need not be and, insofar as he is a historian, will not be. But one can go further than this and say that an analogous thing can be said about the future. For analogy often works not only by looking at past analogies, authoritative or otherwise, but by constructing possible future ones which might also help in testing possible answers to the problem case. Thus in *MacLennan v MacLennan*, 1958, S. C. 105 where the question was could the husband be granted a divorce on the grounds of his wife's adultery, the adultery consisting in her having artificial insemination by donor (AID) without his consent. Here, it was held that this did not constitute adultery on the grounds, *inter alia*, that if it was held that it could they might be forced, in a future case, to hold that a dead person could commit adultery. What happens here is that, as it were, a future hypothetical precedent is created in order to show the validity or otherwise of the present decision. Precedent, and therefore analogy, can thus work backwards as well as forwards. The difference is one of weight or, as Dworkin (1986) says, gravitational force. The past has more than the future. But what is important to note here is how the future cooperates with the past in solving the problems of the present. The future is just as much the future in the present as the past is the past in the present.

(iii) There need also be means of transmitting the past over the generations. This means that tradition is a social thing, not something for individuals alone. The means of transmission and those entrusted with it will play a crucial part in determining the form of that tradition. Traditions where the transmission is entrusted to a caste of experts will be different from those where it is entrusted to a single sacred book available to all. One has only to contrast the Roman Catholic church with its emphasis on the "teaching authority" of the church, i.e. the hierarchy and the Protestant tradition with its emphasis on the sole authority of the Bible.

Why have tradition and why have a legal tradition? One answer is that we cannot start afresh each time. As Karl Popper said when speaking of science, "If we start afresh, then, when we die, we shall be about as far as Adam and Eve were when they died (or, if you prefer, as far as Neanderthal Man)" (1969, p. 126). We cannot operate in a vacuum. We cannot, as revolutions often have, start from a "year one" and create a totally new society without reference at all to the old. We cannot effect even more minor social reforms *de novo* ignoring the social and economic context that the solution has to be placed in. Moral philosophy and economic theory can never be determinate enough to give answers to all the problems that lawyers must solve. They must go back to tradition.

> So what is it that lawyers know that philosophers and economists do not? The answer is simple: the law. There really is a distinct and special subject matter for our profession. And there is a distinct method... It is the method of analogy and precedent... The discipline of analogy fills in the gaps left by more general theory, gaps which must be filled because choices must be made and action taken. (Fried, p. 57)

This is also supported by many views of legal reasoning that ultimately base the acceptability and rationality of legal reasoning on the fact that it takes place within a particular audience or group and it is only because of the cohesiveness of the groups that choices which might seem arbitrary do not become so. Thus John Bell 1986 shows how the constraints within which legal reasoning operates are defined not merely by the logical structure of the logical procedures adopted for performing the task but also by the socially developed criteria of what is acceptable. Canons of acceptable argument embrace both rules defining the logical character of legal discourse and standards of acceptability developed by the principal group within the audience to which reasons are addressed. Rationality, predictability and accountability work within this mode. Thus there is an interlocking network of reasons, principles, rules, standards, analogies which go to make up the tradition and quite often the process of justifying a decision at law will be a mixture of articulated and unarticulated arguments and assumptions which constitute the tradition and thus give coherence and rationality to it.

Here is also where legal scientists can play an important part for they can make clear the interrelations and coherences in the tradition which the practitioners might just *know*. It is this knowing how of the practitioner which comes through socialisation, a knowledge of the correct answer without necessarily being well versed in the structure of the argument, which is often evidence of a tradition. Their work in doing this adds to and affects the tradition. But one must be careful not to assume that it is these principles of coherence etc. that give the theory of the tradition. They are rather part of the form of life of that tradition, instantiating and presupposing the moral values of that form. As Nigel Simmonds puts it:

> Legal and political theories are not descriptions of brute fact. Nor are they merely postulated ideals or aspirations. Theories reflect and are reflected in our social relationships. And the historical development of our social life is itself a part of the intellectual evolution of our ideas... And if understanding a moral or political concept is a matter of understanding the "form of life" to which it belongs, an articulation of this or that conception may well require attention to its history. Moral and political values thus cannot and should not be discussed in isolation from the institutions and social histories that shape them. (1984, p. 13)

We have so far seen how analogical reasoning works in the context of a tradition, which is to say an institution held together by history and argument and their dialectical interplay. Thus the law can only develop within the context of its own tradition. There is no reference outside of the tradition. It is in this way that the version of the "right answer thesis" used by Dworkin in *Law's Empire* can be understood. Dworkin there claims that the right answer is one that is acceptable within the tradition, it makes no sense to ask whether this answer is *really* right. But this seems to lessen the scope for the innovative effect of analogical reasoning within the law since, for any analogy properly to work it must be subsumed within the tradition of the law. So we cannot learn anything new by analogy for the similarity always exists within the tradition and we find that we knew it all along. We cannot make great leaps of the imagination.

At the base of the system of reasoning I have been describing lies the ineffable, the creative leap of the imagination "This is like *that*." But this is domesticated within the tradition or discourse and so loses its capacity to surprise, radically to change direction, to transcend. One can see examples of this in the law where parables are used as analogies by the judges and transform the fierce messages they contain into doctrines of the common law. Thus the parable of the good Samaritan in *Donoghue*

> The rule that you are to love your neighbour becomes in law: You must not injure your neighbour, and the lawyer's question: Who is my neighbour? receives a restricted reply. You must take reasonable care to avoid acts or omissions which you can reasonably foresee would be likely to injure your neighbour. Who then, in law, is my neighbour? The answer seems to me to be persons who are so closely and directly affected by my act that I ought reasonably to have them in contemplation as being so affected when I am directing my mind to the acts or omissions which are called in question. This appears to me to be the doctrine in *Heaven v Pender* as laid down by Lord Esher.

Commenting on this dictum in *Home Office v Dorset Yacht Company* (1970) 2 All E. R at 310 Viscount Dilhorne said,

> Lord Atkin's answer to the question "Who, then, in law is my neighbour?" while very relevant to determine to whom a duty of care is owed, cannot determine, in my opinion, the question whether a duty of care exists,

or as Lord Diplock said in the same case,

> The very parable of the good Samaritan which was evoked by Lord Atkin in *Donoghue v Stevenson* illustrates, in the conduct of the priest and of the Levite who passed by on the other side, an omission which was likely to have as its reasonable and probable consequence damage to the health of the victim of the thieves, but for which the priest and the Levite would have incurred no civil liability in English law. Examples could be multiplied... one need not warn him of a risk of physical danger to which he is about to expose himself unless there is some special relationship between one and him such as that of occupier of land and visitor; one may watch one's neighbour's goods being ruined by a thunderstorm although the slightest effort on one's part could protect them from the rain and one may do so with impunity unless there is some relationship between one and him such as that of bailor and bailee (p. 326)

In the case of *Race Relations Board v Charter* (1972) 1 All E. R 556, an Indian who was an active Conservative and member of the local association applied for membership of the local conservative club and was turned down by reason of his colour. It was held that the club was concerned with providing facilities to a section of the public since the members of the club themselves constituted a section of the public since they were not numerically negligible and the quality that distinguished them from the public at large, that they were conservatives, was essentially impersonal. This being so, discrimination contrary to the Race Relations Act had occurred. The question in this case was whether the East Ham Conservative Club was a genuine private club, thus not "providing facilities to a section of the public" and thus in the position of a private householder. The parable of the guests at the wedding feast is used as an analogy to help us understand what "public" means.

> The guests bidden to supper in the parable did not seek to obtain or use their host's food and drink, still less did those who on his instructions were compelled to come in from the highways and hedges. Even if those who came in at his first invitation or later under that compulsion were the public or a section of the public... they were not seeking but sought. That is one reason why a private house-

> holder may still lawfully turn a person from his house on grounds of race or colour or national or ethnic origins. (*per* Stephenson LJ 565).

We do not see the "Kingdom of Heaven" here, rather a careful discussion of what counts as our private lives for the purposes of the Race Relations Act. A parable of openness becomes an analogy of closure.

This is not to say that within the tradition analogy does not produce rich and new solutions. But the solution we get to is one which in a sense we already know. For the tradition can be viewed as timeless in the sense that past, present and future are all involved in different ways and with different weights in any decision and so the decision is always already there. It is this, rather than a natural law theory, that, it seems to me, is implied when it is claimed Dworkin assumes that law is "discovered".

What we have been looking at up till now is how analogy works as a mode of reasoning employed by judges and how, ultimately, it cannot tell us anything new because it is always locked into a discourse and a tradition. In this ending however, further questions are inevitably raised. Surely traditions develop and change beyond all recognition? Cannot we see this in history? Are there forms of reasoning based on analogy, employing perhaps allegory or metaphor, that enable us to move beyond a tradition and to import and export ideas between traditions? Are there institutions that serve as bridges to other traditions or that can be seen as windows from the one into the other? Or is it the case that we are all immutably locked into our traditions and discourses with no real way out? I finish then, with a quotation from Kafka who raises, appropriately enough, these questions in a metaphorical and allegorical way.

> Many people complain that the words of the wise men are always only parables but cannot be used in daily life, and this after all is all we have. When the wise man says: "Go over", he does not mean that we should go over to the other side, which we could do if it were worth it. He means some mythical Beyond, something that we do not know and that he cannot describe in any more detail and that cannot help us here. All these parables really say is that what cannot be grasped cannot be grasped and we knew that anyway. The things that concern us in our daily lives are different.

One man said: "What's stopping you? If you were to follow the parables you would become parables yourselves and thus be freed from the troubles of daily life."

The second said: "I bet that that's a parable too"

The first said: "You won!"

The second said: "But unfortunately only in the parable."

The first said: "No, in reality: you lost in the parable."

REFERENCES

BELL, J. (1986), "The Acceptability of Legal Argument" in *The Legal Mind,* pp. 44-65 (eds.) MacCormick, D. N. and Birks, P. Oxford University Press, Oxford.

DETMOLD, M J. (1984), *The Unity of Law and Morality*, Routledge and Kegan Paul, London.

DWORKIN, R. (1986), *Law's Empire*, Fontana, London.

FISHER, H (ed.), *The Collected Papers of Frederic William Maitland,* Cambridge University Press, Cambridge.

FRIED, C. (1982), "The Artificial Reason of the Law or : What Lawyers Know", in *Texas Law Review*, 60, 1982, pp. 35-58.

GOLDING, M. (1984) *Legal Reasoning*, Borzoi Books, New York.

HART, H. L. A. (1961) *The Concept of Law,* The Clarendon Press, Oxford.

HAY, D. (1984) "The Criminal Prosecution in England and its Historians" in *Modern Law Review,* pp. 1-29.

KAFKA, (1946) "Von den Gleichnissen" in Brod, M. (ed.), *Beschreibung eines Kampfes, Novellen, Skizzen, Aphorismen aus dem Nachlaß*, Fischer Verlag, Frankfurt am Main.

KRIPKE, S. (1982), *Wittgenstein, On Rules and Private Language*, Blackwell, Oxford.

POPPER, K (1969) "Towards a Rational Theory of Tradition" in *Conjectures and Refutations*, Routledge and Kegan Paul, London.

POSTEMA, G. (1987), "The Roots of Our Notion of Precedent" in Goldstein, L. (ed.) *Precedent in Law*, The Clarendon Press, Oxford.

SIMMONDS N. (1984), *The Decline of Juridical Reason*, Manchester University Press, Manchester.

ANALOGY IN THE LAW

JAN M. BROEKMAN

There is only one analogy in the law, namely the analogy between legal reality and non-legal reality. "Law and Reality" is in that regard a tricky expression: the conjunction is likely to deceive us, because it conceals the analogy. But the analogy remains a basic operation which establishes the legal discourse.

ANALOGY: A BASIC DOCTRINAL OPERATION

Analogy is in more than one respect a basic doctrinal operation:

- to say, how "something is" by means of the appropriate legal expression implies that the analogy is silently taken as a presupposition of such a legal expression;
- the presupposition regards a translation, or shift of meaning from ordinary language into legal doctrinal language. Such a semantic shift always regards "the facts". Legal facts come into (legal) reality by the act of translation itself. The analogy between non-legal reality and legal reality remains a fundamental presupposition;
- facts of the law do consequently always fit into a doctrinal framework, i.e. they are always analogous to a specific doctrinal rule or a legal dogma. If that analogy is not immediately visible, then it has to be constructed by infinite refinements of the legal argument;

- analogies of the legal doctrine are deduced from and legitimated by the fundamental analogy between law and reality. Reality is "presented" in legal cases. Legal analogy refers continuously to such cases.

Cases and analogies form intertextual chains. Reference holds these chains together; procedure is the prescription for such a referential activity. Dworkin has expressed his understanding of this intertextuality in the law with the help of the idea that the law is a "chain novel". Law is a novel of doctrine, according to Dworkin, rendering interpretive judgments concerning which reading of legal texts fits best and, at the same time, demonstrate the best political morality[1].

- legal translations and, consequently, constructions of legal facts present themselves as a representation of the founding analogy between reality and the law. The underlying semantic operation: the translation and the presentation of the facts[2], is one of the most significant instruments for the maintenance of the legal discourse itself. That operation has of course been defined in terms of the legal doctrine, namely as "legal qualification". This qualification governs the transition from reality to the law. The transition can however only take place if there is a prior acceptance of the basic analogy between reality and law;
- consequently, legal qualifications are subject of a doctrinal analysis. The leading issues are, formulated in non-doctrinal terminologies: how and why have legal qualifications to be constructed, how can jurists determine the correctness of their qualifications and how can they provide the necessary justification and legitimation for them.

[1] R. Dworkin: "Law as Interpretation", in: W. Mitchell, ed.: *The Politics of Interpretation,* 1983. p. 249. Jan M. Broekman: "Recht en Structuralisme" in *R & R, Rechtsfilosofie en Rechtstheorie*, 1973. II, Nr 2.

[2] Jan M. Broekman: "Text als Institution", in: *Recht als Sinn und als Institution,* Beiheft 6 *Rechtstheorie*, Mayer-Maly, Weinberger, Strasser (eds), 1984, p. 158f. - id. -: "Zur Ontologie des juristischen Sprechakts", in: *Formalismus und Phänomenologie im Rechtsdenken der Gegenwart,* Festgabe für Alois Troller, Krawietz & Ott (eds), Berlin, 1987, p. 237f.

ANALOGY AS AN EVENT

These observations lead us to a more philosophical perspective on analogy. Its main feature is this: analogy is not a thing, and not a method, but an *event!* Consequently, one has to keep in mind that *it occurs* that a reality is analogous to another reality; we *suddenly are aware* that such and such an analogy comes to the fore. The result of this "sudden awareness" is, that the unforeseeable becomes foreseeable or foreseen. This is clearly a figure of the cartesian light-metaphor, the "light"[3] which necessarily goes with "seeing" and "fore-seeing". In law or theology, the "pre-script", the "pre-cedent" and the "ex-ample" have been related to this metaphor. But these expressions and their ontological implications include uncertainty, unforeseeableness, ambiguity. The analogy in modern formalized law however needs a different understanding, namely no longer as "an-alogy", but as a positive reliable "fundamental existential foundation" (the German: "Letztbegründung"). This dominates today the general philosophical foundation of the dogmatization, formalization and functionalization of the legal discourse. Such developments have shaped our contemporary law. In our contemporary positive law, everything is foreseen. Our legislation gives an extreme example in that regard: things have to be foreseen, even before they occur! This indicates the positivism of the law, as well as the law's rationality and its inherent representational character.

The fascination of the unique position of analogy in the law, the doctrinal consequences of its function and the philosophical context of analogy are the main sources of inspiration with regard to the following considerations.

(1) The first issue is the jurist and the many ways in which he constructs, makes use of, instrumentalizes and legitimizes analogy;

(2) The second is the epistemological implication of such a legal activity;

[3] K. Hedwig: *Sphaera lucis*. "Studien zur Intelligibilität des Seienden im Kontext der Mittelalterlichen Lichtspekulation", Münster, 1980, and: A. Abécassis: *La Lumière dans la Pensée Juive*, Paris, 1988.

(3) The third regards a philosophical question, namely: in what way is reality presented in the legal discourse?

That final question is fully justified. It connects the analogy with a traditional representationalist view. Modern law suggests that it *represents* an image (the essence of analogy) where a philosophical analysis brings to the fore that the legal discourse *constructs* an image which it does not want to present as such, but as a particular *representation*[4].

I

The traditional approach to analogy in the legal discourse implies that the jurist starts from an ontological statement. That statement is, in his eyes, self-evident. It could be formulated as: there is reality on the one hand, and law on the other. All legal expressions presuppose a separation of law and reality. That separation is to the lawyer as evident as the subject-object duality of our traditional epistemology. Analogous reasoning is the preferred way to connect the two. That connection should, according to the demands of legal doctrine, be carefully constructed. Such constructions are therefore object of permanent doctrinal reconsideration.

Analogy and precedent

The doctrinal carefulness is sufficiently guaranteed. One analogy in the law is in principle always preceded by another legal analogy. Legal cases are always preceded by prior cases: the "chain novel"– motive is doctrinally coercive and governs the construction of the legal discourse. No wonder then, that a jurist tends to direct his analogous reasoning towards precedent. That is the function of tradition in all legal systems, and this type of tradition is essential. A change of the legal paradigm is only imaginable within this

4 Jan M. Broekman: "Sprechakt, Norm und Institution", in: *Theorie der Normen.* Festgabe für Ota Weinberger, Krawietz, Schelsky, Winkler, Schramm (eds), Berlin, 1984, p. 26f. - id. -: "Juristischer Diskurs und Rechtstheorie" in: *Rechtstheorie*, Bd 11, Nr 1, 1980.

specific tradition and textuality[5]. Legal reasoning by analogy is consequently a particular case of legal intertextuality. This form of intertextuality however is in the legal doctrine discussed as the problem of precedent.

In his famous *Precedent in English Law*, Cross determines legal reasoning by analogy.

A first type of analogy refers to the situation with a single precedent. "When a single precedent is concerned it is possible to point to three stages in judicial reasoning by analogy although it is not suggested that they are always separated in practice. First comes the perception of relevant likenesses between the previous case and the one before the court. Next there is the determination of the *ratio decidendi* of the previous case and finally there is the decision to apply that *ratio* to the instant case". Analogy is, according to Cross, only relevant to the first and the third stages. The most important is the third, when the judge has to decide about his application of the *ratio* to the instant case, that is: when he finally has to make a decision.

A second type of analogy refers to a situation with many precedents. That situation is the normal doctrinal situation. "When several decisions are involved the reasoning consists of four stages: the perception of analogies (which may frequently conflict) between the instant case and a number of previous ones, the determination of the *rationes decidendi* of the previous cases, the construction of a rule or rules from those *rationes* and the decision to apply the rule, or one of the rules, to the instant case"[6]. According to Cross, both the first and the second type of analogy have in common that the perception of relevant likenesses and the decision of rule-application determines the analogy.

5 M. Krygier: "Law as Tradition", in: *Philosophy of Law and History of Human Thought*, IVR World Congress, Athens, 1985, Panou et al. (eds), *ARSP*, Suppl. II, 1988, p. 179f.

6 R. Cross: *Precedent in English Law*, Oxford, 1979, pp. 183, 188.

Epistemology

Cross' observations and descriptions require some epistemological comments.

1. The most general comment is that analogy in the law regards the totality of the legal discourse, and not only some particular segments of doctrine. This is clearly visible in Cross' reasoning. The epistemological apparatus which is involved in his considerations includes all decisive elements of legal epistemology as such. None of his factors to determine analogy are specifically coined for judicial analogy. Let us reconsider the situation with more than one precedent. The first determinative factor is an ensemble of perception, contextuality, and relevance. The second brings together elements of judicial rationality. The third refers to the problem of the rule and the last to the rule-based decision. Legal knowledge in general relies on these basic operations. This lack of specificity reveals that the analogy is not a matter of legal doctrine. Analogy is *elsewhere*, and it could very well be that analogy regards the totality of the legal doctrine, its foundation in our culture. Hence our introductory remark, that there is only one analogy, namely the analogy between legal- and non-legal reality.

2. A second comment is closely related to the first. Analogy in the law is unthinkable without legal cases. This reveals an important feature of the entire legal discourse. That discourse is to a very great extent determined by the construction of legal cases. Legal history is specifically a case history. However cases can not be regarded as natural facts. They are doctrinally determined constellations of legal facts. Legal facts are by no means equivalent to natural facts. This gives an exclusively textual character to legal cases. Analogy in the law is therefore an analogy between legal texts. This perspective on law and analogy makes it understandable why perception, contextuality and relevance are so important in this regard. Cross's perception of relevant likenesses is a textual operation. The perception is not a, let us say, visual perception. Legal likeness is embedded in the act of writing, and above all, in the act of reading. The conclusion that A is analogous to B is the result of an act of reading and therefore the strategy of the discourse itself.

3. The process of selection and determination of relevance, as described by Cross, indicates how analogy in the law results from the construction and reconstruction of legal cases. It is characteristic for the legal discourse that legal cases are presented as life-factual constellations of social facts. Analogy is consequently presented as the result of an immediate vision on social reality. But our analysis shows how legal analogy, on the contrary, results from the constructive legal mind.

Several features are important here. The dimension of time in legal thought is involved: legal analogies are only possible under the condition of a perfectly foreseeable future of legally qualified circumstances. This foresight is one of the main aspects of the rationality of the law. The construction and safeguarding of that foresight touches on the existence of the legal discourse in its entirety. Law can exist only if legal foresight is guaranteed. Such a guarantee has to be constructed and enforced; it is never a given natural datum. Life is unforeseeable and not entirely understandable in terms of the lawyer's rationality. Semantic transformations have therefore continuously to take place in order to realize legal meanings. Analogies are instruments of that type of legal realizations. Identities and differences are, furthermore, the backbone of analogy in the law. Cross points out that the identities and also the differences do exist as products of the legal mind. Every lawyer, both of the common law and the continental legal system, is able to separate relevant and non-relevant factors of the case. And in doing so, lawyers create, perhaps unknowingly, the main features of the legal discourse. Analogy is an instrument of that discourse. Analogy in the legal doctrine is in principle always instrumental.

Some generally debated doctrinal problems show this clearly. Judges are not always free to decide whether they are or they are not going to apply the *ratio decidendi* of prior cases. In case they can decide, other questions arise. Jurists frequently have different opinions concerning the legal meaning and possible legal interpretation of differences and identities between prior cases and the case at hand. So the judge's attitude becomes of utmost importance: is he going to expand the rules of decision, or restrict them? This is the vital question, and analogy plays its instrumental role again. The instrumental character of analogy is demonstrated by the fact that the problem appears in doctrinal discussion as a problem of the implicit reasonableness that is inherent to the legal decision.

Were the principles involved in *Donoghue v Stevenson* applicable in *Haseldine v Daw* ? In the case of the snail in the bottle of ginger beer (*Donoghue v Stevenson*, 1932), there is a general opinion concerning the *ratio decidendi*. It says, in the words of Cross, that a manufacturer of products, which he sells in such a form as to show that he intends them to reach the ultimate consumer in the form in which they left him, with no reasonable possibility of intermediate examination, and with the knowledge that the absence of reasonable care in the preparation or putting up of the products will result in an injury to the consumer's life or property, owes a duty to the consumer to take that reasonable care.

Reasonableness

Analogy is thus connected with another doctrinal concept, namely "reasonable care". But one has to keep in mind, that "reasonable care" refers to "reasonable expectation" (of behaviour). The latter regards always future behaviour and is therefore related to the general idea that the legal discourse deals with foreseeable reality in all its aspects.[7] It is the application of legal rationality which demands this foreseeable character of the law. The construction of analogy maintains a foreseeable, that is basically rational future for all legal activities in our society.

Coming back to legal doctrine, we have to ask whether the principles of *Donoghue v Stevenson* are useful to the construction of analogy in the case of *Haseldine v Daw*. It is NOT the question, whether the first case IS analogous to the latter, but in how far the construction of analogy is useful in the latter case. There are differences between the cases: they are not identical! In the latter case, personal damage was the result of a crashing elevator. The elevator was repaired shortly before the accident and the crash was related to that reparation. "Repairers" were involved, and not "manufacturers".

[7] Jan M. Broekman: "Norm en redelijke verwachting", in: *Rechtstheorie & Rechtsfilosophie*, R. & R., 1987, Nr. 3; - id -: "Racionalidad juridica, norma y accion", in: *Boletin Asociacion Argentina de Filosofia del Derecho*, 1987, V, no. 46, p. 1.

And, secondly, a control of the repair was possible. That was not the case in Donoghue. The rule of Donoghue was however applied, and the analogy constructed. Why? The answer can be found in a more encompassing view on the common law, not in a specific feature of the law that has to do with analogy. There are apparently no such specific features in legal dogmatics. As already stated earlier, analogy is governed by general constitutive principles of the legal discourse. And so it is here. L. J. Goddart had formulated the relevant principle in a prior case, namely: "the common law must expand to keep abreast of modern life"[8]. Expanding the law is understood here as an expansion of the possibilities to construct legal analogies. It is important to notice how this reasoning relies more and more on the legal rule, its formulation and application. Is analogy a means to a certain end, namely to increase and enrich doctrinal rule-following? Such considerations already lead us to the second type of reflections, namely the epistemological. It is evident how they follow from the purely doctrinal analysis.

Stare decisis

But let us for the moment remain within the realm of doctrinal thinking. A consequence of the doctrinal mechanism which produces legal analogies is what Cross describes as conceptualism. The Anglo-Saxon warning not to get lost in conceptualism is remarkably parallel to the German warnings not to lose one's way in the "Begriffsjurisprudenz". Legal reasoning can indeed get lost in a game of easy analogies. At the end, every analogy looks acceptable. An infinite regress *ad analogiam* is possible, as long as the rules which are entangled in the analogy fit into the case. But when rules fit into a case, do they therefore automatically fit into the concrete social context of the case? Cross reminds his readers that rules have to be qualified. One should not accept the constructions of ineffective or abstruse analogies which could arise from a formal system of precedents. That does not imply any negligence of the consistency of the legal system and the uses of precedent in the law. To accept the requirements of consistency in the law does

8 L. J. Goddard: Hansen v. Wearmouth Coal Co. , 1939, 3 All E. R. , 47, p. 54, Cross; *op. cit.* p. 188.

not mean that one identifies the legal system as a logical code. But such remarks do imply several epistemological questions. The most important of them is perhaps the hidden and silent identification of the "doctrinal rule" and the "*ratio decidendi*. of the prior case". Two problems are interrelated with that observation. First, one has to ask in what regard the *ratio decidendi*. of a prior case is taken as a rule. Is that not a deeply rooted decisionism in the law, with all its positivist consequences? One has doctrinally to decide that the *ratio decidendi*. of the prior case is a rule in the case at hand. But the judge does not overtly expose the rule of a particular decision in his legitimation and qualification of the applied rule. It is his conviction that he has to lay down that rule because of the authoritative character of the prior case. The latter idea is of utmost ontological importance. This is our second problem. Rules are considered "to be" there, and only in need of "being well established".

These two problems regard the philosophical implications of the principle of *stare decisis*. Cross refers here to Levi's *Introduction into legal Reasoning* and points out that there are important differences between the doctrine of precedent in England and the United States. Cross describes the activity of the American judge in terms of Levi's "Introduction": "... the judge perceives resemblances between the instant and a past case and proceeds to formulate a rule to govern both of them. He is not bound by the *ratio decidendi*. of the past case, and the third stage is unimportant because it consists in the application of a rule which has already been formulated with reference to the instant case. Levi does not recognize that there may be situations in which the judge has no choice but to apply the *ratio decidendi*. of a past case, or where he is obliged to do so unless he can point to a reasonable ground for holding that it does not apply. Reasoning by analogy would thus appear to play a more significant role in the American judicial process that it does in our own (The English)." A quotation from Levi's "Introduction" clarifies what is at stake: "Where case-law is considered, and there is no statute, he (the judge) is not bound by the statement of the rule of law made by the prior judge even in the controlling case. The statement is mere dictum, and this means that the judge in the present case may find irrelevant the existence or absence of facts which prior judges thought important... It is not alone that he could not see the law through the eyes of another, for he could at least try to do so. It is rather that the doctrine of dictum forces him to make his own decision"[9].

Two issues in this quotation refer again to the ontological basis of precedent, analogy and *stare decisis*. The first is enveloped in the expression: "to see the law through the eyes of another". That is an appealing formulation of analogy. But the formula is not informative about its essence. To see the law is: to see what? What is seen, in case one sees the law? What IS the law as an object of perception? To see the law – is that not precisely to see rules and analogies leading to applications? That is an ontological problem of the first order. A second reference is in the expression: "the doctrine of dictum". Such a doctrine can only be a representative speech-act. But what is represented in this speech-act? That really is a vital question to the doctrinal speech of every judge. What do his speech-acts represent other than his own speech and the related legal construction of reality?

II

Such considerations lead us to the epistemological implications of precedent and analogy in the law. Let us for the moment determine legal analogy. To understand the difference between English and American law is important and does not exclude Continental legal theory, as we could see from the parallel between Anglo-Saxon conceptualism and German "Begriffsjurisprudenz". Atiyah and Summers, in their *Form and Substance in Anglo-American Law* [10], determine the difference between English and American legal reasoning as differences of style. The first is more "formal", the latter more "substantive" reasoning. The authors argue that the system of precedent leads to formal reasoning. Even in America, where the doctrine of *stare decisis* is looser than in the U. K., lower courts have to bow before

9 Cross, *op. cit.* , pp. 182, 183. See: Edward H. Levi: *An Introduction to Legal Reasoning*, Chicago, 1949.

10 P. S. Atiyah & R. S. Summers: *Form and Substance in Anglo-American Law. A Comparative Study in Legal Reasoning, Legal Theory and Legal Institutions*, Oxford, Clarendon Press, 1987.

higher court decisions without any real possibility of evading them. Precedents are normatively formal sources of law, binding everyone unless and until other courts pronounce themselves on the issues (p. 9). It is clear from the beginning that such a broader framework of consideration (let us call it the framework of "legal theory") provides many possibilities to judge the inherent epistemological issues of analogy in the law. The "why" and "how" of precedent and the doctrine of *stare decisis* contribute to widen this field.

Law as an institution

To embrace the principle of *stare decisis* does not imply the creation of a legal slot machine. The formal character of *stare decisis* will not lead to a mechanistic rule-following machinery. One of the reasons is that a case which is qualified as a legal precedent must be taken as an authoritative case by other judges. This fact is important for its epistemological implications. Let us have a closer look at this problem.

Why does the *stare decisis* principle not lead to an overall formalism and mechanism in the law? An answer is provided by Atiyah and Summers in their "Form and Substance". Their answer appears to be an *institutional* explanation. A first type of reference in this regard is made to the judges and their professional attitude towards the law. "... most judges probably perceive their primary role to be that of loyalty to the law, and to the principle of *stare decisis*. Most judges ... acknowledge a secondary but more active role, which may be seen as one of 'keeping the law up to date', or of 'interstitial legislation', or simply as that of being a 'law-maker' ". And it is finally a reference to the professional behaviour of judges both in the U. K. and the U. S. A., when the authors conclude that "... American courts of last resort (are) in general far more activist than English courts, and also far less technically rule-bound or formal in their approach to *stare decisis*, as well as to other forms of law such as statutes and judgements"[11]. Thus far the institutional behaviour of judges, which is an encompassing theme of the entire book. A second type of reference to institutional factors regards

11 Atiyah and Summers, *op. cit.* , p. 117f.

the role of authoritativeness of prior case decisions. The argument relies on the institutional structure of the law. Our above formulation, that legal history is a case history, refers to the intertwinement of the legal decision making process and the law making process on the one hand, and the institutional functioning of law in society on the other. Again Atiyah and Summers: "If a decided case is to qualify as a legal precedent and thus as a formal reason for deciding a later case, then it must first of all be taken as authoritative by appropriate classes of subsequent judges, for example by judges of lower courts. It must thus have what we call authoritative formality ... if a prior case is to qualify as a source of formal reasoning, it is also necessary that the subsequent judges for whom it is authoritatively binding accord it some degree of mandatory formality. That is, the subsequent judges must treat the earlier decision as excluding or overriding or diminishing the weight of countervailing substantive reasons arising out of the circumstances of the later case. *Stare decisis*, then, generates formal reasons out of precedents which later courts invoke *because they are the law*." "... some obligation on lower courts to observe higher court rulings is regarded as almost a necessity in common law countries. Other things being equal, it is generally assumed that even higher courts are likely to follow their own previous decisions, so it seems a logical corollary of appeal processes that lower courts should be bound to follow higher court precedents."[12]

These descriptions of institutional facts and reasons are convincing and clear. They represent the thought-pattern and style of Atiyah and Summers' entire book, its richness and complexity, its originality and theoretical scope. But their contribution shows also the limits of institutional explanations in general. Such explanations may refer to epistemological grounds, but they do not clarify them. The epistemological grounds for *stare decisis* and *analogy* in legal thought cannot be found in the institutional organisation of the law, but in the specific textual and semantic character of the law. That character remains unclarified. The *stare decisis* principle is a textual principle: a prescription as to how legal texts have to be written and understood in order to be law! Dworkin's proposal to understand the law as a "chain novel" is a first attempt to understand such doctrinal principles as *stare decisis* and *analogy* in these terms. Intertextuality should be the catch-

[12] Atiyah and Summers, *op. cit.*, p. 115f.

word for understanding them. Institutional features cannot elucidate those principles. Atiyah and Summers' book is for this reason, despite its doctrinal depth and richness of doctrinal analyses, essentially historical and descriptive, not an analytical study. Their investigations do not reveal the basic epistemological presuppositions of the law.

This is essentially the same conclusion as was made with regard to Cross' analysis of precedent. The lack of specific instruments to determine the principle of *analogy* is evident in the book of Atiyah and Summers, as well as in the study of Cross. And all authors rely on methodological instruments and arguments which are determinant for the legal discourse in its entirety. No specific features can be found in legal doctrine or legal theory. It is interesting to notice how Atiyah and Summers refer to "general substantive reasons" for the legitimation of the practice of *stare decisis*. The authors do not give a limited list of determined reasons, since these reasons are to their opinion numerous. They only provide some examples: "(1) the practice secures equality before the law at least in the sense that like cases are treated alike; (2) it limits the scope for bias, arbitrariness, and the like; (3) it facilitates planning and reliance on the part of the private parties by providing a reasonably predictable and stable legal framework within which to make decisions; (4) it helps secure legal compliance on the part of losing parties, for they are more likely to see that decisions are not made against them personally, but apply to a class falling under a rule; (5) it serves efficiency by saving resources that would go into examining each case afresh, and by discouraging potential litigants from bringing lawsuits or appealing; (6) it brings home to the judges their responsibilities by forcing them when deciding entirely new issues to consider the various possibilities more carefully"[13].

13 Atiyah and Summers, *op. cit.*, p. 116.

Analogy, Liberalism and Legalism

Three comments have to be made. The first is that these general reasons for *stare decisis* do not differ from the classical legitimation themes within the philosophical framework of social contract theories. Equality before the law, exclusion of arbitrariness, foreseeable future within the scope of the law, neutrality, efficiency of the law and completeness in the sense that there should not be any realm of society outside the law: these themes make clear, why lawyers have to refer to existing legal material, that is: why precedents are important. It also entails why lawyers regard their behaviour along these lines of reasoning as doctrinally "correct" behaviour. But it also becomes clear that there is, in the case of the principles of *stare decisis* and *analogy*, no specific doctrinal or legal theoretical methodology or argumentation. The principles are apparently principles of the legal discourse as such, and they do not regard *analogy* in particular. The specificity of analogy in the law is not in the body of legal doctrine.

A second comment concerns the question of how lawyers materialize their reference to the preceding legal material. The different answers to this question, realized either in the U. K. or the U. S. A., depend on a variety of semantic, epistemological and political arguments. The three are united in embracing a *minimum of positivism*[14]. What binds a judge in the *stare decisis*? There is a general agreement on the fact that the "*ratio decidendi.*" (in America: the "holding") of the decision has to be determined as the binding element. It is important, that lawyers regard their "*ratio decidendi.*" as semantically, epistemologically and politically *neutral*. And this neutral element is, in addition, *formally* interpreted and practised. Differences between the English and American law do not do away with that minimum formality. The general opinion says, furthermore, that the *ratio decidendi.* should have the form of a narrow *rule*. The *material facts* of the prior case in court determine that rule. These ideas are intertwined with the basic conviction that precedents are binding *because of* their "authoritativeness". The authoritative formality is ascribed to rules in cases by judges, but this particular

14 Jan M. Broekman: "The Minimum Content of Positivism" in: *Rechtstheorie*, 1985, Nr. 16, p. 349f.

history of legal qualification is erased from the legal memory as soon as the case starts to function as a precedent, and becomes a source of formal reasoning.

A third comment returns us to Cross and his thesis that the *analogy* between a prior case and the case in court does not play a role on the level of the determination of the *ratio decidendi*.. What type of semantics is behind this observation? If there is legal analogy, then it is analogy between cases. "In" the cases are *rationes decidendi* and therefore also rules. Cases, rules and *rationes* are regarded as autonomous entities, interrelated in such a way, that they finally form the legal discourse in its entirety. The thought-pattern behind it has clearly a Renaissance *more-geometrico* character. Analogy is embedded in a linear and sequential order. The entities which allow reasoning by analogy are altogether separate entities before they are bound together by the analogy. It is the legal mind which causes their interrelationship. In fact these patterns of interrelationship do not, in the first place, aim at *analogy* but at *identity*. That is clear from Cross's argumentation. The final decision which the judge has to take is, according to his argument, the decision to apply the *ratio decidendi*. (in the form of a rule) of the prior case to the later case. It is the identity which counts in the doctrinal reasoning, and the analogy is an instrument of this identity.

The three issues of our comments are interrelated. They are precisely the thought-pattern which is criticized by the Critical Legal Studies Movement. The target is this interrelationship of formalism, determinism, rationality, authoritativeness, objectivism and positivism which forms the described epistemological pattern of the doctrinal principle of *analogy*. The catchwords for this target of the CLSM are: liberalism and legalism. Unger explains, in this context, how doctrinal considerations tacitly imply presuppositions about social, political and epistemological questions. Their absence in theoretical considerations of legal doctrine has a particular meaning! The remark does not witness a need for loose speculations; it has, on the contrary, a precise meaning. Legal semantics start from this point. One should not only consider what is said or written, but also what is kept away or hidden in silence – consciously or unconsciously. This is what Unger refers to in his criticism to what the CLSM generally labelled as "formalism of the law". That "formalism" represents a political ideology, namely legalism and liberalism. "The starting point of our argument is the idea that every branch of doctrine must rely tacitly if not explicitly upon some picture of the forms of social life with which it deals. For example, a constitutional lawyer needs a theory of the democratic republic that describes the proper relation between state and society or the essential features of social organization and individual entitlement that government must protect, come what may. Without such a guiding vision, legal reasoning seems condemned to a game of easy analogies. It will always be possible to find, retrospectively, more or less convincing ways to make a set of distinctions, or failures to distinguish, look credible. A common experience testifies to this possibility; every thoughtful law student or lawyer has had the disquieting sense of being able to argue too well or too easily for too many conflicting solutions. Because everything can be defended, nothing can; the analogy-mongering must be brought to a halt. It must be possible to reject some of the received understandings and decisions as mistaken and to do so by appealing to a background normative theory of the branch of law in question or of the realm of social practice governed by that part of the law."[15]

So what is pointed out here does not only regard a certain silence about what could be said or written. It also regards the context of reasoning and of facts. Doctrinal principles such as *analogy* are neither neutral nor without a specific context. Translated in epistemological terms, it means that analogy in the law cannot be understood in a purely doctrinal way, but only hermeneutically. That is what forms the main argument of J.Esser's important book on "Vorverständnis und Methodenwahl". Esser demonstrates how analogy in the law is embedded in the hermeneutic understanding of reality. Unger's "guiding visions", that explain the legal analogy, are often not or only fragmentarily formulated. The judge, according to Esser, "hat bei seinem Entschluß, eine Norm analog anzuwenden, bereits aus anderen Gesichtspunkten vorentschieden. Im Analogieurteil wird dies nur formal ausgewertet und bis zur Erprobung der Ergebnis-Brauchbarkeit durchgeführt. Das verführt freilich leicht dazu, den Grund der Analogiebildung ... nur unzureichend mitzuteilen..."[16]. One particular element of Esser's considera-

15 R. M. Unger: *The Critical Legal Studies Movement*, Harvard U. P., 1985, p. 8.

16 J. Esser: *Vorverständnis und Methodenwahl in der Rechtsfindung*, Frankfurt/M., 1970, p. 107.

tions is that some doubt is correct about the question whether analogy in the law is ever anything else but "formal"! Can analogy be "substantive" at all? This is in the hermeneutic perspective extremely doubtful.

Formal or Substantive

It is worth considering that the American lawyer looks for the "substantive reasons" of a precedent rather than for the "rule" of a prior case. This suggests the opposite of what was said before, namely that analogy in the law could very well be "formal" by essence and definition. The idea according to which the law is not something that simply exists, but that law is in need of a substantial persuasiveness (Atiyah and Summers) in order to be binding, reinforces a certain substantive character of analogy. The same is true for the above quoted argument of Levi. Analogous reasoning in the law is the creation of a circular movement. Rules of prior cases are reformulated in the light of new facts and a new case.

Two arguments, however, weigh in in favour of the doubt whether analogy in the law can be "substantive" at all. The first is that the doctrinal counter-arguments do not indicate how the determination of the persuasive character of substantive reasons come into life. How is it decided, and who decides? How is a precedent given its appropriate weight? How do precedents receive their proper "gravitational force" (Dworkin)? The second argument is embedded in Unger's criticism of legal doctrine as such. "No matter what the content of the background theory, it is, if taken seriously and pursued to its ultimate conclusions, unlikely to prove compatible with a broad range of the received understandings. Yet such a compatibility seems to be required by a doctrinal practice that defines itself by contrast to open-ended ideology. For it would be strange if the results of a coherent, richly developed normative theory were to coincide with a major portion of any extended branch of law. The many conflicts of interest and vision that law-making involves, fought out by countless minds and wills working at cross-purposes, would have to be the vehicle of an immanent moral rationality whose message could be articulated by a single cohesive theory."[17]

[17] R. M. Unger, *op. cit.*, p. 9.

It is clear from Atiyah and Summers' work that an institutional theory of the legal system does not provide good answers to those various objections. Even the recourse to the institutional idea that an understanding of the judicial process entails the cognition of a nexus of conduct, is not enough. And even Levi's recognition of the circular character of *analogy* in the law does not do away with another silent presupposition of the doctrinal understanding of the law, namely that all movements of the legal mind are compatible with criteria of *reasonableness*[18]. That is the foundation of the idea according to which the analogy in the law *can be substantive*, and is not necessarily formal in its doctrinal appearance. But in this case, one has to bring to the fore that the concept of reasonableness is formal in its essence. Only a formally understood reasonableness is convincing at first sight both for the legal subject as for the judge and the court. That definitively limits the legal practice. Its inherent reasonableness legitimizes that practice as the social institution which makes final decisions in conflictive situations. And that institution has the power to impose its decisions. The legal practice shows an axiologically determined systematicity which fulfils the requirements of scientific criteria, such as coherence, consistency and unity of discourse. The only accepted debate is on *values*. Do values refer to consensus, to considered deliberate judgments, to the acceptance of the "auditoire universelle" (Perelman) or to principles such as justice, fairness and procedural due process (Dworkin)? In what doctrinal ways does the lawyer and the law serve the best constructive interpretation of the community's legal practice? That is the doctrinal question in which *analogy* is embedded. And so is precedent, and so is the principle of *stare decisis*.

[18] Jan M. Broekman: "Recht en Redelijkheid", in: H. Parret (ed.): *In alle Redelijkheid*, Boom, Meppel & Amsterdam, 1989, p. 153f.

III

Analogy transforms the thinker into a prisoner of creativity. His expansion of knowledge, science and perception seems to be bound by analogy as an instrument. What appears as a great light turns out to be a shadow. The will to endlessly expand knowledge is tamed by the rigour of the *analogon* .

Analogon and Autopoetikon

Facts are codified, parallels take away an unlimited view on reality. The knowledge of reality is determined by the engraving of thought patterns and is not the result of a free mind. Social relations are judged along the lines of those engravings, that is according to norms and prefixed patterns of value orientation.

Why do we strive for analogous reasoning and for expansion of our knowledge in terms of analogy? Is it because we have to take risks and avoid them by the *analogon* ? The legal doctrine gives an example in that regard. Legal analogy transforms risks into acceptable risks, and uncertainty into reasonable expectations. Vision and insight are apparently brought to a symbiosis in the light of the metaphor of light, which is finally the *analogon* . Analogy creates a total resemblance of the entire world: everything resembles everything. The endless variability of nature seems in the light of analogy a false appearance. Is life itself the only antithesis to the death of analogy? Is analogy an appearance of death?

Legal doctrine operates with analogy. But every fragment of legal meaning implies virtually all possible meanings of the legal discourse. That implication regards legal rationality and normativity. The doctrinal *analogon* only mirrors that analogy, which is law itself in its circular character. *Analogon* and *autopoetikon* are analogous appearances.

That is not an easy game with concepts and expressions. The analogy is closely related with the foundations of contemporary epistemology. *Analogon* and *autopoetikon* have a different character. There could not exist an analogy between the two if it were not the case. But is it a difference of style or a difference in essence?

The act of representation is common to both concepts. But this already leads to the question of how reality is represented in them. And such a consideration is of immediate importance for the presence of reality in the law. One should consider the following issues:

1. The *analogon* needs referential activity. And its referential activity is in need of an ontologically determined concept of reality in order to function. Functioning references, however, do not *a priori* and fully determine their object. Shifts and changes of object, and therefore also of meaning and names, remain possible. Patterns of analogy regard a multitude of referents. An infinite number of realities, or referents, can become involved in the referential activity within the *analogon* itself. The answer to the question: *what* reality is appropriated by *what* reference, can only be answered *after* the act of reference has taken place. Such a structure is essential for the representation of reality in the *analogon* .

2. The *autopoetikon* also needs reference. But the referential structure here does not regard an infinite reality, a plurality of names and referential possibilities. There is only one reference, namely the one in view of a reality which, already, before all naming, bears a name: the "auton" or "self". An appropriation took place *before* the representation by means of a referential activity came into life.

So the difference between *analogon* and *autopoetikon* is not only a matter of style. It regards the order of appropriation by the act of *naming* a world of realities which has to become the object of reference. A world of realities which is named by concepts and meanings of the natural language, its ambiguities and metaphors, is represented in the *analogon* ; a named world of a univocal, doctrinally conceptualized reality is represented in the *autopoetikon.* That is indeed a fundamental difference. It is, in particular, the difference between the general discourse of a culture and the specific discourse of the law.

There are, as far as our considerations are concerned, two types of *analogy* in general, and two diverse structures of representation within them. One was called the *analogon* , the other the *autopoetikon*. In one type of representation, that of analogy in general, *names* and determinations of what could be an object of representation are not fixed or definitively determined. This is, however, not so in the case of the legal discourse. Analogy in the law is founded in the whole complex of *names* that are already given by the legal doctrine. Analogy in the law refers therefore to a reality which has already a name. Reality is already presented by the law *before* the law represents reality in all its legal acts. Important is here, that we have to keep in mind how all the names which legal doctrine has given to reality and which in doing so became object of legal reference, are finally gathered in *one name: law*! It is this structure of representation that finally determines the analogy in the law. Analogy in the law serves the *autopoetikon*. This is the deeper meaning of the conclusion, drawn from the analysis of the doctrinal function of analogy, according to which the analogy is an instrument within the doctrinal body of the legal discourse.

So in the law, the *analogon* transforms itself into the *autopoetikon*. Analogy in the law is always preceded by the NAME which is LAW, the presence of law, the self-presentation which has to be presented by means of representation. In receiving a NAME, reality is given an identity and a conceptual framework of meaning. The reality of everyday-life has become a fixed identity in the eyes of the law. The fixation took place along the lines of the founding features of the doctrinal body, the corpus of precedents, the leading issues of jurisprudence, the conceptual scheme of the history of legal cases. It is in this regard quite understandable that analogy in the law aims at identities rather than at parallels. A sufficiently reliable legal reasoning is only supported by an identity of legal cases. The same is true for legal rationality and for a reasonable legitimation of the legal practice. The NAME which is LAW is the precedent which preceeds all precedents and cases. Precisely this precedent forms the definitive context for the *stare decisis* principle in the law.

Reference and Institution

The NAME which is LAW designates not only the source of all legal meanings but also the law as an *institution*. THE NAME IS THE INSTITUTION. Legal meanings and legal speech-acts are institutional meanings and acts. What does this imply? One has to say: "the legal discourse is an institution", and not: "there is an institution which pronounces itself as "the legal discourse". There is not an institution which *precedes* the legal discourse. The institution is neither the speaker nor the subject of the legal discourse. The legal discourse is, in other words, not a discourse *of* an institution. The discourse is not possessed by an institution. That is precisely the identity of all legal identities: the discourse is an institution in itself. Whenever the law speaks up, the institution pronounces itself.

Analogous reasoning takes place in the institution; the legal analogy *is* institutional in its own right. That also regards the professional aspects of the construction of analogy. Analogy in the law does not in the first place appear as a theoretical problem! Analogy in the law belongs to professional practices. The construction of analogy is essential to the practice of the law. These constructions are not identical with the pattern of doctrinal rules. Analogy belongs indeed to that system of rules, rule-applications and doctrinal methods. This does not imply an identity with that system of rules and doctrines which jurists identify as the legal institution. It is indeed necessary for the legal practice that the *formal* reference in the case of analogous constructions is correct; *substantive* features are, however, not brought to the fore! The question has been posed before: can analogy be substantive? Cross, and also Atiyah and Summers, can only write their books because of the non-identification of the system of doctrinal rules which constitute the analogy on the one hand, and the legal system as an institution on the other.

Analogy can very well be the result of a strictly rule-following doctrinal procedure. Most analogies in the law are, however, created in the course of the practice of the law. Such analogies do not result from the application of a legal theory. They come into life as particular instruments which belong to the strategies of the legal practice. Skills and particular purposes of the legal practitioner are based upon such instruments. As a consequence, legal analogies derive from the law as an *institution*.

Critique of the institution

Doctrinal descriptions of the legal practice in general and of the related analogies, precedents and *stare decisis* do not only elucidate the law as an institution. Descriptions are in this regard not only descriptions and textual representations. They create the institution and its basic functions, rather than describe them. Or better: their creation appears as a description. That insight in the essence of an institution is, however, not brought to the fore. The books of Cross, Atiyah and Summers, and others mentioned before, are good examples of this approach. Our criticism focused on the absence of an epistemological understanding of the institutional mechanisms of law, since analogy was determined as one of the most important mechanisms. The authors equalized two different questions, namely "what happens within an institution" and "what is an institution", and they did not clarify how the two questions are functionally dependent on each other. That is a common feature of the so-called "institutional theory of law"[19].

Is it ever possible to criticize an institution, and what are the limits of explanatory statements concerning an institution? Can the latter ever reach the grounds of an institution, since any institution is deeply rooted in society and history of a culture, without any possibility of a rational and causal explanation for the existence of that particular institution and its specific forms in a given culture? Hence there is the idea that expressions and determinations of a natural language always function within a type of institution. And this is the more so for artificial languages. A critique of an institution is in this perspective at its best a play with inter-institutional and hence intertextual concepts. The legal discourse is a very strong force in society. All legal expressions have virtually a common denominator; they all say what they say and have as a further inherent meaning: "... and this is (valid) law." So again: can there be a possibility of enhancing the epistemological presuppositions of the law as an institution? Can one free oneself from the described determinative forces? Analogy certainly does not indicate such a direction. On the contrary: analogy functions as a repetition, as a reproduction of the institution in the heart of legal cases.

Behind all those considerations functions the objectivist thought-pattern. That is an epistemological position which in itself forms a representationalist view on reality. In short: one cannot be free from any institutional ties in order to be able to understand its epistemological and ideological force. Such a freedom does not exist in the human and social world. But is this the final justification of a critical position in view of Cross, or Atiyah and Summers, who determine the analogy as an institutional instrument of the law?

19 D. N. MacCormick: *Law as an Institutional fact*, Edinburgh, 1973; O. Weinberger: "Die Norm als Gedanke und Realität", in: *Österreichische Zeitschrift für Öffentliches Recht*, 1970, Nr. 20, p. 203f.; D. N. MacCormick & O. Weinberger: *Grundlagen des Institutionalistischen Rechtspositivismus*,. Berlin, 1985.

What is the core problem of analogy in the law? Analogy appears at a first glance as a theoretical issue, perhaps a the reinforcement of doctrinal reasoning in the law. Then it becomes clear that analogy is a constitutive element of the legal discourse in general and particularly of legal practice. Analogy belongs to a complexity of doctrinal forms, such as precedent, *stare decisis* and law as a totality of cases. These concepts refer to the law in its entirety and there is no theoretical or practical specificity to find in that regard. What is evident for legal analogy, is evident for the entire legal discourse. What is important is that there seems to be an analogy in its own right between the *analogon* and the *autopoetikon*. But analogy in the law abolishes that encompassing analogy. The autopoetic force within the law absorbes the functioning analogy: legal analogies always function in the self-referential practices of law. This determines the analogy as an element of law as an institution. What does that case-history of analogy in the law mean?

The question focuses on the ultimate relevance of the institutional character of the law. It regards the appreciation of the legal discourse in its entirety and not only the analogy. How is reality made apparent in the law, especially according to its basically institutional referential features?

Knowing the Institution

Our analysis developed hitherto the idea that the law presents reality in the form of a specific representation. This representation is the result of the constructive doctrinal and institutional forces which give the law its final shape. Reality is a legal reality in that representation. But legal reality is consequently only a representation, and nothing else. In other words: the law pictures a preceding reality which could be called: the life-factual reality. It is this reality which is transformed into the legal imagination. The legal practitioner holds these representations for more true, more accurate, socially reliable and determined than any other possible representations in a natural language. So these representations serve the institution, but the institution suggests that it serves the representations. In more crude formulations: legal reality serves the law, the legal discourse and the legal institution. But the law suggests that it serves reality. A philosophical consequence is, apart from the ideological factors which are involved here, that the institution has to be seen as *a form of life*.

Knowledge of the institution is (1) knowledge by means of the descriptions and historical analyses of its functions and principles; and (2) concealed knowledge in so far as it has to be a knowledge according to rules, values and basic structures of the institution itself. The self-referentiality plays a dominant role again. Since the law is a strong institution, analogy in the law creates and requires knowledge in the first sense and contributes to conceal knowledge in the second sense. The concealment received its philosophical description in the first lines of this essay's third section.

Knowledge of analogy is firmly embedded in the first sense of the concept. It is extremely difficult to imagine how analogy could serve the second sense of the concept. Analogy is the result of the actions of judges and courts, and the outcome of the functioning of organisational, particularly hierarchical, social structures and the corresponding application of relevant principles.

Current legal studies which include analogy, regard analogy as an outcome of creative institutional forces. They take analogy as the result of courts and judges, and of legal reasoning in general. It means philosophically, that the institution is dominated by a specific form, namely the subjectivity and individuality. Courts and judges are in this regard the dominating subjects of the institution. It is a matter of culture and of legal legitimation, that these subjects appear to dominate and structure the institution. All theories of institutions refer to the subject. It remains concealed, however, that the subject is created in the course of cultural history and of the development of relevant values in such a way that it became the most natural category of all epistemological thought-patterns. The reference to the subject is a reference to the institution, because the institution "created" the subject, and not the subject the institution! The legal institution represents itself as the result of actions of a subject (Courts, Judges). This representation is an act of creation: in doing so, the institution (re)creates itself.It conceals the fact, that the subject, which is placed in the role of the creator of the institution, is a creation of the institution. The epistemological pattern of subjectivity is so strongly determining our thoughts, that even this conclusion can not free itself from a linguistic pattern which is dominated by the subject as its main category. To conclude: all institutional knowledge is presented as knowledge of a subject. To study the knowledge of a subject and to interprete that knowledge as subjective knowledge serves the prolongation of the institution in which the subject is embedded. Analogy is the instrument of judges and courts? Yes and no. The legal representation of reality is in itself the presentation of a legal reality.

Legal thinking is presented as analogous thinking. This is particularly true for the legal practice. But how is the relation between the overt knowledge and the concealed knowledge of the institution present in the law? It is suggested in legal thinking that the analogy serves the coherence, the consistency and unity of the law. In other words: the analogy is one of the determining forces of the legal practice, its regularity and its reasonableness. The supposed reasonableness of the legal discourse conceals the concealment of the institution of the presupposed basic analogy between legal and non-legal reality. Rationality of the law, and its inherent reasonableness make it acceptable that legal meanings are given to life facts. This can only be the case if there is the basic analogy between law and reality. The thought-pattern of analogy is a phenomenon of a philosophical pattern which is determined by the act of identification (Adorno). It is for this reason, that legal theory does not take into account how the reconstruction of an institutional rationality serves a preceding identity of law and reality. This presupposed identity, the question whether "there is" an entity called "law" and another called "reality", and whether one could then, as a second step, declare an analogous relation to exist between the two, is not an issue in legal theory. This was criticized in saying that legal theory only describes the institution as a source for analogy. This concealment of the basic analogy is a main challenge for legal theory in general and for the study of analogy in the law in particular.

Law and Philosophy Library

Publications:

1. E. Bulygin, J.-L. Gardies and I. Niiniluoto (eds.): *Man, Law and Modern Forms of Life*. With an Introduction by M. D. Bayles. 1985 ISBN 90-277-1869-5
2. W. Sadurski: *Giving Desert Its Due*. Social Justice and Legal Theory. 1985 ISBN 90-277-1941-1
3. N. MacCormick and O. Weinberger: *An Institutional Theory of Law*. New Approaches to Legal Positivism. 1986 ISBN 90-277-2079-7
4. A. Aarnio: *The Rational as Reasonable*. A Treatise on Legal Justification. 1987 ISBN 90-277-2276-5
5. M. D. Bayles: *Principles of Law*. A Normative Analysis. 1987 ISBN Hb: 90-277-2412-1; Pb: 90-277-2413-X
6. A. Soeteman: *Logic in Law*. Remarks on Logic and Rationality in Normative Reasoning, Especially in Law. 1989 ISBN 0-7923-0042-4
7. C. T. Sistare: *Responsibility and Criminal Liability*. 1989 ISBN 0-7923-0396-2
8. A. Peczenik: *On Law and Reason*. 1989 ISBN 0-7923-0444-6
9. W. Sadurski: *Moral Pluralism and Legal Neutrality*. 1990 ISBN 0-7923-0565-5
10. M. D. Bayles: *Procedural Justice*. Allocating to Individuals. 1990 ISBN 0-7923-0567-1
11. P. Nerhot (ed.): *Law, Interpretation and Reality*. Essays in Epistemology, Hermeneutics and Jurisprudence. 1990 ISBN 0-7923-0593-0
12. A.W. Norrie: *Law, Ideology and Punishment*. Retrieval and Critique of the Liberal Ideal of Criminal Justice. 1991 ISBN 0-7923-1013-6
13. P. Nerhot (ed.): *Legal Knowledge and Analogy*. Fragments of Legal Epistemology, Hermeneutics and Linguistics. 1991 ISBN 0-7923-1065-9